CRESCENT MOON PAINTERS

KURT JACKSON

KURT JACKSON
Painting-Sea-Sky-Light-Land-Cornwall

Jeremy Mark Robinson

Crescent Moon

Crescent Moon Publishing
P.O. Box 1312, Maidstone,
Kent, ME14 5XU, Great Britain
www.crmoon.com

First published 2009, 2010, 2013. Reprinted 2018.
© Jeremy Mark Robinson 2009, 2010, 2013, 2018.

Printed and bound in the U.S.A.
Set in Rotis Serif and Gills Sans Light.
Designed by Radiance Graphics.

British Library Cataloguing in Publication data.

Robinson, Jeremy
    Kurt Jackson: Painting-Sea-Sky-Light-Land-Cornwall
    (Painters Series)
    1. Jackson, Kurt – Criticism and interpretation
    I. Title
    759.2

ISBN-13 9781861713100 (Pbk)
ISBN-13 9781861714480 (Hbk)
ISBN-13 9781861716712 (Pbk)
ISBN-13 9781861717481 (Pbk)

CONTENTS

ACKNOWLEDGEMENTS

Thanks to Michael Jay. Martin Val Baker. Bob Devereux. Paul Evans. Stewart Edmondson. Tom Rickman. Pamela and Noel Betowski.
Special thanks to Tony Maestri.

Great Atlantic Map Works Gallery, St Just. Rainyday Gallery, Penzance. Penwith Gallery, St Ives. Tate Gallery, St Ives. Newlyn Art Gallery, Newlyn. White Lane Press, Plymouth.

To the authors and publishers quoted.

ABBREVIATIONS

P   *Paintings of Cornwall and the Scillies*, 2000

PREFACE

This book is a study of the art of the British painter Kurt Jackson. I hope to share some of my enthusiasm for Jackson's work with other readers and admirers.

The statements about Kurt Jackson's career and works are accurate, as far as I can tell: the biographical facts and information about Jackson's career are drawn from published interviews and articles, which can be found in newspapers and magazines, exhibition catalogues, and websites (see bibliography). The book *Paintings of Cornwall and the Scillies* is a good place to start for further research.

I have also drawn on conversations and correspondence with other artists, critics and gallery owners.

Jeremy Mark Robinson
2009/ 2013

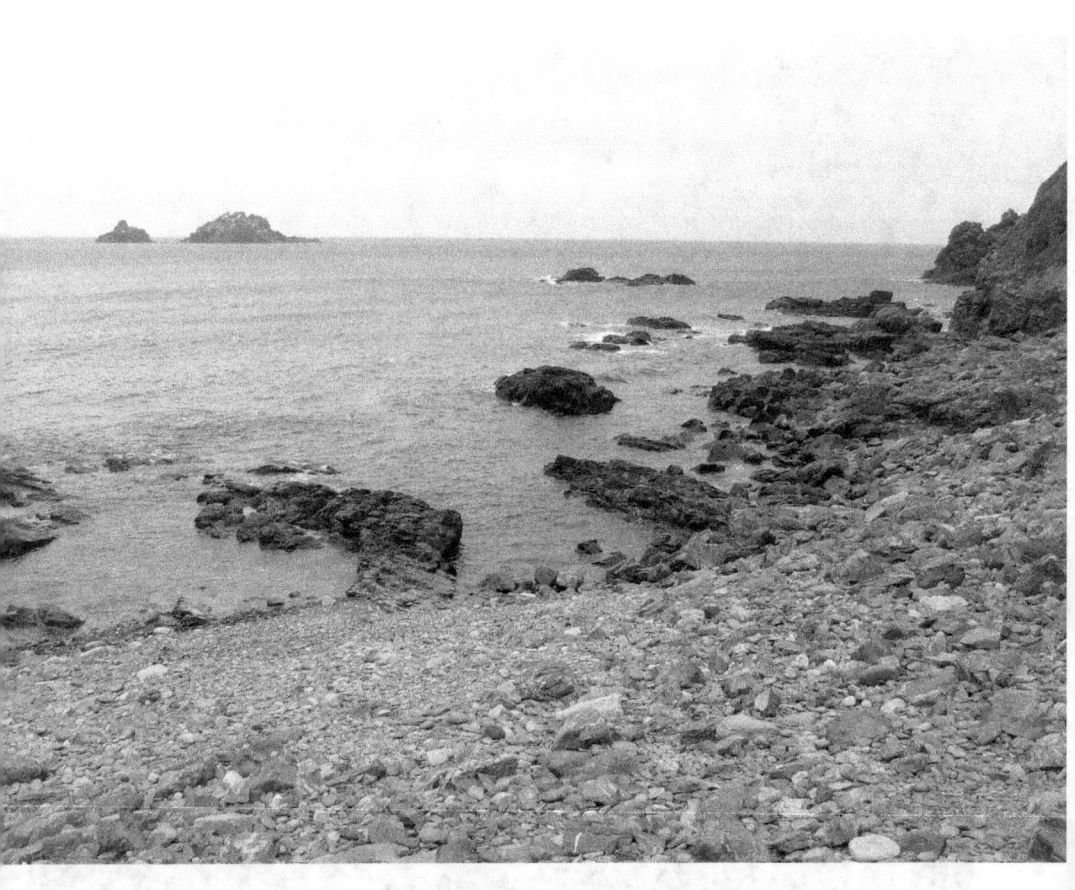

The heart of Kurt Jackson's art: Priest Cove near St Just in West Cornwall.

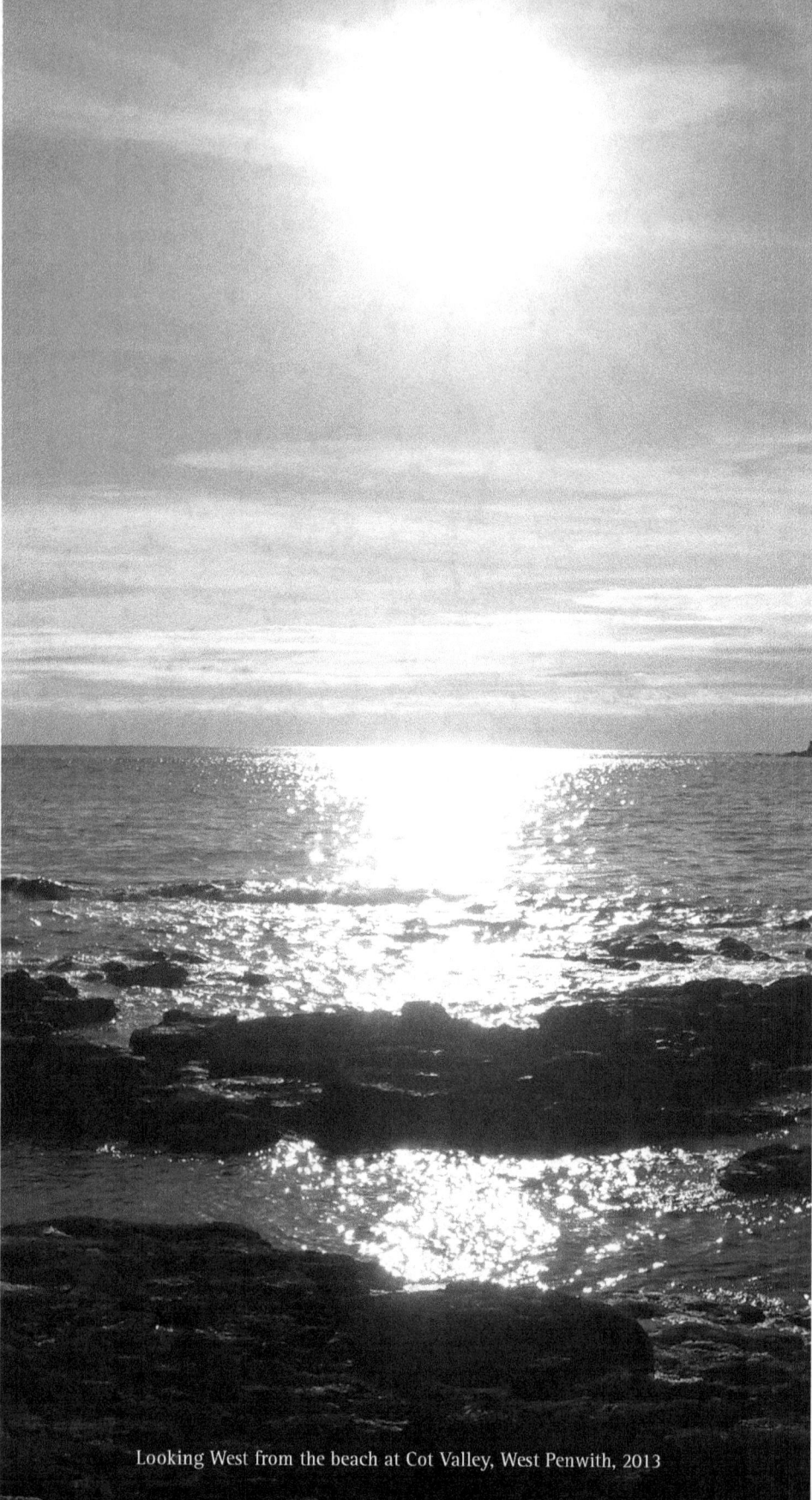

Looking West from the beach at Cot Valley, West Penwith, 2013

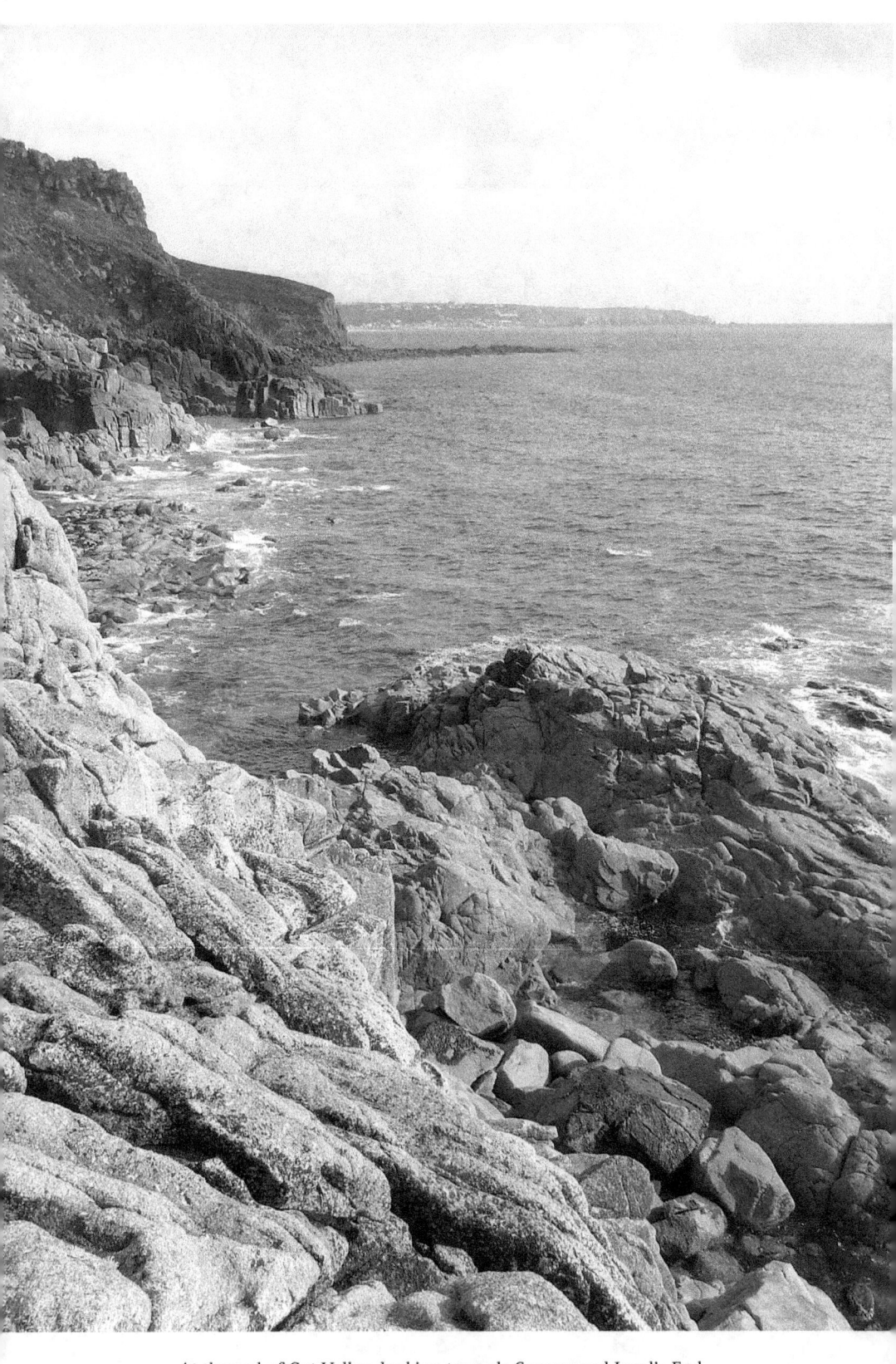

At the end of Cot Valley, looking towards Sennen and Land's End

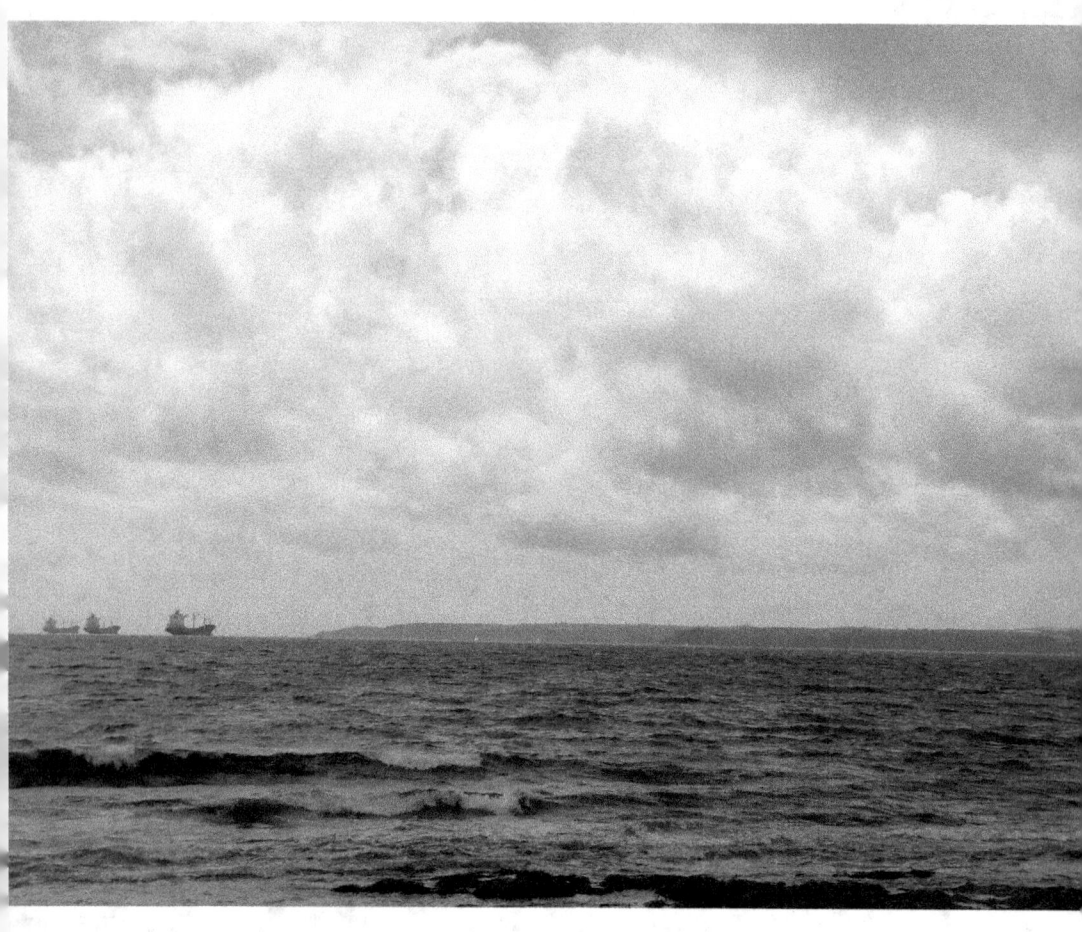

The Lizard from Falmouth

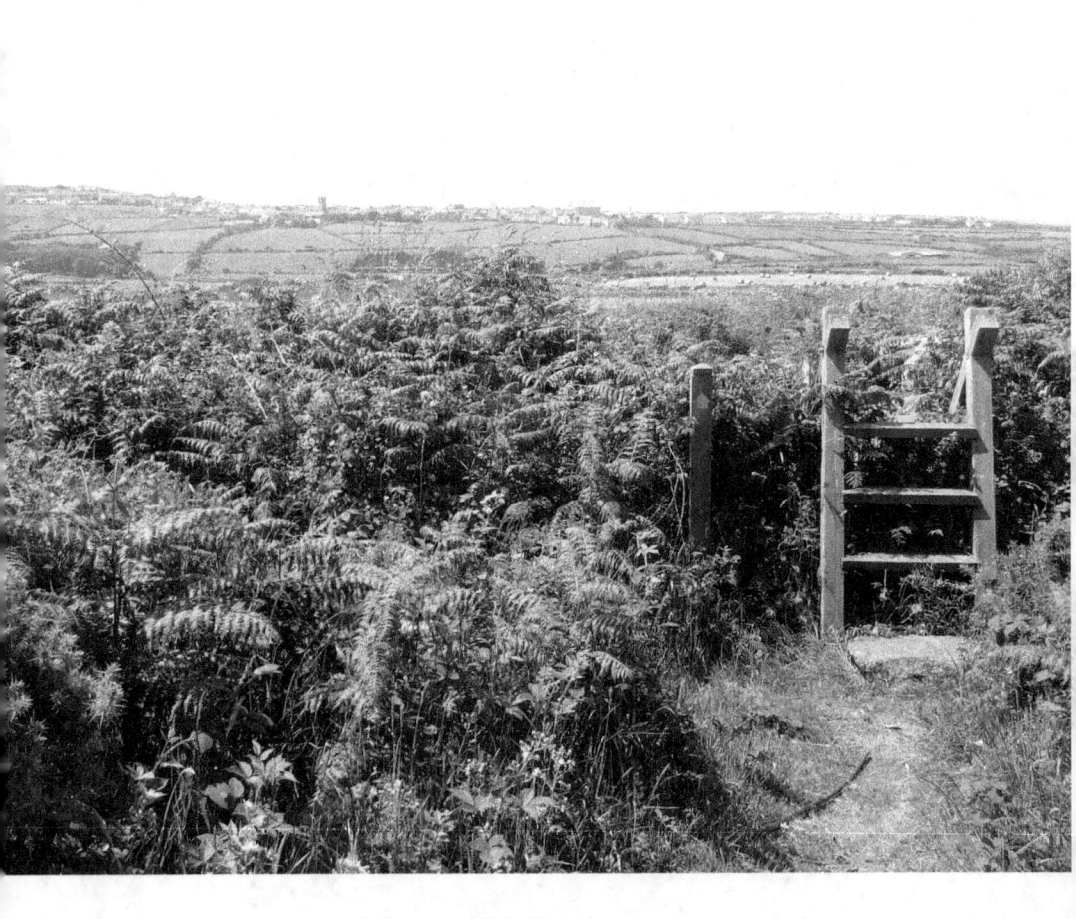

St Just seen from Kenython

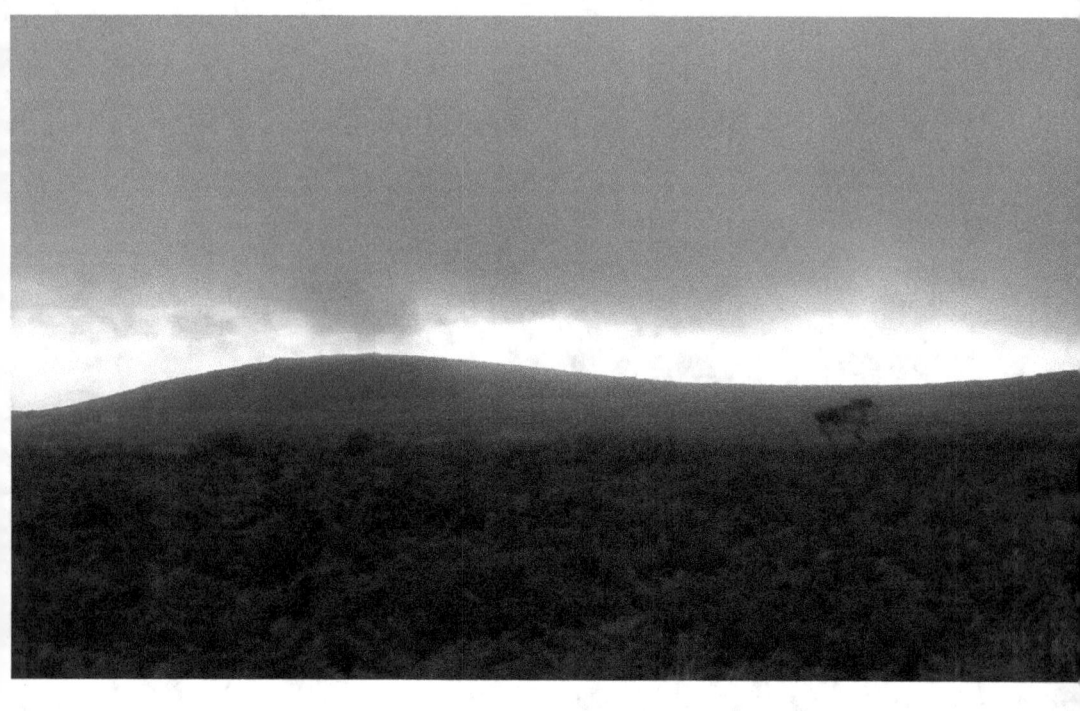

Looking towards Carn Brea, West Penwith, at sunset, 2013

INTRODUCTION

I first met Kurt Jackson in 1996, while on holiday in West Penwith in Cornwall. Actually, it was an odd sort of meeting. I'd been visiting the art galleries in the area (as usual), and had come across Kurt Jackson's paintings in a group show (with Bo Hilton and Louise McClary) at Rainyday Gallery in Penzance (run by Martin Val Baker, one of the best galleries in the area). Val Baker told me that the art scene was thriving in West Cornwall, and he was putting on shows. The group show had opened a couple of days earlier (on May 4, 1996), and a lot of people had attended the private view (although Val Baker hadn't sold any work yet).

I was struck by Kurt Jackson's landscape and semi-abstract paint-ings, which seemed to be in the West Penwith/ St Ives/ Newlyn painterly abstract style – roughly painted areas of blues, greys and whites: seascapes. The sensuality and clarity of the painterly approach was very appealing, and of course they were paintings of the sea, which was always a good start for me.

But I was also hooked by the titles and the particular places that Kurt Jackson was painting: Priest's Cove, Cape Cornwall, Cot Valley and the area around St Just. This was a part of Cornwall I'd enjoyed visiting for some time, and liked very much, so it was interesting to see art that was centred on this particular, very special, very atmospheric part of Cornwall.

Cot Valley was the first part of the area I got to know really well – with its tiny gurgling stream winding through, and the orangey-browns of the bracken, the triangle of the shining sea at the end of the valley, and the absolute quiet. The vivid orange of the vegetation combined with golden sunlight creates a radiant red-orange in the Cot Valley which Vincent van Gogh would have loved – especially towards sundown, when the sun's at the West end of the valley (Kurt Jackson has painted the valley many times, often using the stream as a centrepiece). The light blasts along this valley towards the later part of the day, and the way it reflects off the ocean and is framed by the cliffs on either side is very appealing. It's a readymade painter's view – and you get plenty of time to look at as you approach along a path for half a mile, following the Cot stream.

The small beach of Nanven at the end of the valley is also a favourite spot of mine, with its distinctive egg-shaped white granite stones, and the feeling of being secretly enclosed by cliffs on three sides. Nanven, facing West, is completely dominated by the sea and the sky; like Priest's Cove half a mile up the coast to the North, it seems to have been built as a viewing space for the sky and the sea.

Kurt Jackson's views of the tranquil Cot Valley, usually with the stream winding through the lower centre of the composition, include *Cot Valley Stream* (1998), *Low Sunlight, Cot Valley* (1998), *Cot Valley* (1995), *Cot Valley, Sunshine On a Rainy Day* (1995), *Sun & Shade, Cot Stream* (1999), *Cot Stream* (1995), and *Late Afternoon, Cot Valley* (1998). And the distinctive image of the 'V' shape of the valley with the sea at the end and orange-brown vegetation also occurs in Jackson's pictures of nearby Kenidjack (as in *Cold, Wind, Warm Sun*, 1998, or

Kenidjack Valley, 1997, which also includes the disused chimney at Kenidjack).[1]

Apart from Kurt Jackson, many other painters have used Cot Valley, Kenidjack Valley, Cape Cornwall or Priest Cove, including Paul Lewin, Tom Rickman, Gary Long, Gill Watkiss, Paul Evans, Neil Davies and Neil Pinkett (these artists were included in the exhibition about the area, *Cot, Cape and Kenidjack,* at the Great Atlantic Map Works Gallery in St Just).

A few days later I was in St Ives, talking to artists and gallery owners (I remember Bob Devereux reciting a poem about the Netherlands in his gallery, with me as an audience of one), and found out more about Kurt Jackson.

The people at Penwith Galleries gave me his telephone number and I called him from the call box outside the Tate Gallery. This isn't something I usually do, calling people I don't know at all out of the blue. The only thing I had to go on was that I really liked his paintings, and I'd read that he was at Ruskin College in the early 1980s, where a friend of mine, Bridget Downing, had also studied.[2]

Kurt Jackson was friendly, and we arranged to meet later at his local pub, the Star pub in the middle of St Just, where he appeared with his family (Jackson sports a T-shirt of the Star Inn in one of his self-portraits, *Cove Dancer*, 2003. In that painting, it's a real T-shirt). He is a stocky guy with a shaved head and jewellery piercings.

At the time, it seemed as if Kurt Jackson had an amazing life, with his wife, Caroline and kids (Chloë, Zinzi and Seth) in a comfy house in St Just, and he was painting pretty much full-time (he said he's had only one or two jobs, and has worked pretty much full-time as an artist since those early jobs).

Later we went back to his house in Chapel Street (all wood furniture and floor, hippy hangings, colourful coverings, upright piano), where Kurt Jackson showed me his oil, watercolour and acrylic paintings, his studio, the attic full of frames, paintings and a plan chest). As we sat talking (drinking whisky and listening to the divine Natacha Atlas

1 Kurt Jackson has acknowledged that two shapes recur in his art: the horizon line of sea and sky, and the foreshore, and the 'V' of the valleys near St Just (P, 29).
2 Kurt Jackson took art classes at Ruskin, but his degree was in zoology. At Oxford he met Caroline, his future wife, who was in the year above him (P, 10).

and world music), I thought that Jackson seemed to be having a good time – making art and living with his family in the most wonderful part of Britain.

❖

In this book I will be discussing Cornwall itself – partly for self-indulgent reasons, but really because Kurt Jackson continually emphasizes the significance of Cornwall in his art. In the catalogue of his first London show he wrote:

> *I prefer to focus in on a specific area and explore it repeatedly through a number of paintings* and, even though I travel about a great deal, I still try and use this approach. (1998; my italics)

That area is of course West Cornwall – Jackson's landscape of the soul, his homeground. (But I won't be looking at the history of art in Cornwall, or the life and times of Cornish artists, or much on how Kurt Jackson's painting relates to art in Cornwall. Cornish art has attracted quite a bit of critical attention; there are plenty of studies of it around)

❖

When I first became aware of Kurt Jackson's art, in the mid-Nineties, he was showing work in galleries like White Lane Gallery and New Street Gallery in Plymouth, Porthmeor Gallery, St Ives, and Beside the Wave in Falmouth, and participating in many group shows – for example, at Visions and Journeys in St Just, Rainyday Gallery in Penzance, and the Newlyn Society of Artists shows. At the time, Jackson was exhibiting in small, commercial art galleries, and his paintings were modestly priced. The price list from the show with Bo Hilton and Louise McClary at the Rainyday Gallery (Penzance) in 1996 has Jackson's paintings between £200 ($300) and £280 ($420) for smaller works (watercolours and acrylics), and £1,200 ($1,800) for larger (oil) works.

The rise in Kurt Jackson's popularity seemed to occur in the late

Nineties, between 1998 and 2000.[3] That was when Jackson had his first major London show (at David Messum's Gallery), in the heart of the British art world, Cork Street. His prices increased accordingly, to £650 ($975) for small watercolours (11 by 11 inches) and £2850 (4275) for larger pieces (29 by 43 inches).

By the mid-2000s, the smallest of Kurt Jackson's paintings were selling for £1,000 ($1,500), i.e., for a seven-inch square acrylic painting, with a typical price of £4,500 ($6,750) for a 22 x 25 inch painting. The big oil and mixed media canvases were going for £9,850 ($14,775), £14,500 ($21,750), £18,500 (27,750), rising to £50,000 ($75,000). Now I wish I'd bought some of the early pieces! (I did ask Jackson if he'd give me a painting when I visited his studio; he declined, wisely).

I knew that Kurt Jackson's art was becoming popular when I was marking a bunch of essays by art students at Canterbury art college and they were writing essays like "Kurt Jackson and Tracey Emin". When an artist is being written about by art students, you know they've made a pretty big impression.

Why?

When asked why people liked his art, Kurt Jackson didn't know – what artist does?

> That constantly surprises me. I have always painted exactly what I've wanted to paint, but whatever I choose to paint it seems that someone always wants it. (P, 21)

Nobody knows quite why people took to Kurt Jackson's art in the late 1990s and early 2000s, and not that of 100s of other artists. It's a mystery, like the *Harry Potter* phenomenon. Because if there was a formula, everyone would be following it!

For me Kurt Jackson is a fundamentally conservative artist who produces attractive art that can be regarded as 'pretty pictures'. But it

---

3 The success that Kurt Jackson has enjoyed has created (perhaps inevitably) some resentment and jealousy in the art community of Cornwall. There are too many accounts of bad feeling and acrimony, though, for there not to be some truth behind the stories (there is a fascinating behind-the-scenes story to the Cornish art scene – but nobody wants to tell it – for fear of libel!). I won't point out any examples here, but if you dig around, you will soon find them! Jackson, we must remember, is only one of hundreds of artists who draw inspiration from the Cornish landscape.

contains enough roughness and funky stuff to elevate it above the usual landscape painting and tourist tat of Cornwall.

Around 1997-1998 I suggested to Kurt Jackson that we produce a book together[4] – his paintings combined with my poetry and writings. My idea was to call it *Cape Cornwall*, and it would include mainly his landscape paintings of the area, centring on Priest's Cove. We got quite far along with it (down to me writing part of the book and applying for Arts Council[5] funding for it, because it would be an expensive product, being full colour).

In the end, the project languished (mainly due to the cost). A couple of years later, a version of the *Cape Cornwall* book was published, but with Ronald Gaskell's poetry (the published book was disappointing, the poems undistinguished, and it wasn't what I envisaged).

❖

As a youth, Kurt Jackson visited the Amazon, the Arctic, and hitch-hiked across Africa. Travelling remains important in Jackson's art, a habit picked up from childhood holidays in Mediterranean countries.[6] The Isles of Scilly, Scotland, Greece, and France are regularly visited by the artist. (The sketches show images of mosques and towns in Algeria and the Middle East).[7] But it was always West Cornwall that he returned to: he has said:

> I still get just as much pleasure going down to Priest Cove, into Kenidjack or Cot Valley or down to Botallack Cliff even though I've been working in those places for years and years. (P, 12)

Kurt Jackson moved first, in 1984, to North Cornwall, to the small community (out of season) of Boscastle. The move to St Just (in 1989) came about partly, Jackson recalled, because there seemed to be more

---

4 Before this, I told Kurt Jackson that I was going to write a book about his art – he wrote to me, sending two of his early catalogues (on December 23, 1996): 'I look forward to when you write the definitive work on my painting!!' Well, it's taken a long time – over twelve years!
5 A government body dealing with the arts.
6 Kurt Jackson remarked in 1999 that 'there are landscapes in southern Europe, like the olive grove belts in Greece and Spain, which I get immense satisfaction out of... Some of my earliest memories are of the Greek olive groves, camping wild with my parents' (P, 19). They were places of limestone, red soil, scrubby plants, 'places I just love returning to' (P, 31). You can see them in pictures such as *Olive Grove, Very Hot, Loud Cicadas, Rhodes* (1997).
7 Such as *Hydra* (1993), and *Djenné Mosque* (1984).

happening artistically in West Cornwall ('there was clearly more going on in the west', as he put it [P, 17]).

At Boscastle, Kurt Jackson began the practice of visiting a location time after time – in this case, the River Valency valley. 'When you paint the same location repeatedly there's a deep affinity that develops between you and that place,' Jackson commented (P, 12).

It was 'a very nice challenge to set yourself', Kurt Jackson remarked, going to the same place and painting it again and again. The changes in light, colour, tone, etc, over the days, weeks and seasons, were explored in a way familiar in many artists' work (such as Claude Monet painting his garden, or Robert Smithson going to the American desert).

From time to time Kurt Jackson has explored the passing of time within the same image, producing a variety of views of the same place over successive days, as in *Seven Evenings On Botallack Cliff* (1998), or the eclipse pictures of 1999.

Some of Kurt Jackson's early paintings have an opaque, muted quality, a little reminiscent of Vincent van Gogh's early works – paintings such as *Stannon Stone Circle* (1987) and *Roughtor* (1988). In these pictures, the depiction of radiant light – particularly back-light or South light – that contributes so much the success of Jackson's art – isn't developed yet.

For research resources on the internet there are some art galleries which have (or used to have) information on Kurt Jackson, such as the Lemon Street Gallery site,[8] at:

www.kurtjackson.co.uk,

and the David Messum Gallery[9] site at:

www.kurtjackson.com.

I have tried to give a balanced and fair account of the art of Kurt Jackson, though parts of this book are personal and poetic.[10]

---

8 The Lemon Street Gallery had some useful entries about Kurt Jackson's shows on their website, but since the break with Jackson, they have deleted them all.
9 In 2009, Kurt Jackson announced that he was leaving the David Messum Gallery.
10 The views expressed in this book are mine; they are one person's view of art, and of one artist.

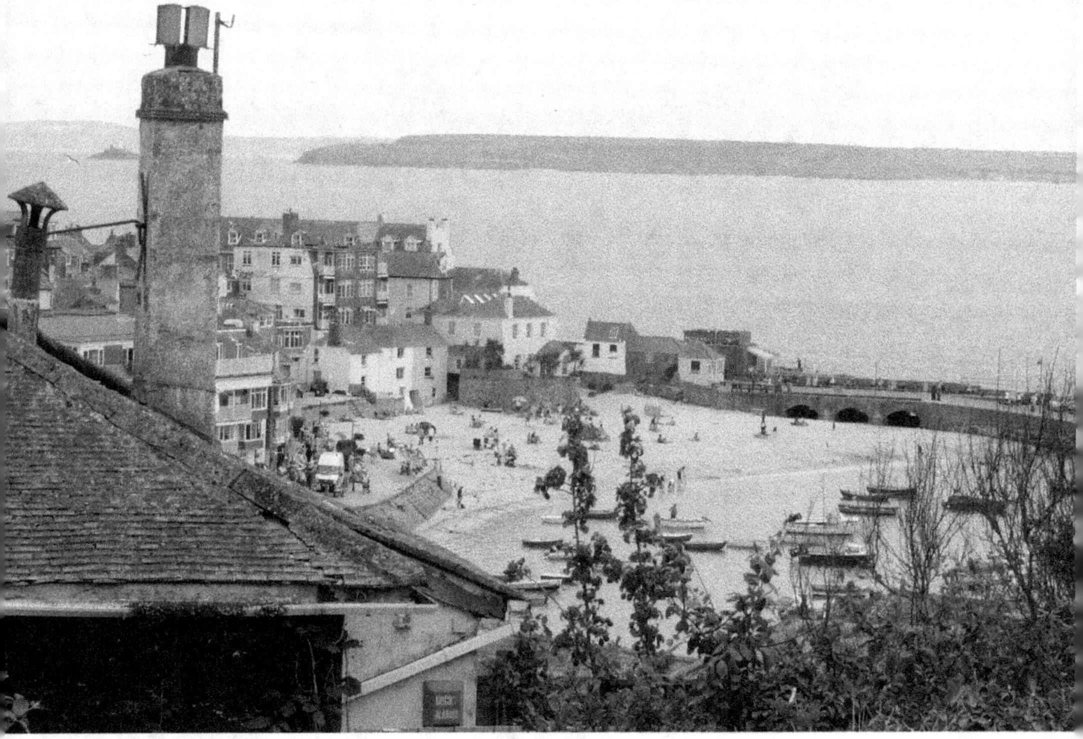

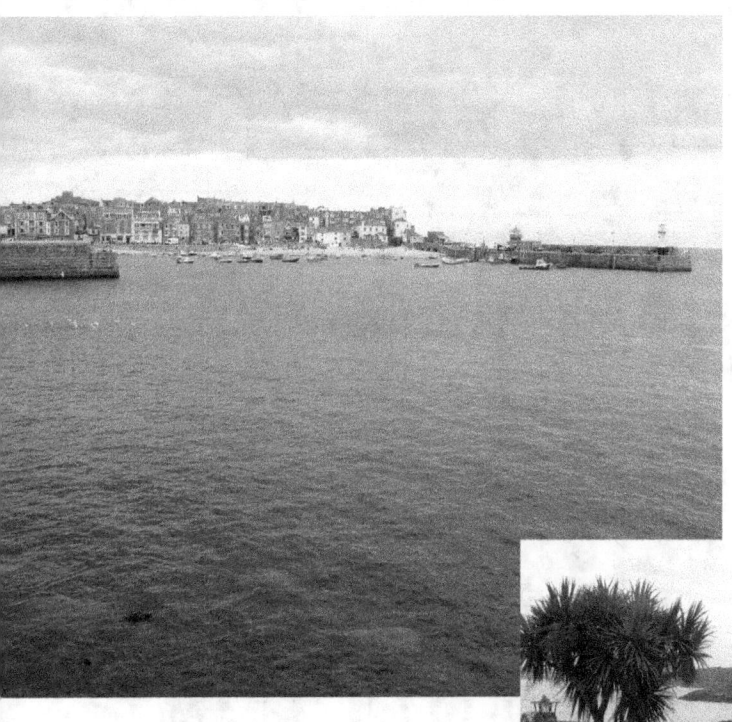

The centre of the art scene in West Cornwall: St Ives.

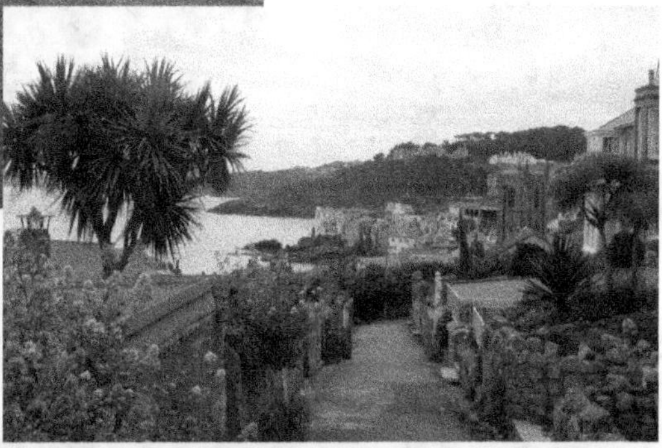

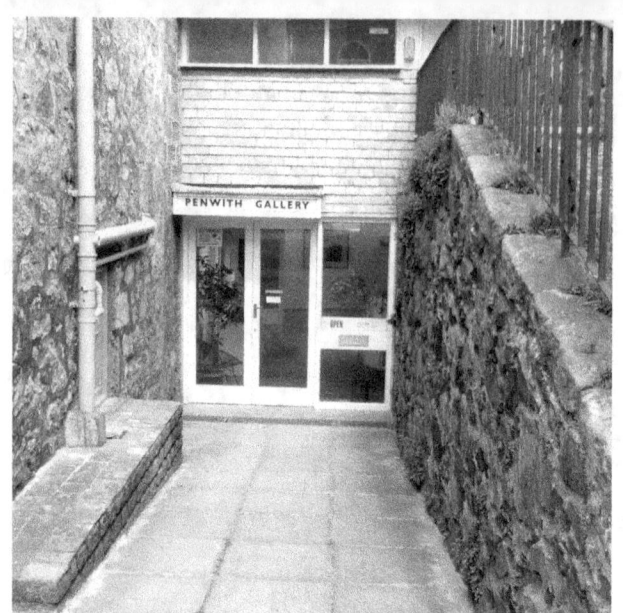

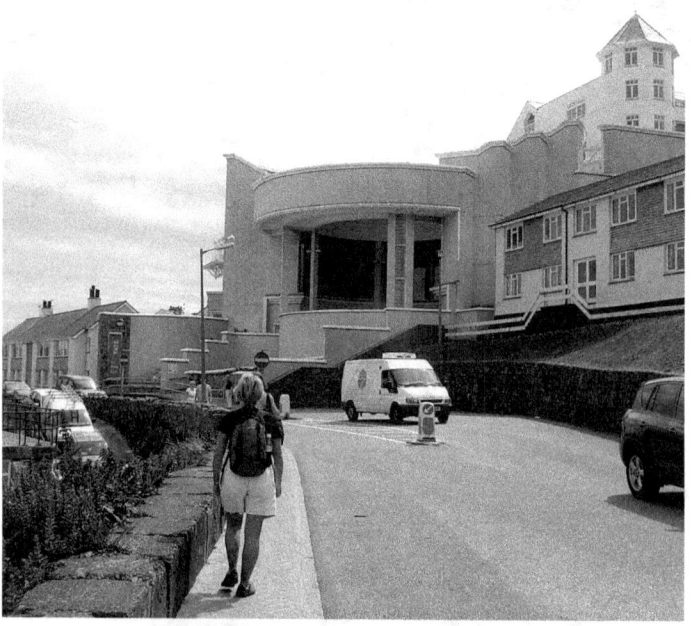

Some of the principal sites in the art scene in Cornwall: the Tate Gallery in St Ives (above), Penwith Gallery, also in St Ives (top), and Rainyday Gallery in Penzance (right).

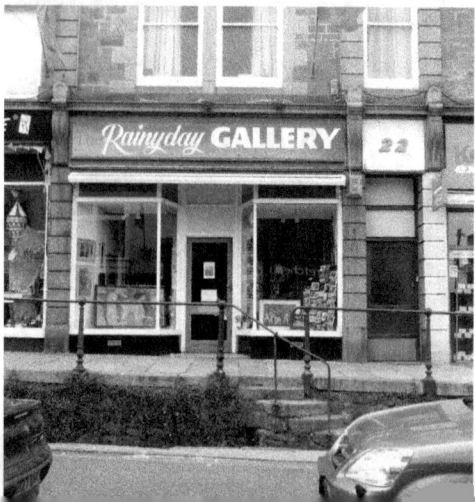

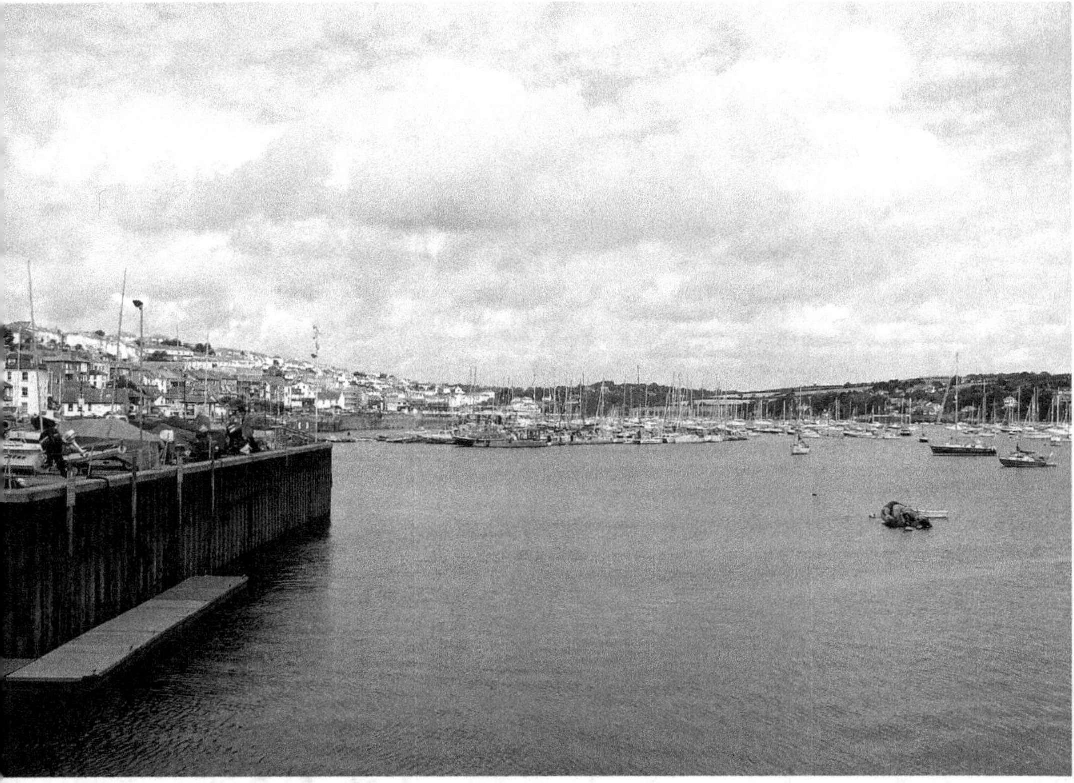

Falmouth harbour

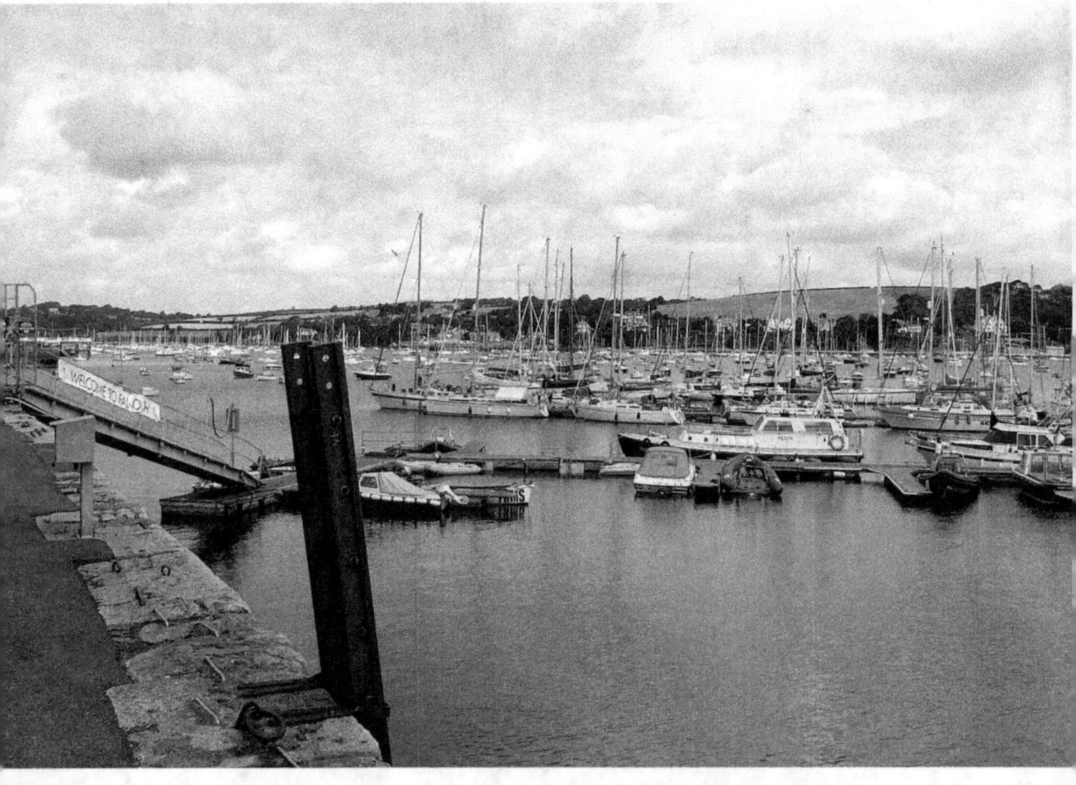

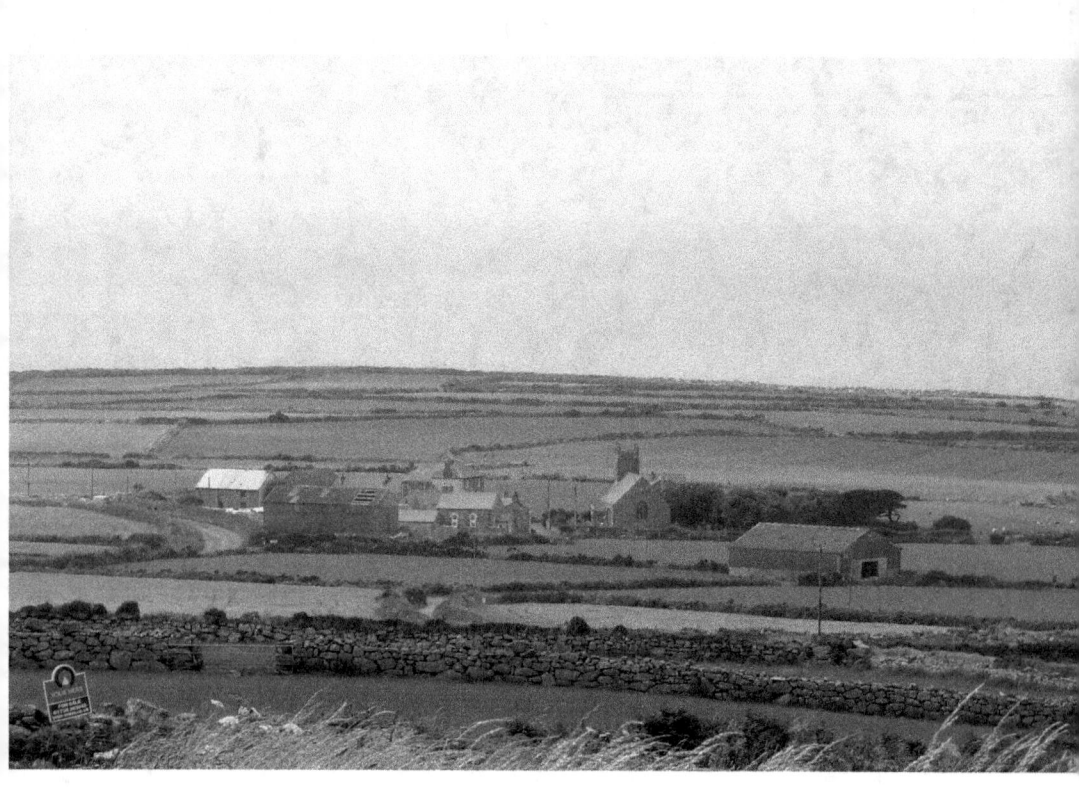

Morvah village, Cornwall

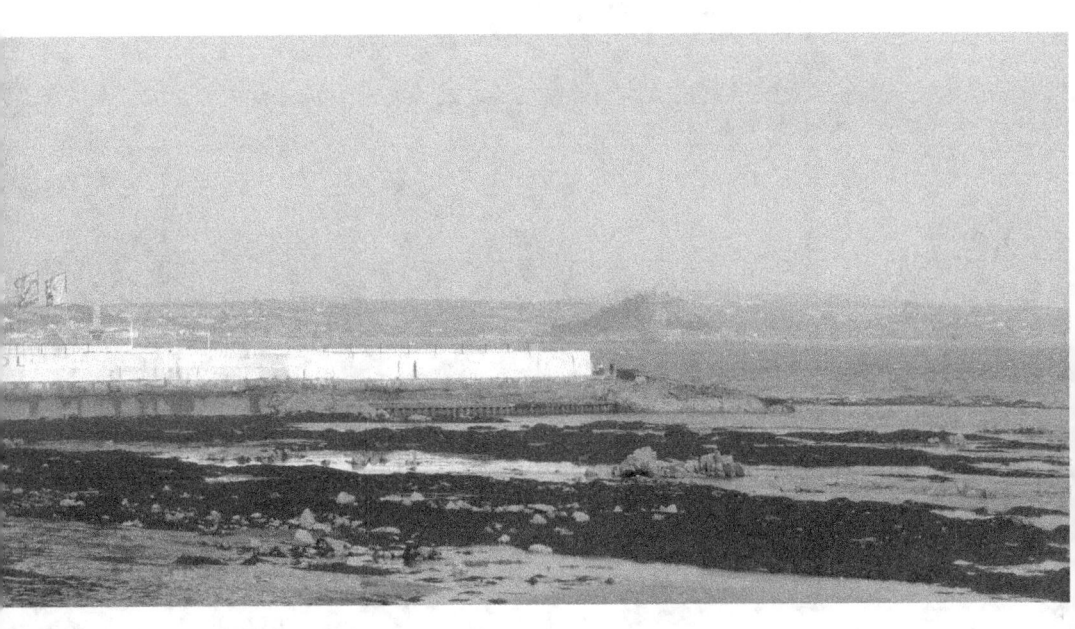

St Michael's Mount from Penzance promenade

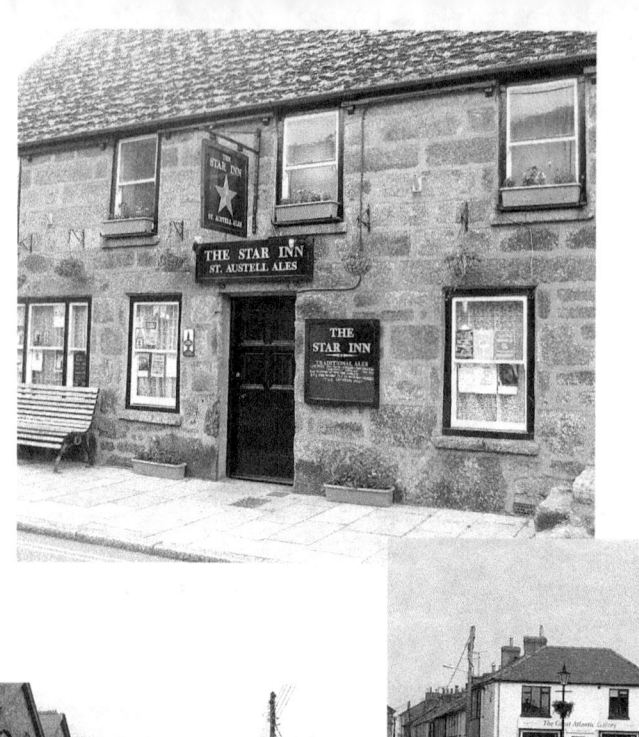

Views of St Just
in Cornwall,
including pubs,
chip shops and
art galleries

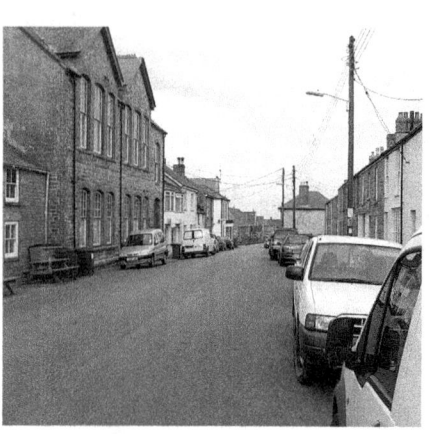

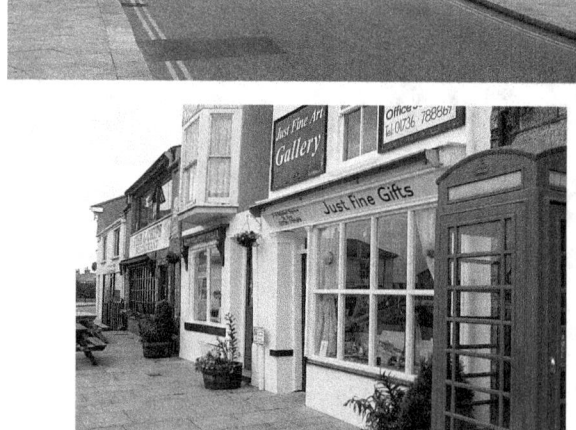

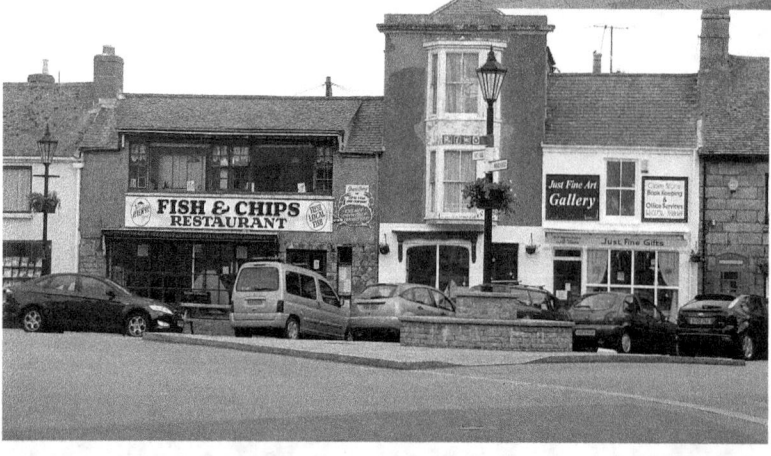

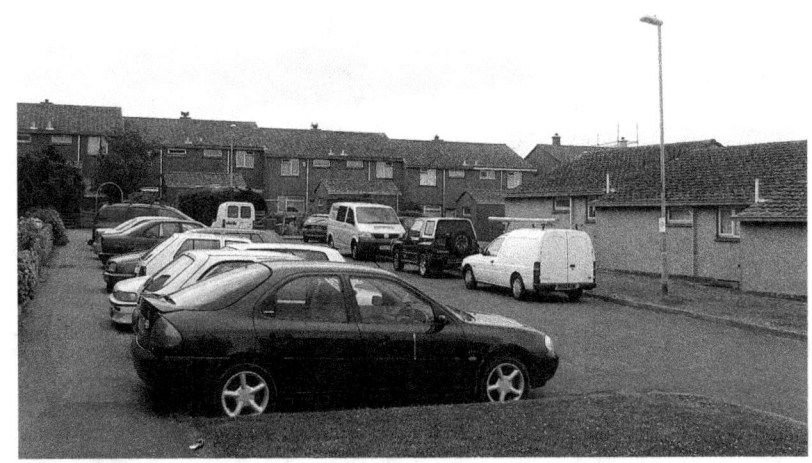

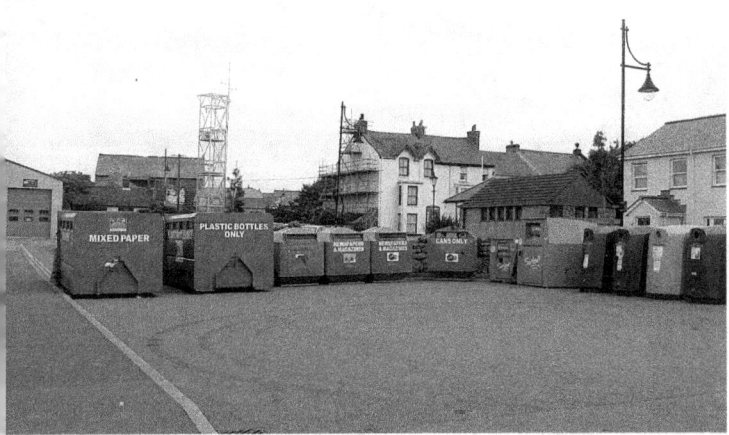

Aspects of St Just that appear in few paintings of the area - such as housing estates and recycling centres.

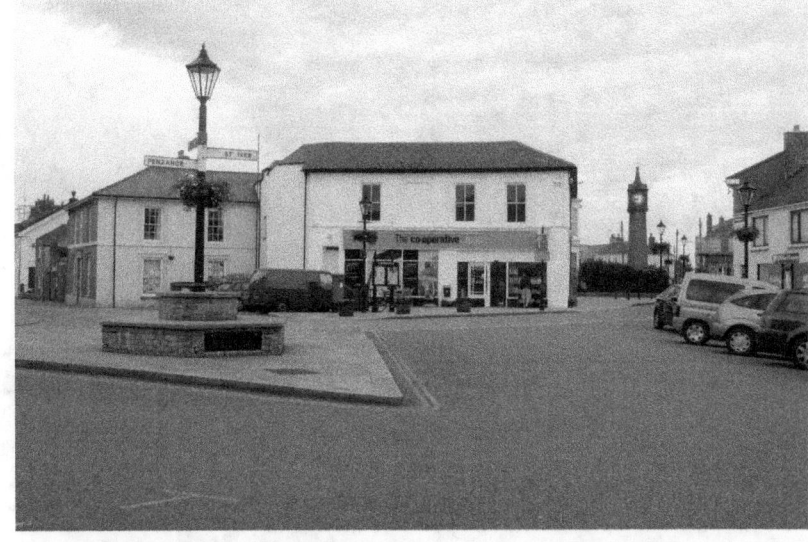

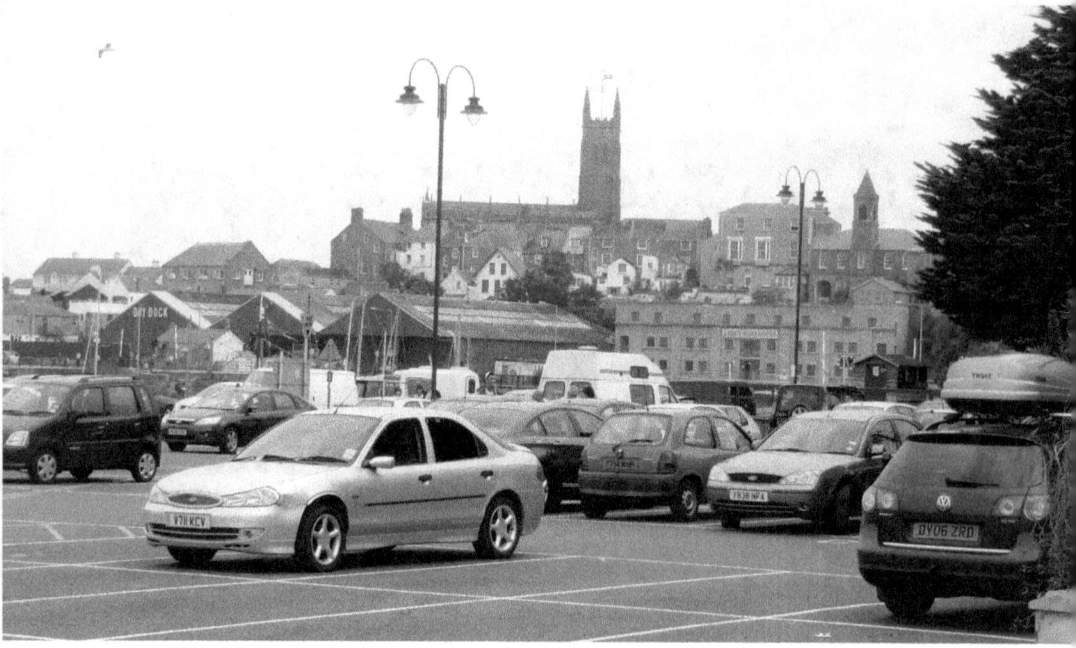

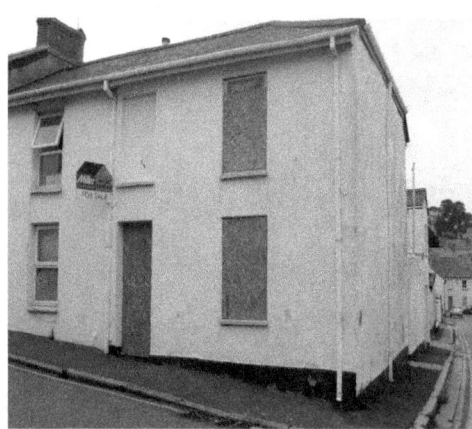

Aspects of West Cornwall you don't often see in paintings of the area: cars, houses and streets in Penzance.

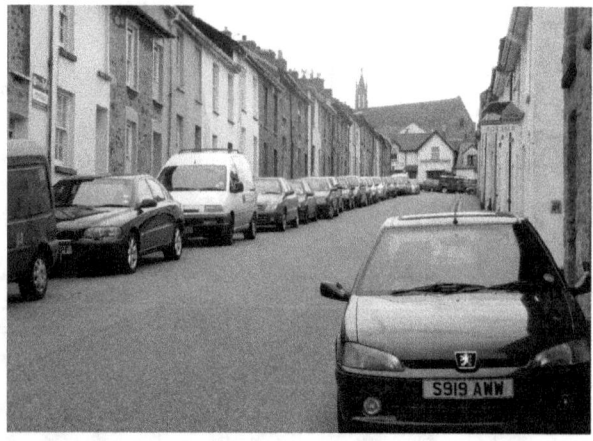

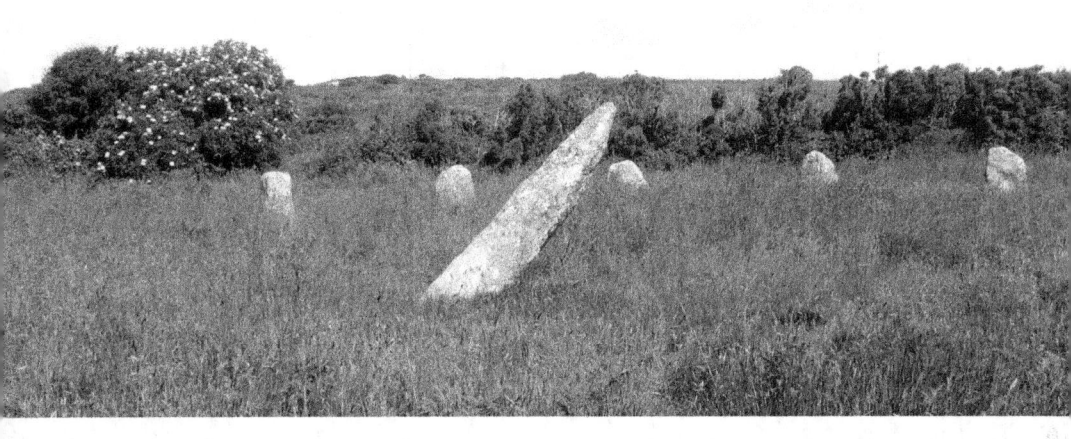

Boscawen-Ûn stone circle, near St Buryan, above.
Bollowall barrow, near Cape Cornwall, below.

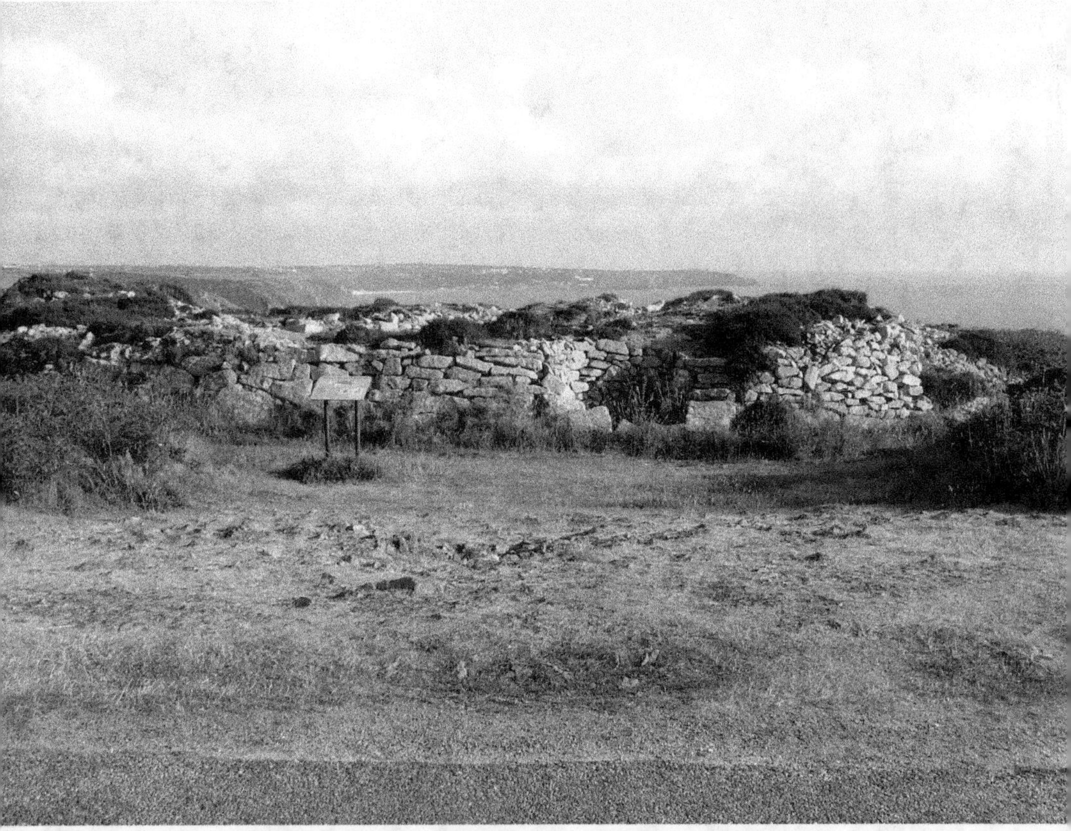

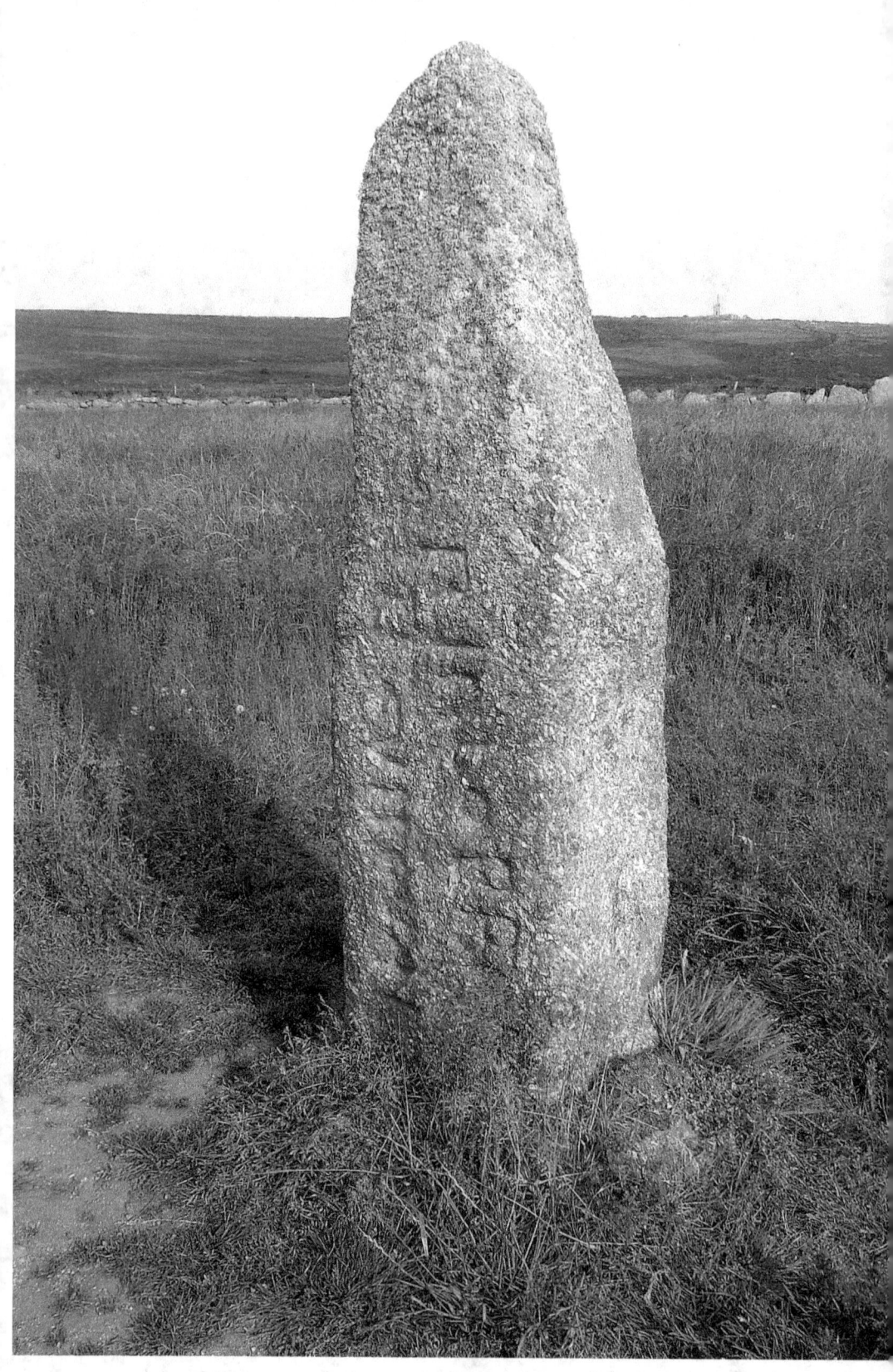

The Mên Scryfa standing stone in West Penwith

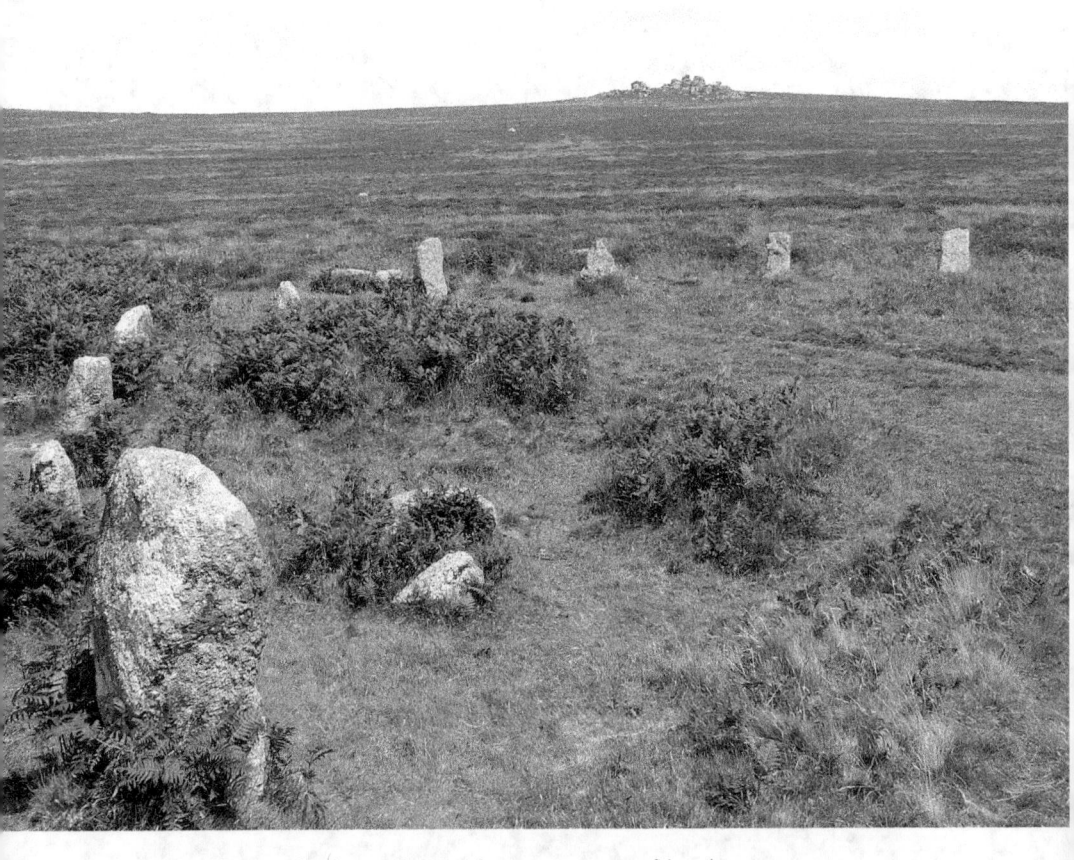

Up on the moorland near St Just, there are many prehistoric monuments,
including Tregeseal stone circle, above.

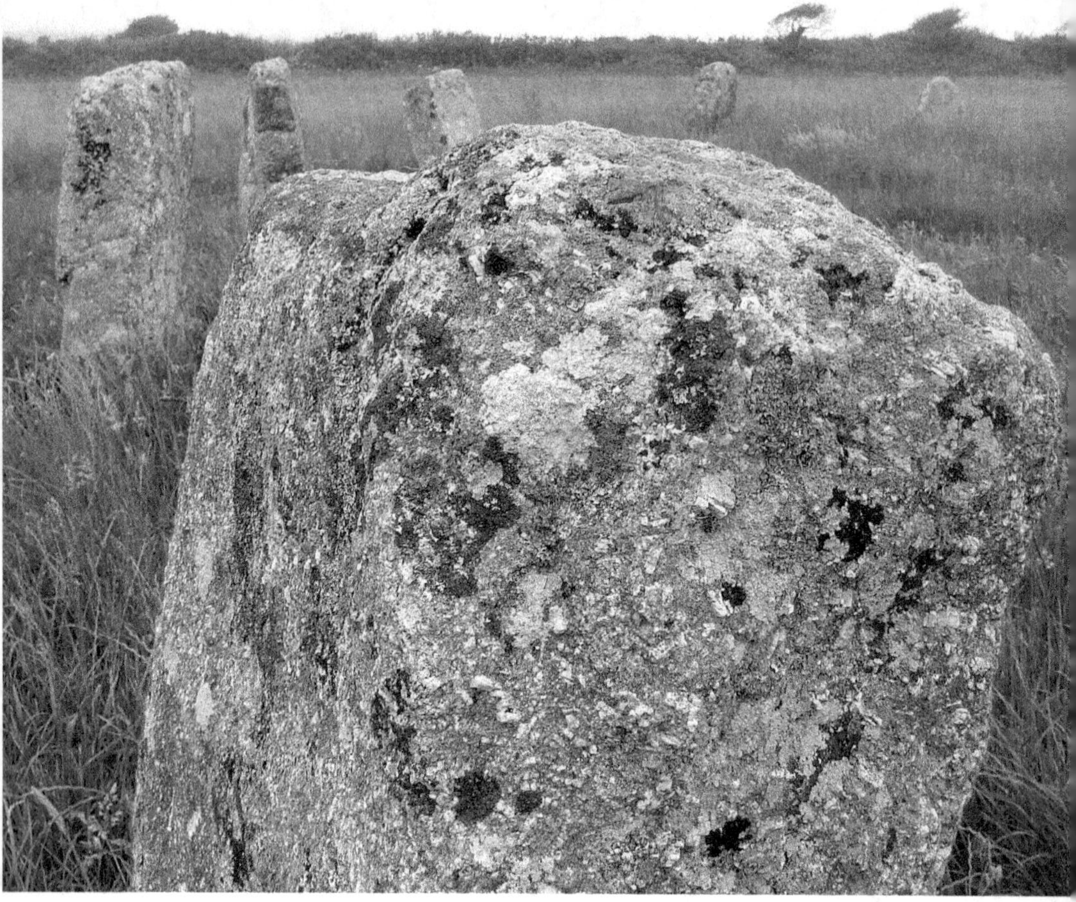

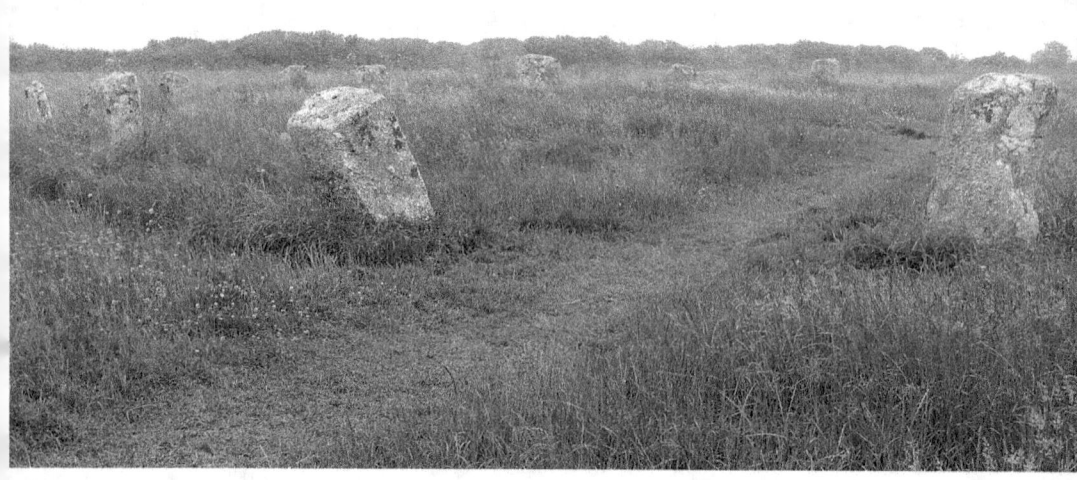

Merry Maidens stone circle, near St Buryan in West Cornwall

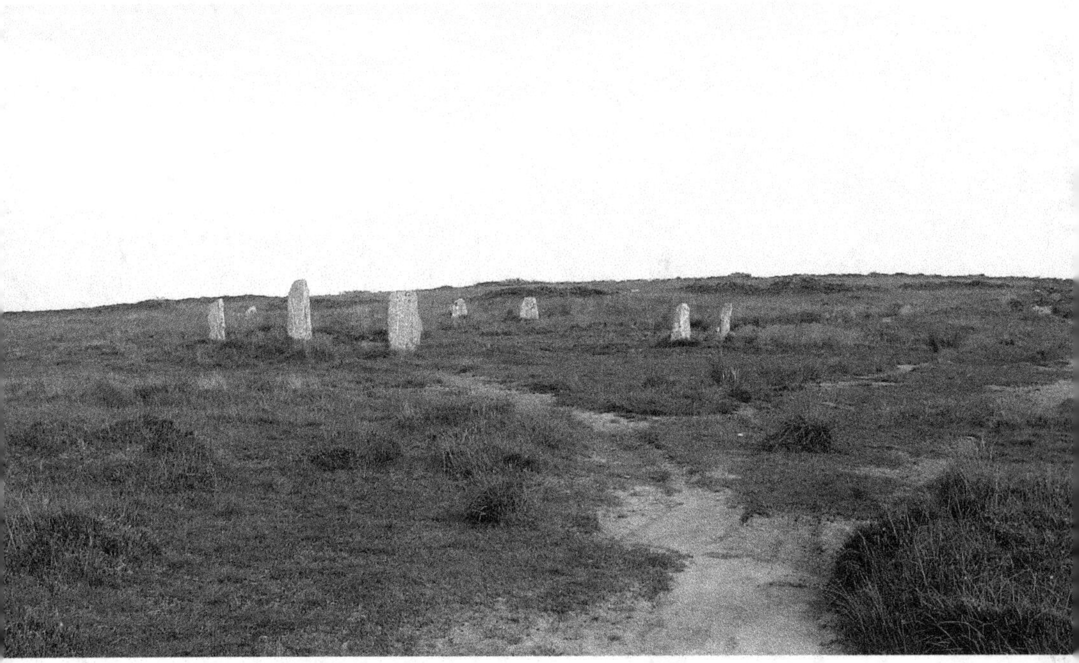

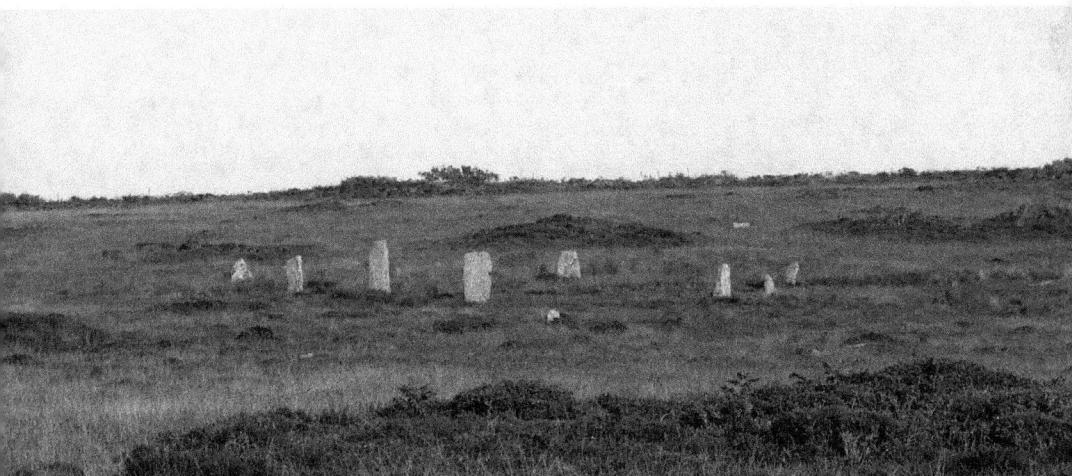

Boskednan Stone Circle (a.k.a. Nine Maidens), in amongst the mines and barrows of the moorland of West Penwith

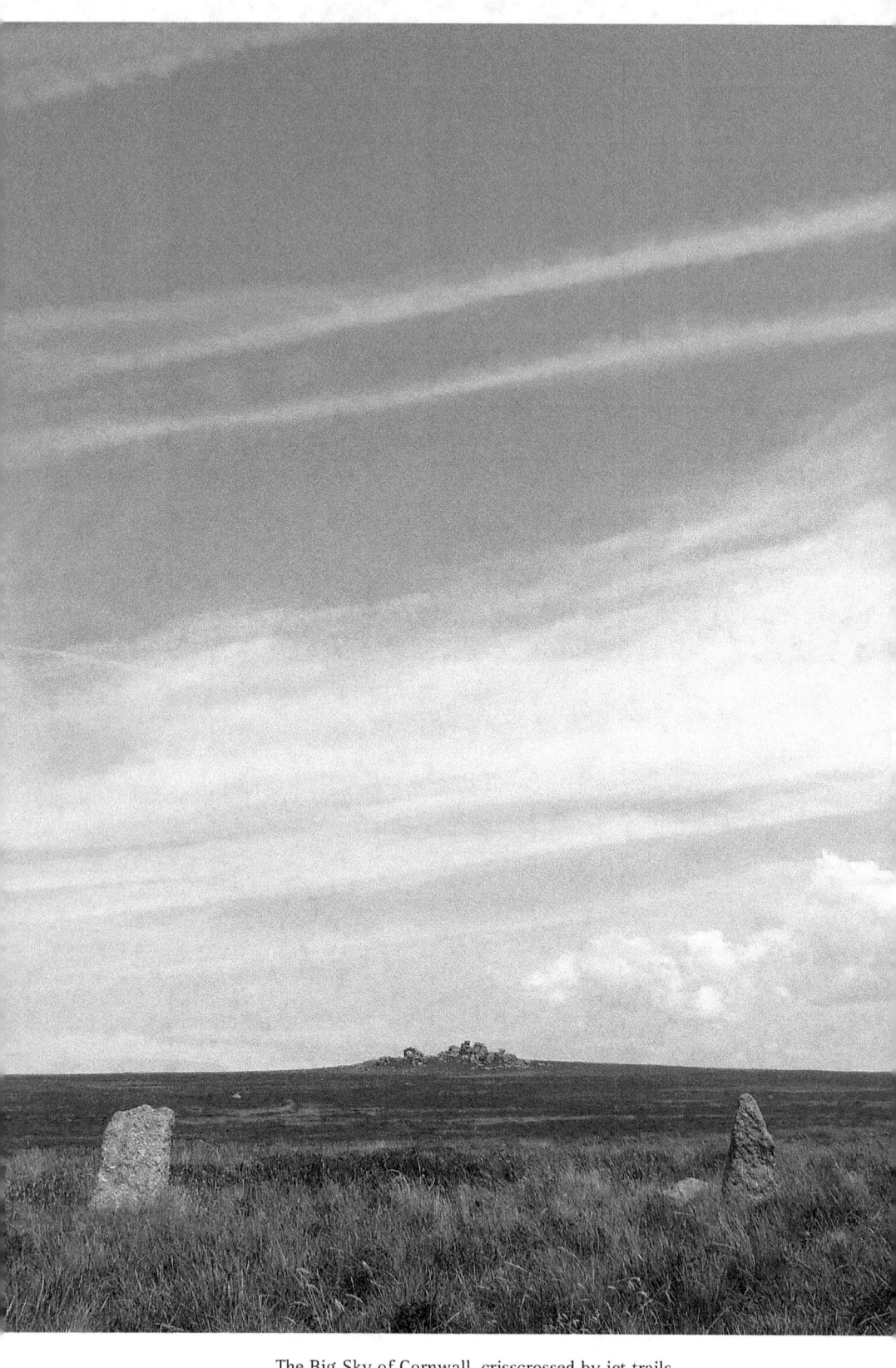

The Big Sky of Cornwall, crisscrossed by jet trails,
at Tregeseal stone circle, looking towards Carn Kenidjack

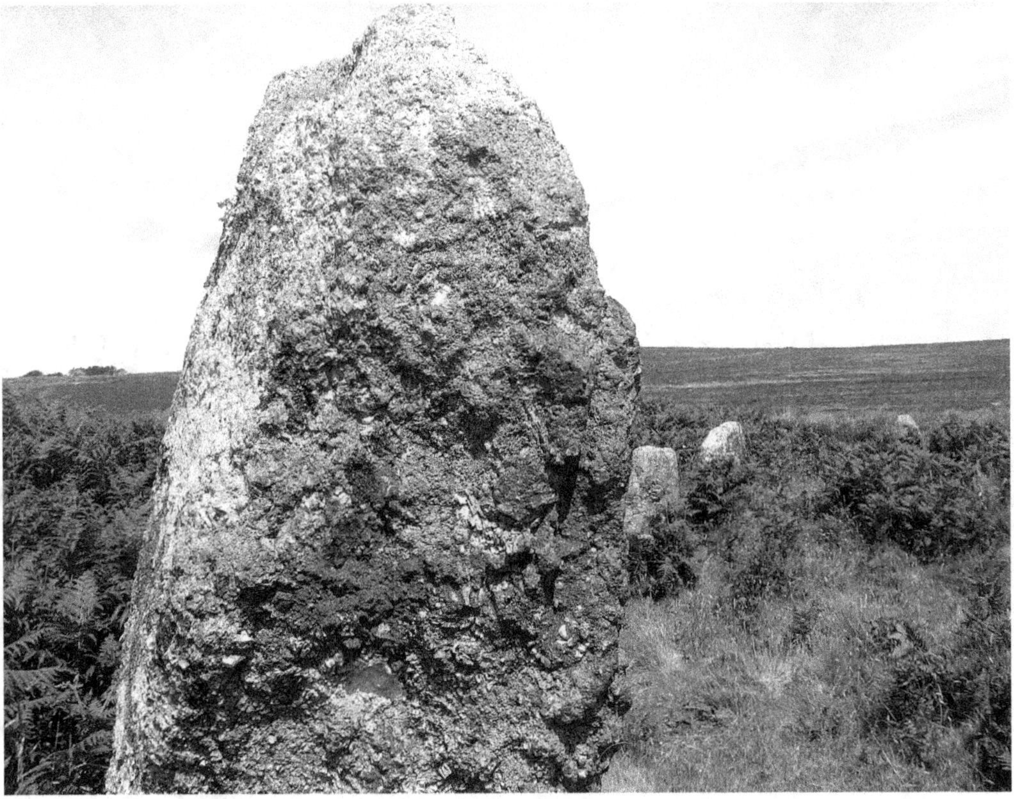

Tregeseal stone circle, above, and nearby, Carn Kenidjack, below.

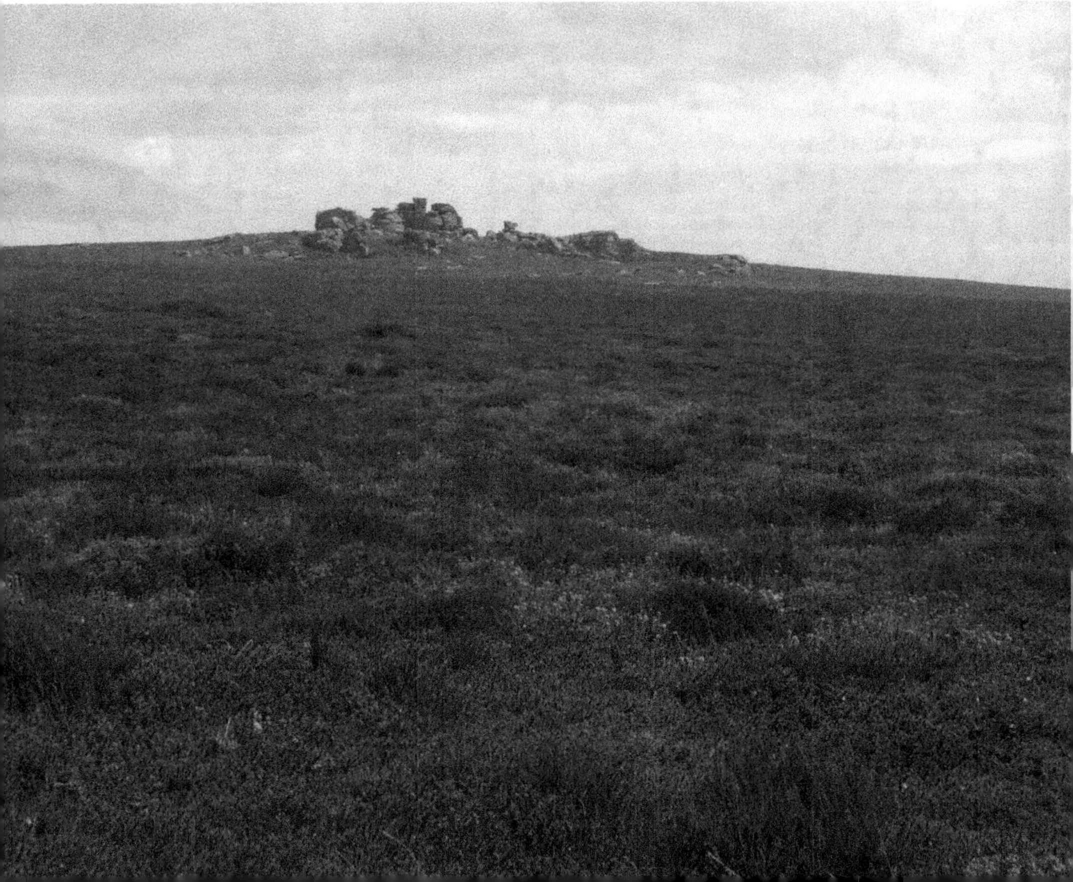

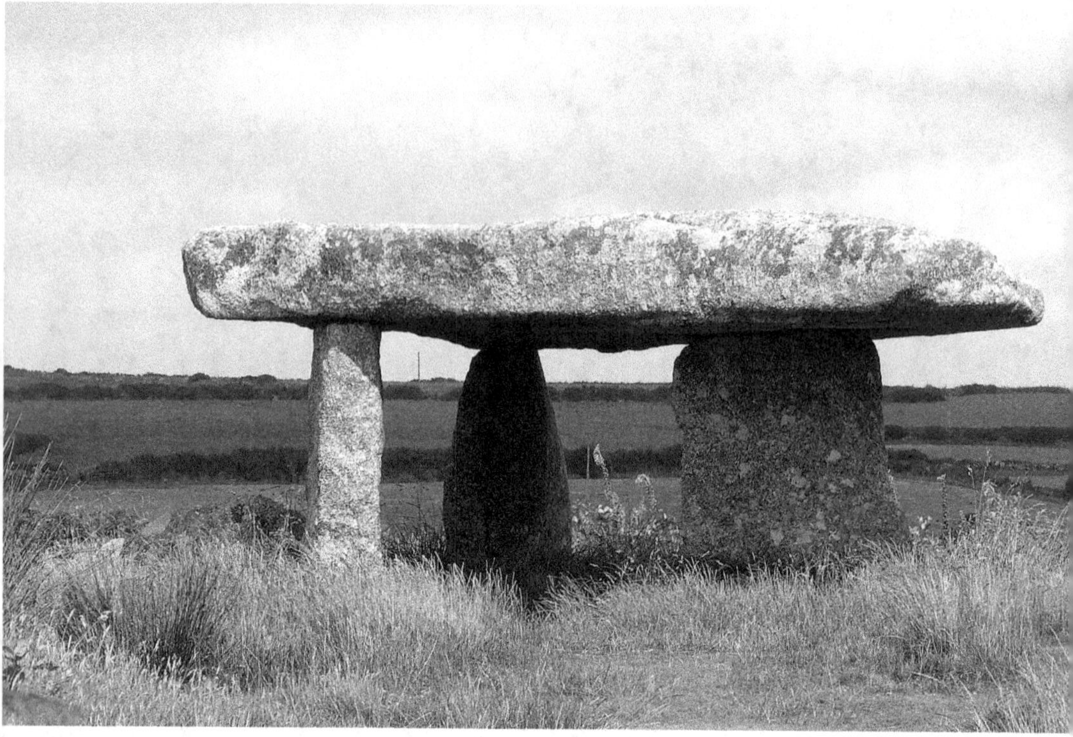

Two of the most famous prehistoric monuments in the West Penwith area:
Lanyon Quoit (above), and Mên-an-Tol, the holed stone (below)

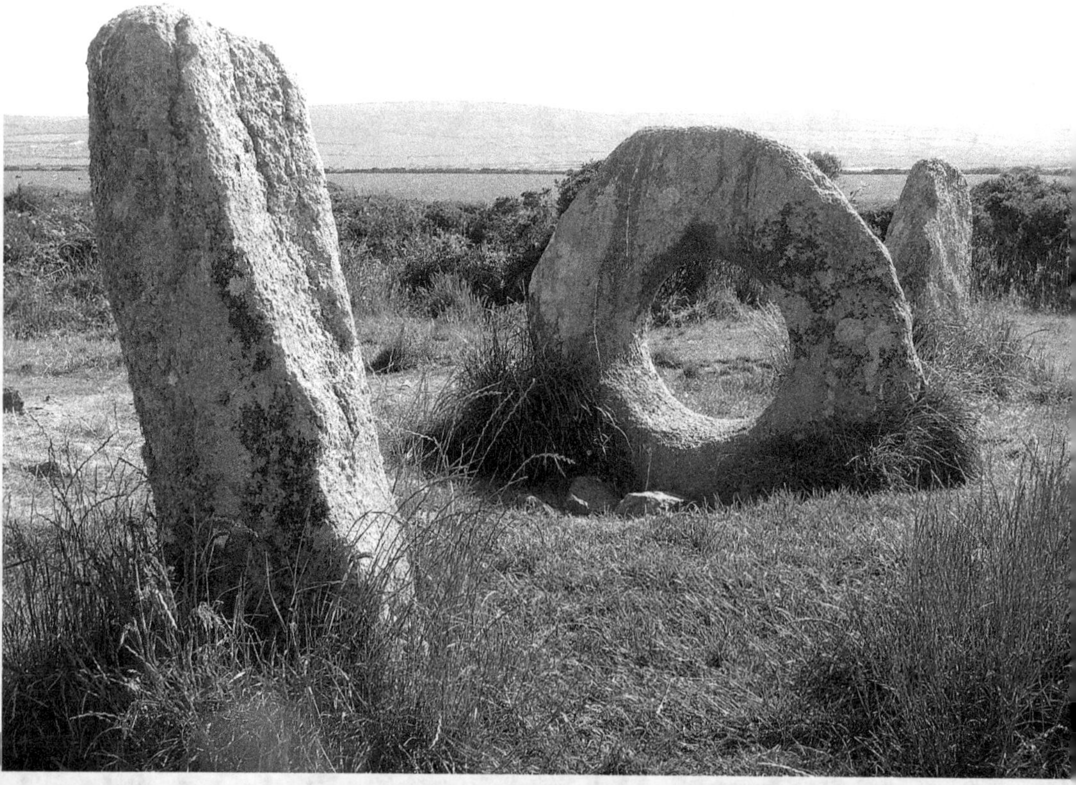

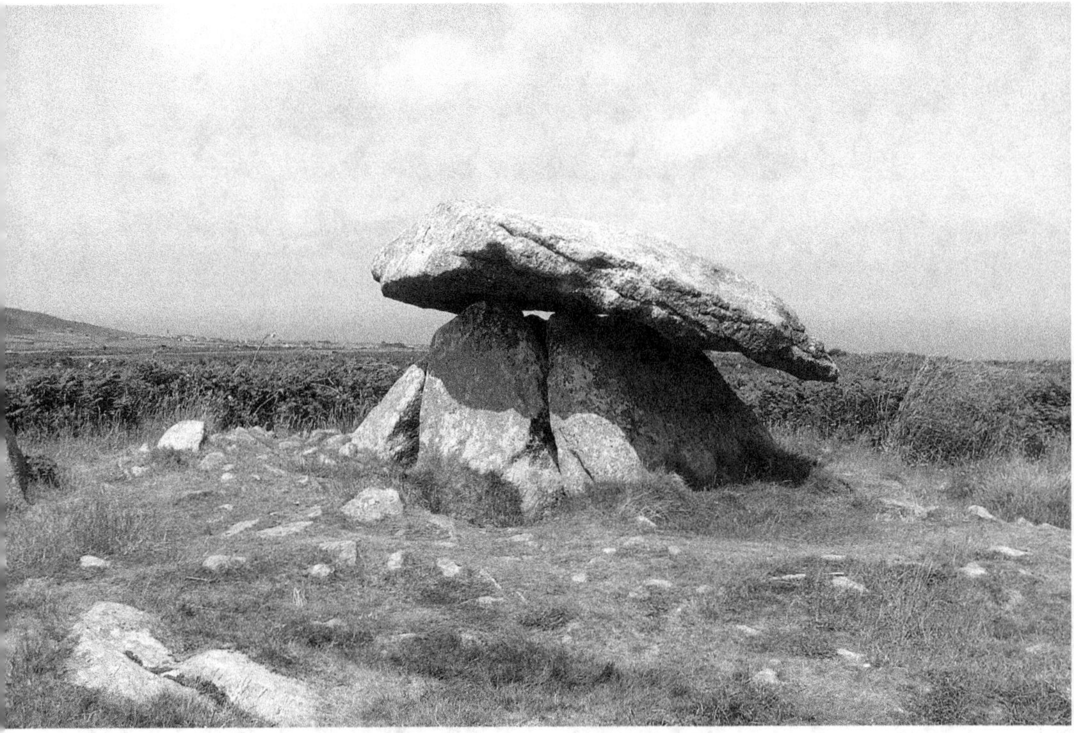

Chûn Quoit, above. Chûn Castle, below.

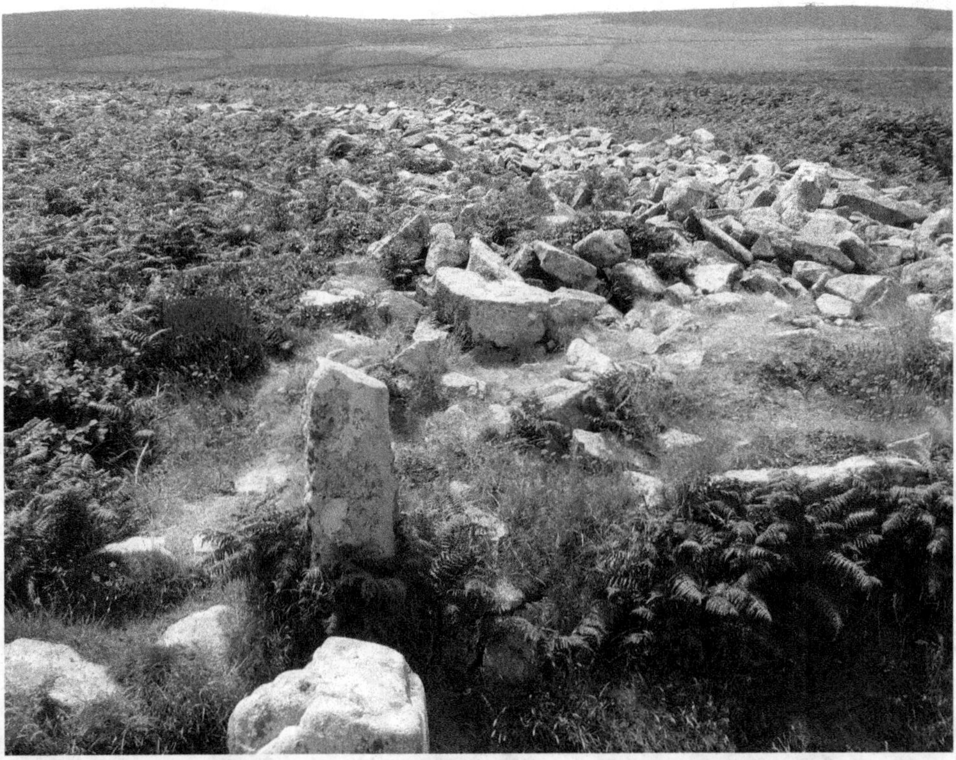

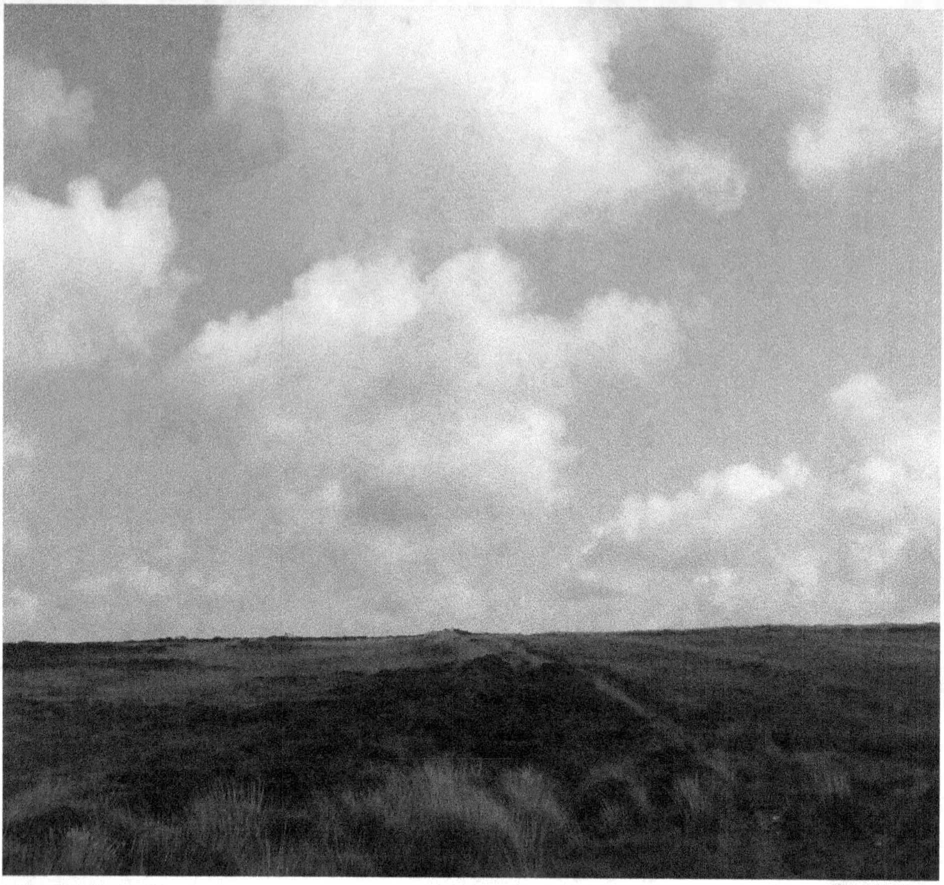

Woon Gumpus, where they do say the Devil will drive you mad
if you dare to dance across the moor widdershins on a Friday at 1.43 p.m.

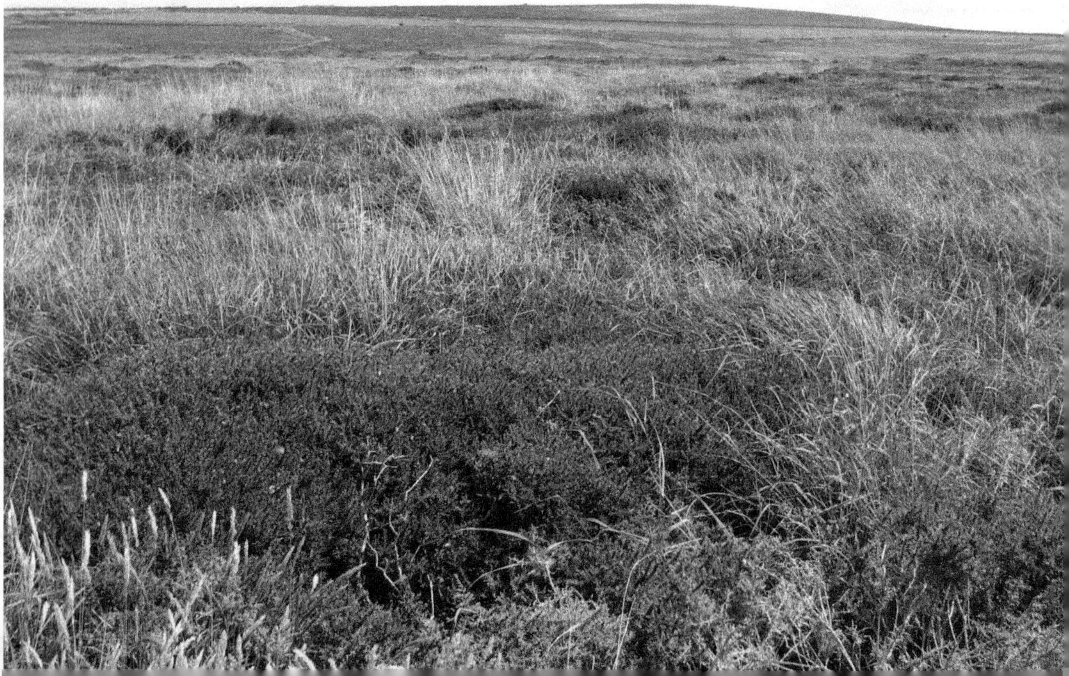

2

CORNWALL

CORNWALL

In cultural stereotyping, Cornwall is the country of surfer dude beach culture of Newquay[9] (subject of the embarrassingly bad 1995 movie *Blue Juice*); coastline (always described as in tourist brochures and travel books 'rugged' or 'rocky'); country houses and gardens; pirates and smugglers; shipwrecks (and ship-wrecking); lighthouses (Virginia Woolf's *To the Lighthouse*); mines; hippies, pagans, New Agers; artists; Cornish cream teas; Cornish ice cream; Land's End; tourism and tourists (tourism remains a hugely important industry in Cornwall. Indeed, art and art galleries in Cornwall can be viewed as just another element in tourism). Then there's the Celtic fringe and the Cornish language, with its nostalgic romanticization of vanished cultures (Kurt

---

[9] Surfing, body boarding, canoeing and wind surfing occurs all along the Northern coast of Cornwall, where the waves are higher and stronger.

Jackson has more recently encouraged the use of the Cornish language by including Cornish translations in his art catalogues, by Craig Weatherhill, as well as noting down Cornish terms in his paintings – words like *mor, kernow* and *porth* recur). Oh, and low wages, un-employment and a depressed economy.[10]

In popular culture, Cornwall means famous holiday destinations: Land's End, above all, and St Ives, Newquay, Falmouth, Fowey, Meva-gissey, Bodmin Moor, the Helford estuary, the Lizard and the Scilly Isles. Not forgetting St Michael's Mount, the Eden project, the Tate Gallery, Tintagel, the Seal Sanctuary, Goonhilly's radio dishes, Culdrose air station, Dobwalls theme park, Cornwall's Crealy Great Adventure Park, Buccaneer Bay, the Blue Reef Aquarium, Poldark Mine, St Austell Brewery Visitor Centre, Pendennis Castle, Wheal Martyn Museum, Lanhydrock, the Minack Theatre, Newquay Zoo, Paradise Park, Jamaica Inn, Glendurgan, Dairyland Farm World, Flambards, Geevor Tin Mine, the National Maritime Museum, etc.

Kurt Jackson does not think of himself as a Cornish painter: he lives in Cornwall, and often paints in Cornwall, and often chooses Cornish subject for his paintings, but that, he admits, doesn't automatically make him a 'Cornish' artist. He wasn't born in Cornwall, and didn't grow up in Cornwall (though he had Cornish connections further back in his family). Kurt Dominc Jackson was born in 1961 in Blandford, a small town in Dorsetshire in Southern England, and grew up in Hert-fordshire (North of Londinium). But as far as the international art trade goes, and contemporary criticism, and for many art lovers, Kurt Jackson *is* a Cornish painter (because that's what they want him to be).

❖

It's St Just, Cape Cornwall, Cot Valley, Kenidjack Valley and that North-Western coastline in Kurt Jackson's paintings, not the much more well-known areas like Newlyn, Penzance or St Ives. Penzance and Newlyn may be only 7 miles away, but in this part of Cornwall, each mile is stretched out, and the differences and changes intensify. West of the Hayle River is different from the rest of Cornwall.

---

10 As Kurt Jackson noted of the fishing and mining industries in Cornwall: 'unfortunately, the local communities have become over-dependent on one or two types of employment so that when one industry declines whole communities are thrown out of work' (P, 18).

Cornwall can feel like an island in many ways (cut off from the rest of England by the River Tamar, for instance, and the distance from the centre). West Penwith is another island inside an island (Cornwall), which's also inside an island (Britain). And, even within West Penwith, there are differences. A mile along a country lane can seem like a different place.[11]

It seems crazy to insist that the area around St Just, Botallack, Pendeen and Trewallard is different from Newlyn, Mousehole and St Buryan, but it is! Just as it is different again from Zennor and Morvah, and different again from St Ives and Caris Bay. The differences are physical, social, maybe even cultural. They can be seen, for instance, in the art of each area.

Critics and visitors may lump all of art in Cornwall together, but cultural and social differences are maintained by artists working in Cornwall between, say, West and East Cornwall. Art on the North-East coast, for instance (at Bude and Boscastle), is not the same as that made in the Lizard. In West Cornwall, the Lizard is different again from West Penwith (Kurt Jackson has made far more art in West Penwith than the Lizard). And the Land's End peninsula is divided up again into areas: St Ives and Newlyn are associated with the famous schools or styles of Cornish painters, for example. If art critics discuss painting in West Cornwall, they always concentrate on St Ives, Newlyn and Penzance. But the areas of St Just, Sennen, Zennor and Porthcurno are different again (and the artists in these small areas can be loyal to their particular corner of Cornwall. For visitors, Penlee House Art Gallery & Museum in Penzance is a good place to start for historical collections of Cornish art, as well as the Tate Gallery at St Ives and the Royal Cornwall Museum in Truro).

There is definitely an aspect of the parochial, small-town or village mentality here, the suspicious view of outsiders (folk from 'up country').[12] So, for the ultra-conservative minded, even a quaint, touristy, former fishing town like St Ives can seem like a sleazy flesh-pot. Or think of it in terms of ever-widening circles: there's your self,

---

11 The population of Cornwall is around half a million; 63,000 in Penwith; 11,000 in St Ives; and 4,690 in St Just.
12 If you visit many areas of South-West Britain, everybody seems over-60, white and grey-haired.

your body, your centre first; beyond that, your home, rooms, and the people close to you; beyond that, the surrounding buildings and land; beyond that, the nearby streets, lanes, fields, trees; beyond that, part of a village or a town; beyond that, the village or city itself; beyond that neighbouring towns. And so on. (The centre in Jackson's art is St Just).

However, Kurt Jackson's art is certainly *international* as well as being very place specific – I don't want to give the impression that his art is parochial, conservative and provincial. But, despite operating in the international art world, I'd say that one of the endearing aspects of Jackson's art is its specificity. It really is an art about *that* particular riverbank or *that* cliff above the ocean.

Kurt Jackson, for instance, has identified himself with the St Just group of artists, and painting in and around St Just is thought to have a different flavour from the art in Penzance, Lamorna or St Ives.[13] We may be talking of distances of only a few miles here, between towns and villages, but the physical aspects are only a small part of the whole picture. Remember that Cornwall has had a high concentration of artists for decades. Remember too that artists have always found it easier to define themselves by what they are *not*, rather than what they *are* (it's for other people to categorize them). Thus, it's easier for artists to say 'we're not *like that'*, to celebrate their differences ('we don't paint in the St Ives manner', say). However, we are also talking about very subtle differences at times, which you'd have to study closely to see at all.

---

13 Kurt Jackson describes St Just as 'very Cornish; very honest and down to earth... a vibrant, active community' (P, 17, 19).

The first impression of St Just-in-Penwith itself and the surrounding area (Botallack, Pendeen and Trewallard) is a place dominated by an industry (mining) that has gone (a town that has seen better days). The housing estates and the look and atmosphere of the town evoke mining. St Just has a pretty church, a bakery (open on Bank Holidays!), a fish and chip shop, two small supermarkets (Spar and Co-op), a newsagents, a village green (Plan-an-Gwarry), a couple of pubs (including the Star), some gift shops, and bus stops behind the square near a car park (free!), and a small library (which was run, Jackson told me, by a couple of witches). Small aircraft buzz overhead continually, flying out from Land's End Aerodrome, a couple of clicks South of St Just (they do scenic flights - highly recommended - they fly out over the ocean).

St Just's fairly typical thus far[14] - but it does also have one or two art galleries, which's very unusual for a British town of this size (the galleries come and go over the years in St Just, like businesses anywhere, but there's usually at least one). Apart from Land's End, St Just has the most Westerly stores in mainland Britain. People in St Just call the town - and Cape Cornwall - the *real* Land's End (years ago, Cape Cornwall was thought to be further West than Land's End). Four miles to the South, Land's End receives far more visitors, but it isn't a particularly appealing place, with its coach parks and gift shops; a really good seaside town is a marvellous experience (Bournemouth, Hastings, Penzance), but Land's End is plasticky and fake, but not in that appealing, tacky way; it's a bourgeois, clinical idea of the vacation experience, a lame resort designed by accountants and lawyers. (Just along the coast path, though, there's an attractive little farm - Carn Greeb. There are hens, ducks, donkeys, pigs, goats, cats, chickens and lambs - it's a little oasis).

Holiday makers and visitors typically pass through St Just on their

14 I would imagine that St Just is hellishly dull if you're a teen looking for action. There's not much to do for teens in St Just: you can't go into the pubs... when it's mizzling nothing's open... and if you haven't got a car you can't get back from the small nightclubs in Penzance or Truro late at night. So the kids hang around the bus shelters, benches and the clocktower, where they drink and laugh at the tourists.

way to St Ives or Land's End, or the beaches of Sennen, Treen and Porthcurno, or maybe the mines of Levant and Geevor[15] which you drive right past on the road to St Ives (St Ives, Penzance and Land's End are easily the biggest draws in this part of Cornwall). So at first sight, St Just-in-Penwith doesn't seem to be a place where tourists might want to stop. St Ives has its holiday parks, its gorgeous back streets, its pier (Smeaton's), its fishing boats and harbour, its many gift shops, its big beaches (the Island, Porthmeor, Porthminster), the Barbara Hepworth Museum and the Tate Gallery, and at the height of the season, it's rammed with people (whereas St Just never feels crowded, even in July and August).

But St Just has a rough-hewn, stony, windblown charm of its own, like a Welsh mining town. There's the sea and the coast, above all, and the moors, the fields, the villages, and the country lanes. But there's also plenty of history and culture in the surrounding area: the prehistoric monuments (stone circles, barrows, quoits, menhirs), the mediæval wells, the churches, the mines. And the art, of course – plenty of art, with an emphasis on landscape and abstraction.

The many prehistoric sites in West Penwith include burial mounds (Ballowall), the Mên-an-Tol holed stone, the quoits or menhirs (Chûn quoit, Mulfra quoit, Lanyon quoit), the prehistoric/ mediæval settlements (Chysauster village, Carn Euny, Bosporthennis), the wells (Madron, Sancreed), the 'fogous' or underground chambers (Euny, Pendeen, Boscaswell, Boleigh), the standing stones (the Pipers, the Blind Fiddler, Mên Scryfa), the stone circles (Tregeseal, Boskednan, Merry Maidens, and one of the great circles in Britain, Boscawen-Ûn stone circle, near St Buryan, an awesome place on a par with Avebury and Stonehenge).

British place names are one of the enduring delights of the British landscape,[16] and West Cornwall doesn't disappoint. Around the coast of St Just-in-Penwith, for instance, you'll find:

---

15 Kurt Jackson showed *The Mining Paintings* at Geevor in 2008.
16 For instance, J.R.R. Tolkien and Joanne Rowling have drawn on British place names extensively in their fantasies *The Lord of the Rings* and the *Harry Potter* books.

*Kenidjack — Letcha — Porth Nanven — Ballowall — Zawn a Bal —
Carn Gloose — Kelynack — Woon Gumpus - Nanquidno Downs —
Botallack*

One of my favourite place names is Crows-an-wra (Witch's Cross).
All of those names, and many more, will be found in the titles or
calligraphy of Kurt Jackson's paintings (they're too good to leave out).
And the names also emphasize that the artworks were made in very
particular places: Gribba Point, for instance, is a few hundred yards
from Maen Dower, but that distance is important.

THE ART SCENE IN CORNWALL

Among painters, artists who worked in Cornwall who have links with
Kurt Jackson's art would include: Wilhelmina Barns-Graham, Terry
Frost, Anthony Frost, Alan Davie, Roger Hilton, Peter Lanyon, Patrick
Heron, Breon O'Casey and Ben Nicholson. There are a bunch of artists
who have often exhibited their work alongside Jackson's or have links
with his art: Gill Watkiss, Bo Hilton, Michael Finn and Jeremy
LeGrice. There's also a bunch of mainly landscape artists who work in
or use West Penwith who are of the same generation as Jackson: Neil
Pinkett, Porl Thompson, Paul Lewin, Robert Jones, Louise McClary, Zoe
Cameron, Laura Wild, Rachel Kantaris, Simon Pooley, Alex Smirnoff,
Richard Nott, Tom Rickman, Bob Vigg, Myles Oxenford, and Paul
Evans.[17]

There are also groups of artists on the Cornish scene who form
artistic dynasties: Peter, Andrew and Matthew Lanyon, Rose, Roger
and Bo Hilton, Bob, Jenny and Zara Devereux, Terry and Anthony
Frost, and so on. The main art school in Cornwall – at Falmouth –

[17] Visiting the New York art galleries in September, 2008, a few painters struck me as
having affinities with Kurt Jackson – Jane Bloodgood-Abrams' golden Hudson River
Valley pictures (at DFN Gallery), Clarence Betleyoun (at Amsterdam Whitney Gallery),
and Eddie Kennedy (at J. Cacciola Gallery).

produces art students who continue to work in Cornwall or use it as subject matter: Jessica Cooper, Jill Chandler, and Robert Jones.

❖

Kurt Jackson wasn't born in Cornwall, but nor were most of the famous Cornish artists in the modern era: Patrick Heron (Leeds), Terry Frost (Leamington Spa), Ben Nicholson (Denham), Roger Hilton (Middlesex), Naum Gabo (Briansk, Russia), Breon O'Casey (London), Alan Davie (Grangemouth), Barbara Hepworth (Wakefield), Wilhelmina Barns-Graham (Fife), etc. Even Alfred Wallis, credited as a key influence in the rise of modern Cornish art, was born in Devonport.

While there has been plenty of art to be found in Cornwall for decades, not all of it is as good as that of Kurt Jackson, Michael Finn, Terry Frost or Barbara Hepworth. Looking round the art galleries and studios in Cornwall, you soon discover which is the really good stuff, and who are the artists worth following. There's a good deal of art in Cornwall which is dull, uninspired work, indistinguishable from the bad crafts, greeting cards, and tourist gifts that surrounds it. Similarly, you rapidly uncover the really interesting art galleries – Avalon, Newlyn, Great Atlantic, Salthouse, Lemon Street, Rainyday, Penwith.

❖

The tradition of painting in Cornwall which Kurt Jackson is part of is fundamentally landscape painting combined with elements of 1910s-1920s Expressionism and mid-20th century abstraction. It's a landscape painting tradition that is essentially modernist, not post-modernist (though, as noted already, it manifests aspects of other artistic styles, including Conceptual art).[18] The chronology of modernism which Jackson's art is steeped in runs up to and includes Abstract Expressionism (in the main).

If one looks at lots of painting and art made in Cornwall over the past century or so, a number of qualities soon emerge: a quasi-abstract, Post-Impressionist approach; loose handling of pigment; plenty of landscapes and seascapes; still-lifes; lots of pottery and pots; and many modest subjects (it's not usually an art of big historical topics, for instance, or a radically political art). All of those elements

---

18 'I see myself as part of the English landscape tradition but I want to go about it in a modern way', Kurt Jackson remarked (P, 20).

can be spotted today on a visit to Penzance, Falmouth or St Ives.

Another visitor to this part of Cornwall was D.H. Lawrence, who famously lived in a cottage at Zennor, not far from where Patrick Heron later lived at Heron's Nest. At Higher Tregerthen near Zennor, the one-up one-down cottage Lawrence and his wife Frieda rented was only £5 ($7.50) per year. The neighbouring house was £16 ($24) a year. The cottages had no running water nor indoor sanitation. This was during the First World War, when the locals were suspicious of the Lawrences, because Frieda was German. It was also the time when regular visitors John Middleton Murry and Katherine Mansfield witnessed some truly amazing and violent arguments between Lorzeno and Frieda.

ART GALLERIES IN CORNWALL

The best of the art galleries in West Cornwall have a particular flavour – they're typically a little roughly hewn, with irregular white-washed walls, uneven stone or wooden floors, and plenty of natural light. The small, low-ceilinged rooms are in old buildings tucked around corners and out-of-the-way alleys. They have small windows, stands of greeting cards and postcards, a rack of artists' prints, and maybe an upstairs gallery reached via rickety wooden stairs. A glimpse of the blue blur of the ocean in between stone cottages. The sound of seagulls and nearby crowds. Or maybe just the wind.

The galleries are more appealing for being constructed in ageing buildings that've had different uses over the years (and they're also part of the socio-economic shift in contemporary British life from the manufacturing and engineering industries to leisure and tourist industries, and Cornwall is very much part of that transformation).

Kurt Jackson has been associated with many of what I regard as the more interesting art galleries in West Cornwall, such as Rainyday

Gallery, New Contemporary Gallery and Wolf At the Door in Penzance; Salthouse Gallery in St Ives (run by the inimitable Bob Devereux); Avalon Art in Marazion; Beside the Wave in Falmouth; and the Lemon Street in Truro. St Just has had its own galleries, which include the Great Atlantic Map Works, Navigator Contemporary Arts (now Over the Moon), Nancherrow Studio, Tregeseal Gallery, Blackbird Barn Studios and Gallery, Old Sunday School and Vision and Journeys (undoubtedly the most significant presence in recent years in St Just is the Great Atlantic Map Works, run by Michael Jay).[19] Some of my favourite galleries were the little ones in out-of-the-way places, such as Ian Cooke's printmaking studio near the Mên-an-Tol (Cooke produced two of the finest books on prehistoric monuments in Cornwall – *Journey To the Stones: Mermaid To Merrymaid* and *Mother and Sun*),[20] or the one in the old school at Kelynack.

Sadly, some of these galleries have gone the way of all things (Wolf At the Door, Visions and Journeys, etc). The art world is a cutthroat business – but only to the same degree that all business, all capitalism is. There are a number of guides to local art galleries and craft centres available, and a good one is produced by Martin Val Baker.

Kurt Jackson has had one-man shows and contributed to group shows at many of the above galleries. From the late 1990s Jackson was showing in London's Cork Street (at David Messum) on a regular (annual) basis (until they parted ways; Jackson has also left his Cornish dealer, Lemon Street. He is now with Redfern in London).

Kurt and Caroline Jackson have their own limited company (called Kurt and Caroline Jackson Ltd),[21] thru which they trade in merchandizing spun off Jackson's art (such as jewellery, prints, postcards,

19 These galleries come and go: in 2004, St Just had Great Atlantic Map Works, Just Fine Art, Just Cornish, the Nancherrow Studio, Navigator, Bob Vigg's Tregeseal Gallery, and , among others.
In 2013, the art galleries included: Tregeseal Gallery, Tremorran Gallery, the Stone Age Studio, Turn of the Tide, the Purple House Gallery, the Artisan, Bank Square Gallery, St Just Art, Morten Gallery, Helen Jay, and Cape Cornwall Studio.
20 I. Cooke: *Journey To the Stones: Mermaid to Merrymaid*, Mên-an-Tol Studio, Penzance, 1987, *Mother and Son*, Mên-an-Tol Studio, Penzance, 1994. The best authority on prehistoric monuments in Britain is probably Aubrey Burl: *Rings of Stone: The Stone Circles of Britain and Ireland*, Francis Lincoln, London, 1979. Craig Weatherhill, who has translated some of Jackson's texts for his catalogues, produced a good guide to West Penwith's prehistory in *Belerion*, Alison Hodge, Penzance, 1981.
21 You can examine the public financial records of the company online. It was founded in 2005 in Penzance by Dr Kurt Dominic Jackson and Mrs Caroline Beata Jane Jackson.

greetings cards, etc). The company is planning to open a gallery in St Just which will sell some of Jackson's and associated works.

Kurt Jackson's work has also been shown in many other galleries in the West Country, such as Plymouth (1988, 1990, 1993), Royal West of England Academy, Bristol (1995, 2000-05), Bath (1989, 2004), Handle House, Devizes (1996), Taunton (1986), Exeter (2004), and North Cornwall Museum, Camelford (1986-1995). Jackson has also shown at many regional galleries in the U.K., such as Hastings, Rye (1994), Ashbourne, Derbyshire (1994, 1995, 1997), Doncaster (1997), Cambridge (1997), Harrogate (2001), Edinburgh (2002, 2004, 2006), and Stow on the Wold (1998).

The most prestigious gallery in Cornwall is of course Tate St Ives, which has certainly boosted art in Cornwall in numerous ways.[22] Before the Tate opened in June, 1993, two of the key galleries on the Western peninsula I reckon were the Newlyn Art Gallery and Penwith Gallery[23] (founded in 1949). Kurt Jackson had his first show (*Porth*) at Newlyn Art Gallery in early 2004.

There have long been plenty of other places to see art in West Cornwall prior to the Tate: the Barbara Hepworth Museum and Garden is probably the stand-out, a setting and display in the heart of St Ives that can hold its own against any other major artist's home museum.[24] Other important sites on the art trail in St Ives include the Leach Pottery, the artists' studios along the Backs, and Penwith Gallery. Outside St Ives, good public spaces in the region include Newlyn Art Gallery, the new Exchange in Penzance (tucked away in a back street – yet again!), Falmouth Art Gallery and the Royal Cornwall Museum in Truro.

Although Cornwall has an extraordinary history of artists working in the area, not all of the art on show in the county is first-rate. There

22 Kurt Jackson has acknowledged the importance of the Tate in Cornwall – new galleries have sprung up, the economy of St Ives has been boosted by the new visitors, art's been taken more seriously by locals, and it's helped artists to get exhibitions (P, 19).
23 If you're disappointed by a visit to the Tate Gallery in St Ives (which seems to promise more than it delivers), go to Penwith Gallery, which features some important Cornish artists.
24 Barbara Hepworth was inspired by the landscape of Cornwall, and said that the natural setting was 'the most tremendously inspiring one to me'. Driving around Cornwall, Hepworth found that it was her personal (bodily) response to particular landscapes that mattered (quoted in W. Forma, *Five British Sculptors*, New York, 1965).

is plenty of what I would class as second-rate or third-rate or tenth-rate or just plain dull art on display, plenty that's twee, bland, and irredeemably conservative. That's partly to do with the way the whole art world is set up: art galleries and dealers prefer art that sells, art that people want to buy. That means the art is going to tend to be inoffensive, familiar, safe. (Why? Because that's how the whole of Western culture is).

On a visit to Cornwall in 2013, the art appeared depressingly bland, wholly geared towards tourism and decoration – pretty but spineless, art eviscerated of all feeling and vitality.

Kurt Jackson doesn't like to associate his art with an art that sees the landscape as 'twee' or 'quaint'. Of course: every eager art student, every artist who takes their work seriously, is keen to distance themselves from anything 'twee' or 'quaint'.

One way to spot Z-rate painting is the amount of *light* it contains or gives out. The French Impressionists have been celebrated as painting light, as capturing the fleeting play of light on water, and so on. I don't agree. Many Impressionist paintings to me are like blank walls rather than windows. The light is dull and opaque. Compare the French Impressionists, for example, with the Early Netherlandish masters – Rogier van der Weyden, Jan van Eyck, Hans Memling, Quentin Massys, Petrus Christus *et al*, and you'll see what exquisite, jewel-like, translucent paintings they created. Thankfully, Kurt Jackson's paintings do give off and transmit light (otherwise we might not be talking about them).

There are plenty of studies of painters and painting in Cornwall, so I won't add to them here. There is one intriguing visit of an artist to Cornwall and the Cornish art scene which deserves a little more attention: the American abstract painter Mark Rothko (1903-70), the manic depressive's favourite artist (along with Vincent van Gogh and Ad Reinhardt). Rothko came over to England in Summer, 1958 and stayed at Little Parc Owles, with Peter Lanyon and his family. Rothko was looking for a suitable chapel which he could decorate. Rothko met some of the St Ives luminaries, such as Patrick Heron. To Linden Travers, the wife of James Holman, chairman of a local engineering firm, Rothko confessed, 'painting is such agony' (M. Whybrow, 150).[25]

The Cornish seaside town of St Ives has a special place in British art history. Taken together, in one broad sweep, the number of talented artists who worked in St Ives and West Penwith at one time or another is quite extraordinary, considering the tiny scale of the place. St Ives is the site – the whole town is a studio space – of a host of celebrated figures in British art: Barbara Hepworth, Ben Nicholson, Patrick Heron, Francis Bacon, Bernard Leach, Alfred Wallis, Terry Frost, Peter Lanyon, Adrian Stokes, Wilhelmina Barns-Graham, David Bomberg, Alan Davie, Roger Hilton, Bryan Wynter and Breon O'Casey.

The roll-call of distinguished visitors to St Ives included Victor Pasmore, Naum Gabo, Laura Knight, and Rothko's fellow New Yorkers, Helen Frankenthaler, Mark Tobey and Larry Rivers. It is odd to think of the big names of the art world descending on the sleepy Cornish harbour town. Somehow, the words New York City, Abstract Expressionism and provincial St Ives seem incongruous.

Yet, when one looks closer at the St Ives art scene, one sees an enormous love of landscape, symbolism, the *avant garde*, Surrealism

---

25 Peter Fuller wrote in his essay "St Ives" of Lanyon, regarded as one of Britain's best postwar abstract artists: 'Lanyon was also developing a reputation in New York. He got to know Mark Rothko well and brought the American over to St Ives in 1958... We need not be surprised if Lanyon, the figurative painter of the vanishing field, finds a soul mate in Rothko, the great abstract painter of the absent figure. Both were struggling for that 'Higher Symbolism' in painting, and both, in different ways, were aware of its virtual impossibility – of the risk of losing everything, including themselves, in the void of sensation and 'pure' abstraction.' (*Artscribe*, 51, June 1985, 110)

and, importantly, abstraction. Painters such as Patrick Heron, Peter Lanyon, Alan Davie, Wilhelmina Barns-Graham and Terry Frost were clearly influenced by American postwar art. The *New American Painting* show at the Tate Gallery in 1956 had inspired and encouraged Lanyon, Heron *et al.*

The surrounding landscape of West Penwith is deeply influential on St Ives painting: the moors, the purple heather, the windswept beaches, the menhirs and stone circles, the little cottages and the (now) disused mineshafts and engine houses.[26] Mark Rothko would have been sympathetic to this landscape, and to the landscape painting tradition, for it was very often already abstract. This Cornish part of the planet is a world away from the grime and noise and skyscraper canyons of Gotham. It's understandable that an artist who sought solitude like Rothko should come to St Ives.

The wonderful studios of St Ives – one of the main attractions of the place – are a world away from the vast, high-ceilinged, white-washed lofts and studios of New York City. One can still wander into some of the Porthmeor Studios, and they are still magical spaces. In New York's studios one looks out onto a grid of busy streets, yellow taxis, fire escapes, giant billboards and enormous skyscrapers in and around Broadway and 42nd Street, Union Square, the Village and the Bowery. In St Ives, the sea dominates the windows of the studios which overlook the beach. The sea is always there – it appears in many of the St Ives artists' works.

The abstract landscape tradition in painting, developed so powerfully by Mark Rothko, Barnett Newman, Clyfford Still, Robert Motherwell and Morris Louis is still going strong in Cornwall. One only has to visit contemporary galleries such as Salthouse Gallery, Penwith Gallery, Great Atlantic Map Works, Avalon and Newlyn Art Gallery, to see that the influence of Rothko and Abstract Expressionism is alive and well.

It is significant that Mark Rothko has been regarded as much more

26 Kurt Jackson remarked that he tried to avoid putting the disused chimneys and mine workings into his paintings, because they were such a cliché of the area. But then he gave in, after painting in the mine at South Crofty, accepting that the chimneys and engine houses were part of Cornwall.
Jackson also consciously avoids: the Brisons, famous tourist spots, green for the sea and straight lines.

important by art critics around the world than almost any of the St Ives artists (such as Peter Lanyon, Patrick Heron, Terry Frost, Anke Petersen, Ben Nicholson, John Wells, Roger Hilton, Breon O'Casey, and Anthony Benjamin). But then, very few postwar British artists have achieved the kind of fame Rothko, Jasper Johns, Andy Warhol and Willem de Kooning have (one thinks of David Hockney, Peter Blake and Francis Bacon). Furthermore, there isn't an abstract painter in 20th century Britain who has been as widely celebrated as Mark Rothko.

POETRY IN CORNWALL

Be not afeard: the isle is full of noises,
Sounds and sweet airs, that give delight and hurt not.

William Shakespeare, *The Tempest* (3.2.147)

There is a long tradition of poetry in Cornwall, but I am going to introduce two poets in particular (I've published their work). One is the U.S. writer Ursula Le Guin and the other is the Cornish poet Peter Redgrove. These poets offer the flavour of Cornwall in verse, and their poems can be seen as poetic links to Kurt Jackson's paintings.

Ursula Le Guin (b. 1929) – for my money the greatest fantasy writer alive, and one of the finest writers in the world – found the Isles of Scilly inspiring. Her marvellous *Earthsea* books drew on the Scillies as well as the Greek archipelago, for the creation of the magical world of islands, Earthsea. There isn't a better evocation of a life lived on islands and surrounded by islands than the *Earthsea* books, a life of boats and tides and journeys between islands, and always dominated by the ever-changing weather. Not only does Le Guin depict a fantasy world as rich and inspiring as any of the famous fantasy realms in the history of literature, she also provides an exploration of philosophical and spiritual issues as profound as any writer you care to mention. And her writing style is lyrical and poetic.

Ursula Le Guin's 1975 book of poetry about a visit to Cornwall (which I have re-published)[27] is a pæan to this particular corner of Britain. This is the first part of Le Guin's poem 'Chûn' (it's too long a poem to quote in full):

> The first day to the high place of Chûn.
> The road goes low between walls
> of spark-strown granite, dry-laid
> by those who cleared the little fields,
> and kept up since, for maybe eighty generations:
> heavy boulders earthset as the base,
> smaller rocks set close and vertical.
> Gorse breaks gold from roots among the rocks.
> The road stinks, till we get past
> a farmer turning muck on his high field.
> The farmyard drive's all liquid mud. Then no road,
> only a grass track up the hill
> and up, and wind a bit, and all the while the land
> rising in long green swells wave-netted by the walls
> that mark the oldest fields in England,
> and up, onto the land into the wind,
> until we realise that this shallow ditch
> between rockheaps and gorse and heather clumps
> is the outer ring, and we have come to Chûn.

Peter Redgrove (1932-2003) is my favourite among the more recent Cornish poets. Like most of the famous Cornish artists, Redgrove wasn't born in Cornwall, but he became deeply associated with it. Cornwall is crucial in Redgrove's poetic world. It is the Cornwall of constantly changing weather, of clouds and storms and bees and orchards and estuaries and mud-flats and mines and stone walls and granite and megaliths and dunes and, of course, the sea, always the sea, on all sides. Redgrove calls it 'the dreaming sea', in so many poems, and of course it is the restless human unconscious (and it feeds his poetry endlessly).

Peter Redgrove is one of Cornwall's very greatest artists, and one could pick hundreds of poems to illustrate how Redgrove used Cornwall, turning it into a magical, nourishing place. There are poems

---

27 U. Le Guin, *Walking In Cornwall*, Crescent Moon, 2008/ 12/ 13.

about alchemical honeymoons in Penzance, many poems about Redgrove's (adopted) home-town of Falmouth, with its docks, boats, and deep estuary (Redgrove taught at the art college for many years), or the witch museum at Boscastle, or the mines (Poldark) at Helston, or the dunes at Perranporth, or the gardens of Tresco and Glendurgan.

Here are some extracts taken from the two books of Peter Redgrove's poesie that I publish: *The Best of Peter Redgrove's Poetry* and *Sex-Magic-Poetry-Cornwall: A Flood of Poems*. The first is 'Sunlight, Moonlight, Stonelight', a poem about the Scilly Isles, a place very dear to Redgrove – as it is to Kurt Jackson:

Sunlight, Moonlight, Stonelight

A heath of turf that bows to the sea at night,
A webwork of sunshine in which the islands are caught;
A black cliff still as a sleeping medium throws out its white cloud-ghost
Miles into the air. The sea contains more lights
Than the sky does, by millions, in fractured waves.

Smaller ghosts are raised on the low rocks
By the continual deaths of the waves
On a beach of stone tied deeply with streams of erosion,
With iron clamps of shadow. Doorways
Open a crack in the stone. There is light within,
But not the kind of light we can see with.
Limpets crawl to bask in it there, the mussels jostle
The barnacles. The sea breaks casks
Of white light that searches and mingles
Into the blacklight cracks of the stone. The light of the sea
Chalked on stone coasts by a stone moon,
By the waves of a stone moon,
The rolling casks full of white spume

Is a reasoning, active light; the light of the stone.

Ponders only one image, that of stone,
Which is presence more than image,
A back-shock and a spindrift cuff, or high and dry
In its massif, voiding a sky-clambering ghost,
Or pelvis of itself, throne of its own foetus,
Squeezed by the tide weeping an electrical note.
The water becomes black and will not send back any images.

A star touches the water, the whole sea
Becomes a cog of tines, a clock of dancing cogs, then the faint-gold

Touch of the star goes and the sea
Is a restless liquid full of self-lighted stones.

The second extract is from 'Round Pylons', another sea poem, which I've chosen because it has a painterly image of the sea hanging out portraits in the hedges, which links to Kurt Jackson's art:

The sheeted sea coming ashore
And hanging its pictures up in the hedges,
Its unsalted portraits,

The surface of the sea doubling
As it opens into sleep,
A source among white sources, cresting.

The third extract is from *An Alchemical Journal* (a.k.a. *In the Esplumeor*), a series of prose poems which abound in Cornish references. It's about one of the mines of Cornwall, the Poldark Mine:[28] Peter Redgrove was acutely conscious of what lay *underneath* the Cornish landscape – not just the many mines, but the minerals and stones embedded in the granite, and the immense energies flowing through the rock (Redgrove was particularly fond of limestone caves that had been hollowed out by water).

Under the black light, mother and daughter, in Poldark Mine, near Helston, the room lined with shelves full of the crystalline minerals bathed in ultra-violet, shining their unnamed colours, like solid fireworks slowly exploding, the mother and daughter, the faces black but the radiant white calcite of the teeth luminous as the million year lump of calcite aglow beside them, the light's tunes played on the rocks, the nails bright in the black hands like night reaching out of the bluely-luminous ocean-foaming sleeves.

---

28 You can go underground in the Poldark Mine; most mines are only open on the surface.

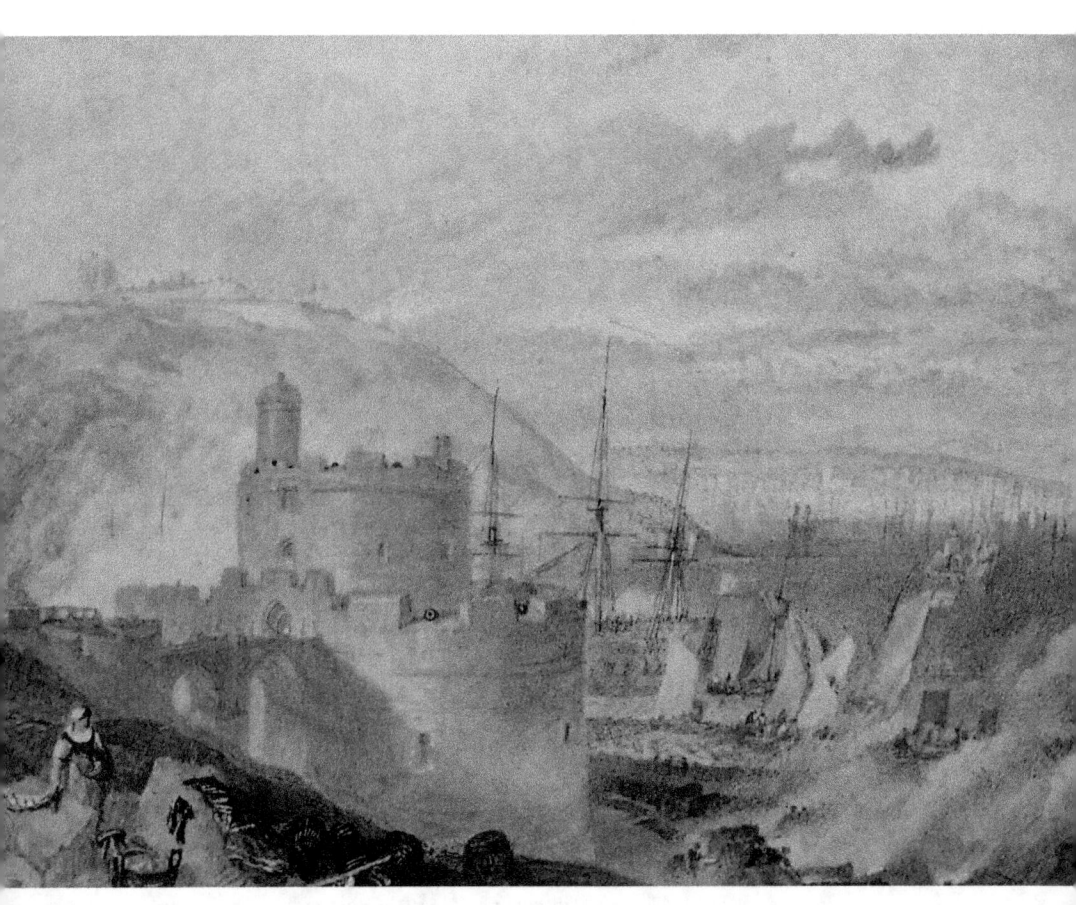

J.M.W. Turner, *Falmouth*, c. 1825, private collection

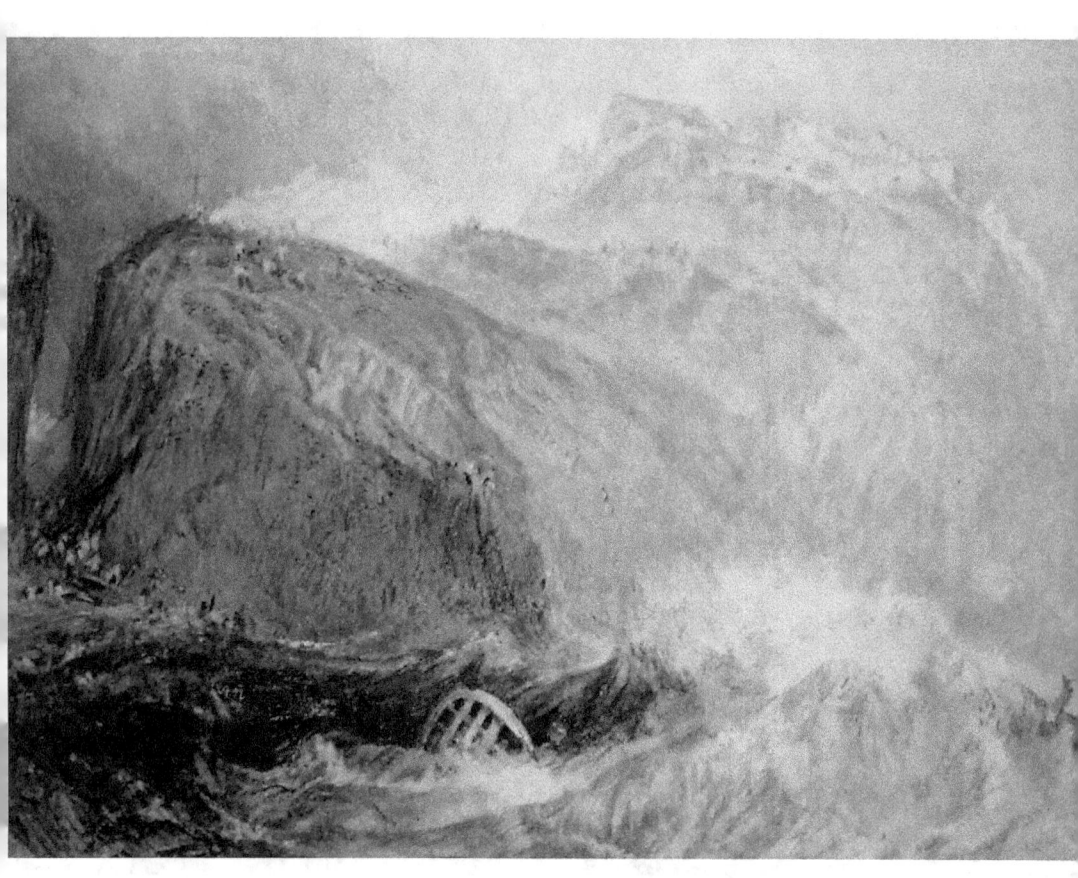

J.M.W. Turner, *Tintagel Castle*, 1815, Boston

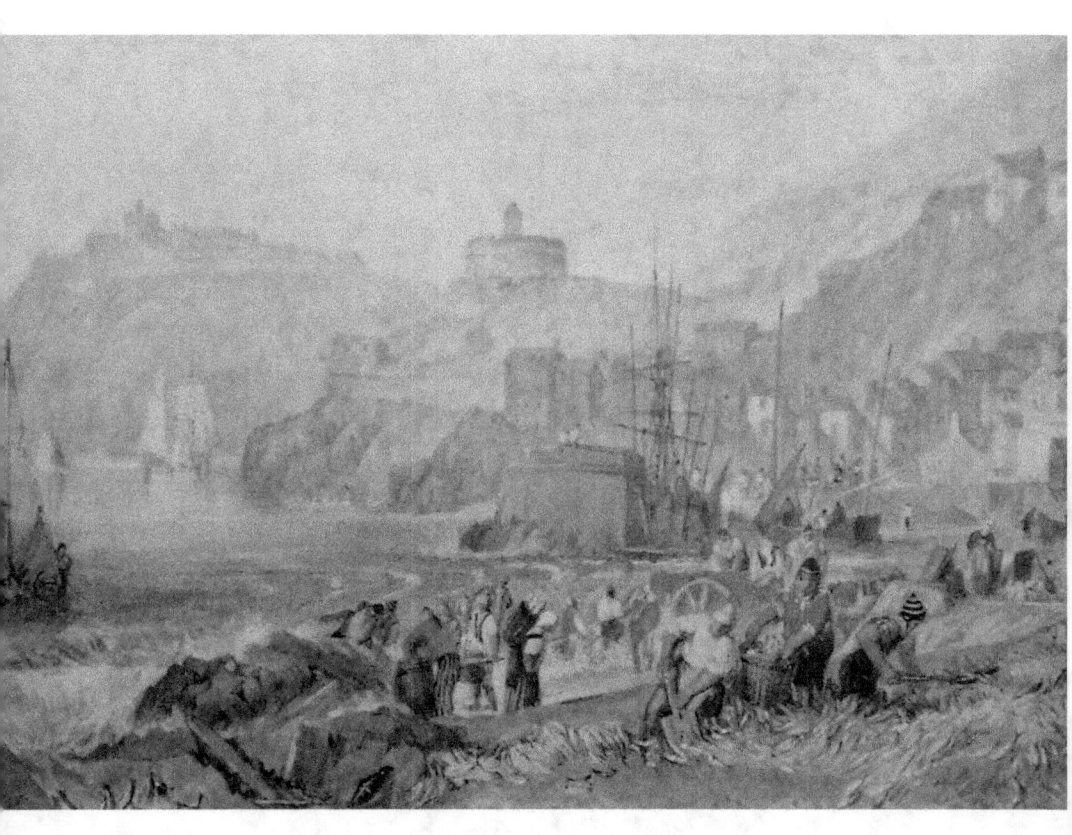

J.M.W. Turner, *St Mawes Castle*, private collection

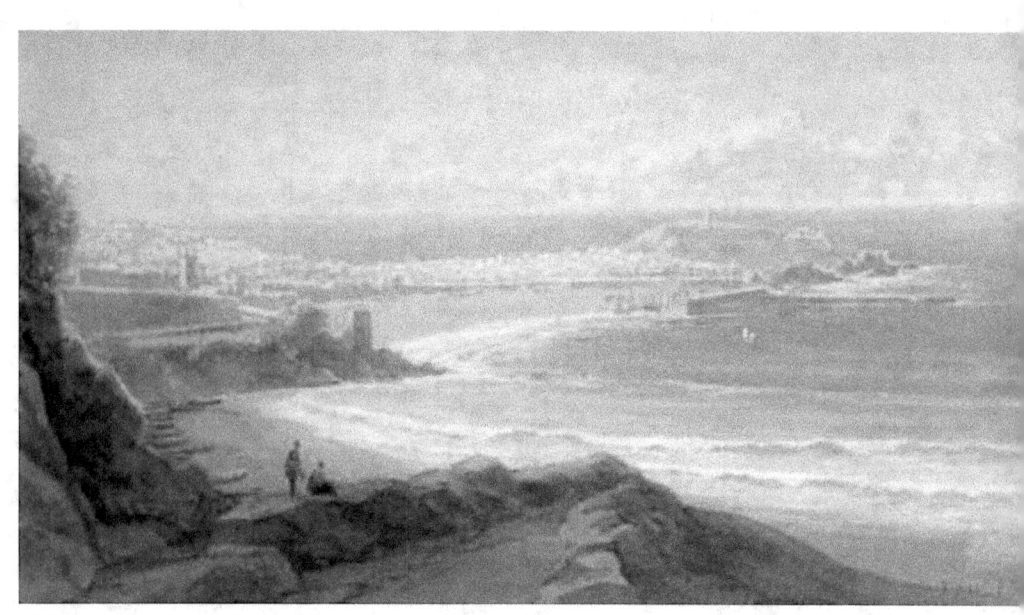

Thomas Hart, *St Ives*, 1870s, private collection

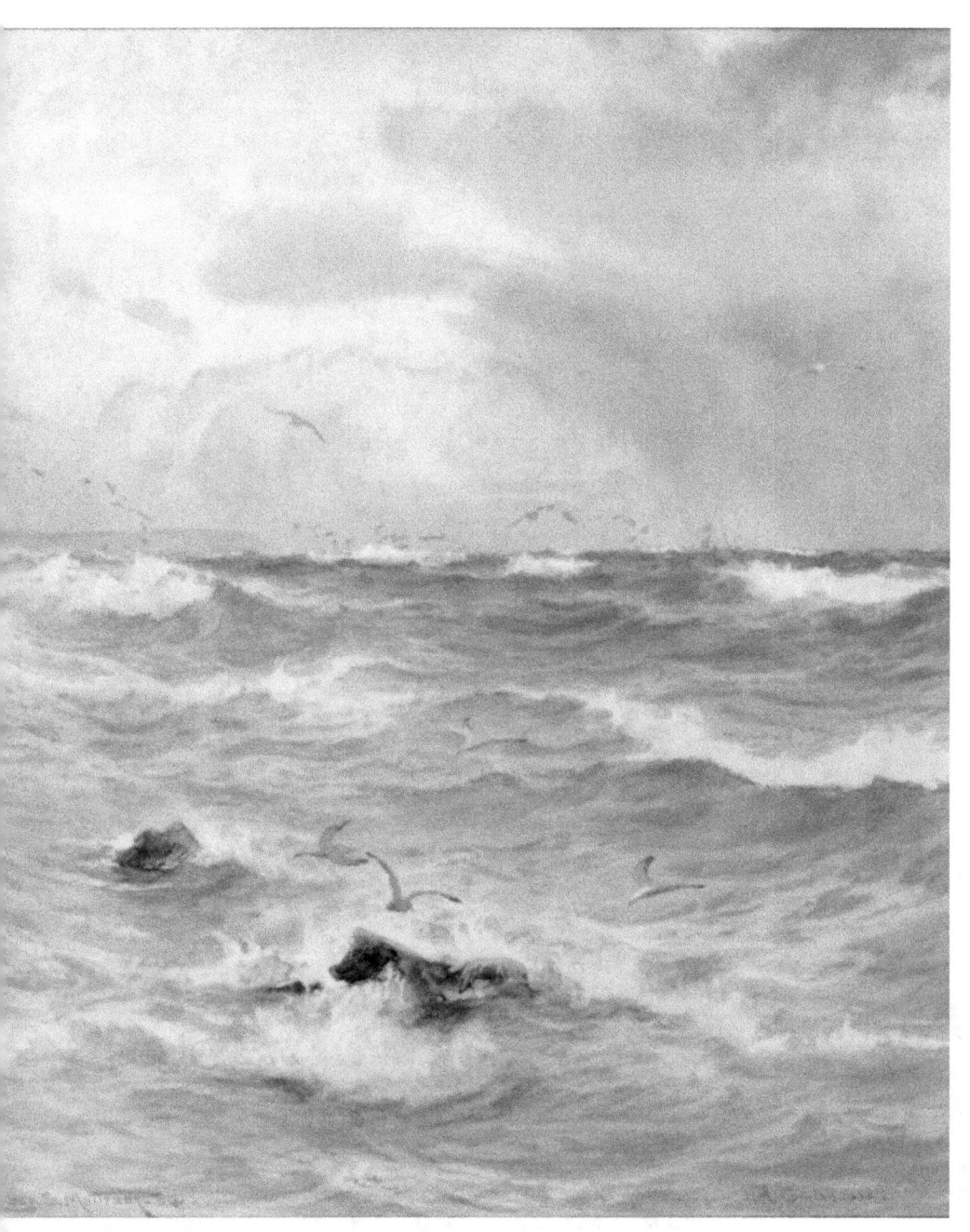

Charles Sim Mottram, *A Cornish Sea*, 1904, private collection

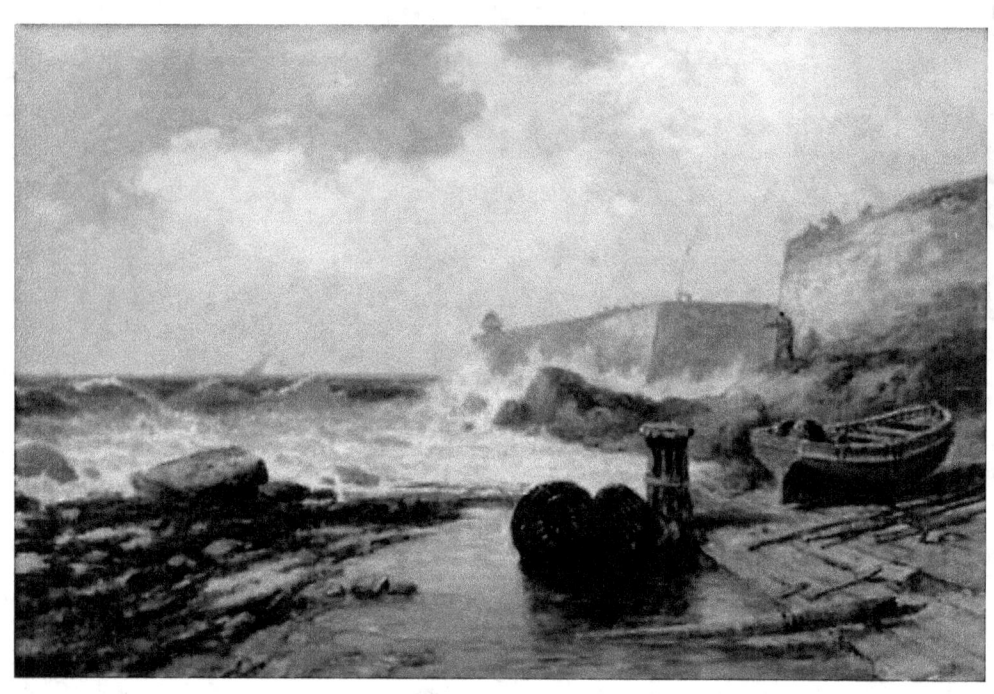

James Hook, *St Ives*, 1860, private collection

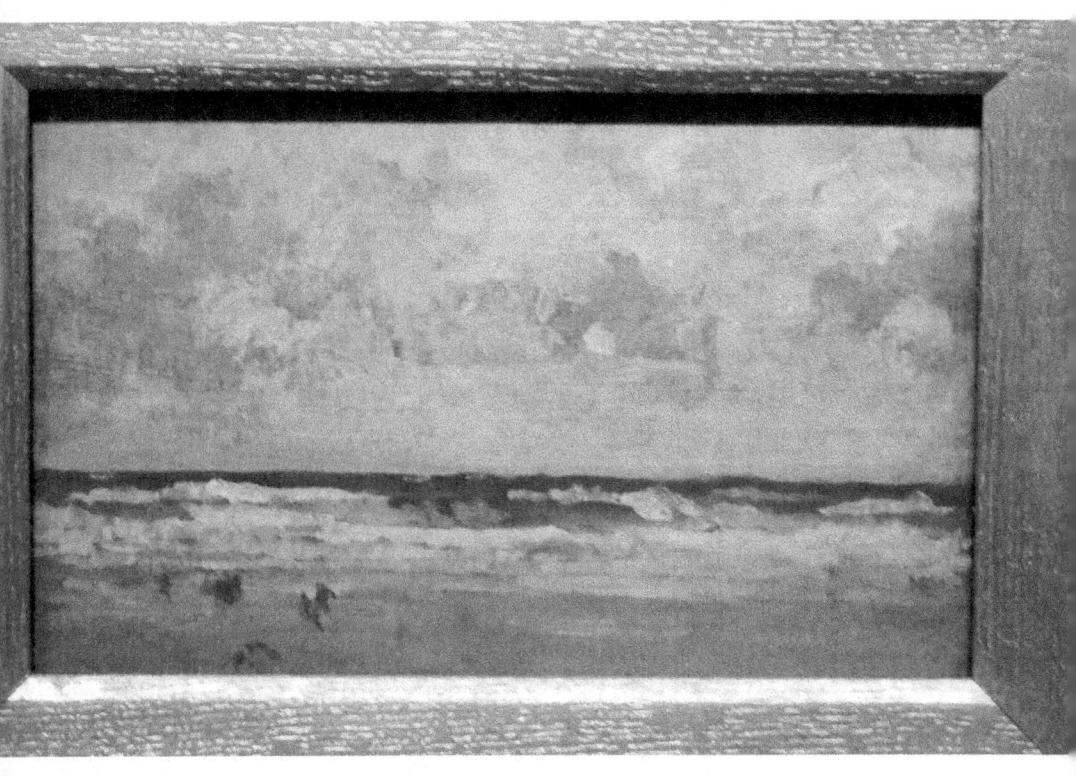

James McNeill Whistler, *St Ives*, Freer Gallery of Art, Washington, DC

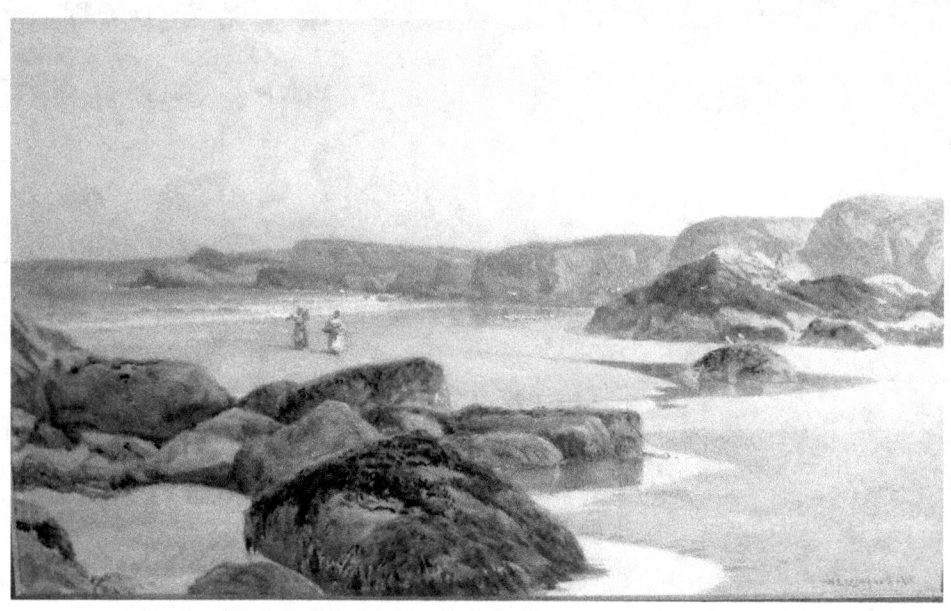

William Edward Croxford, *Newquay Town Beach*, 1916, private collection

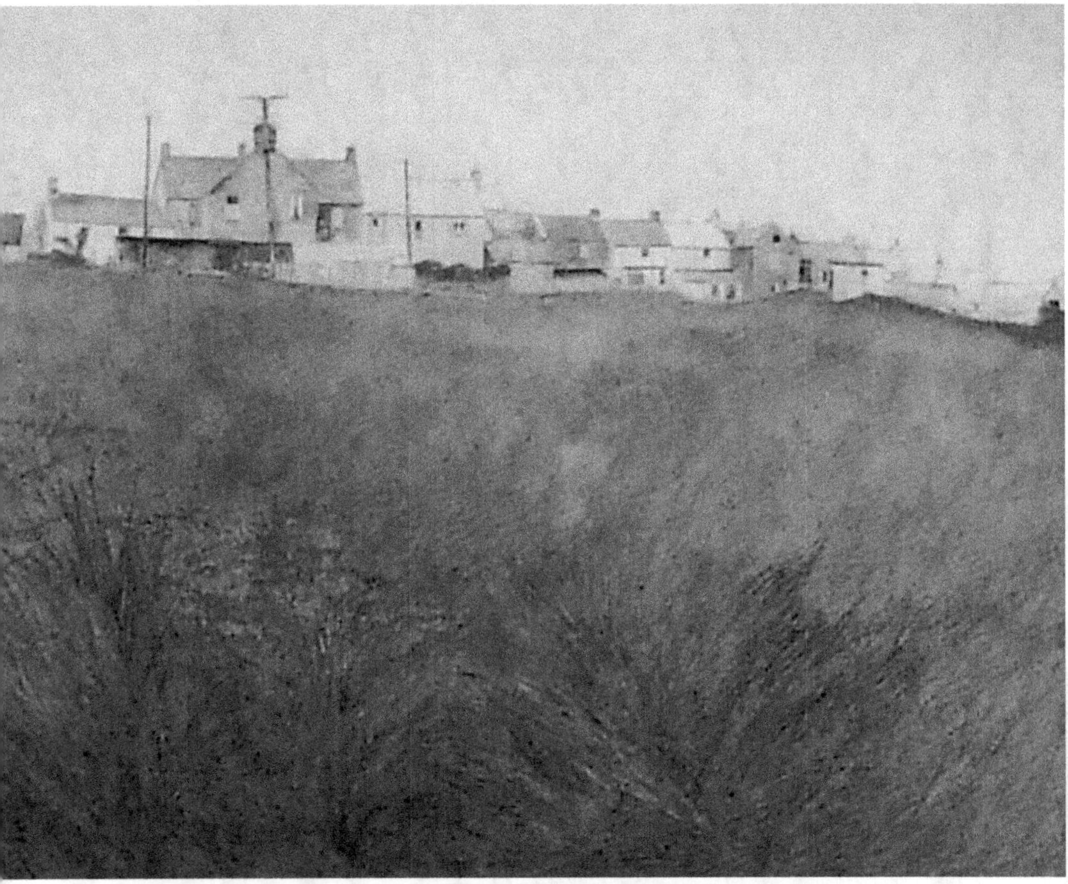

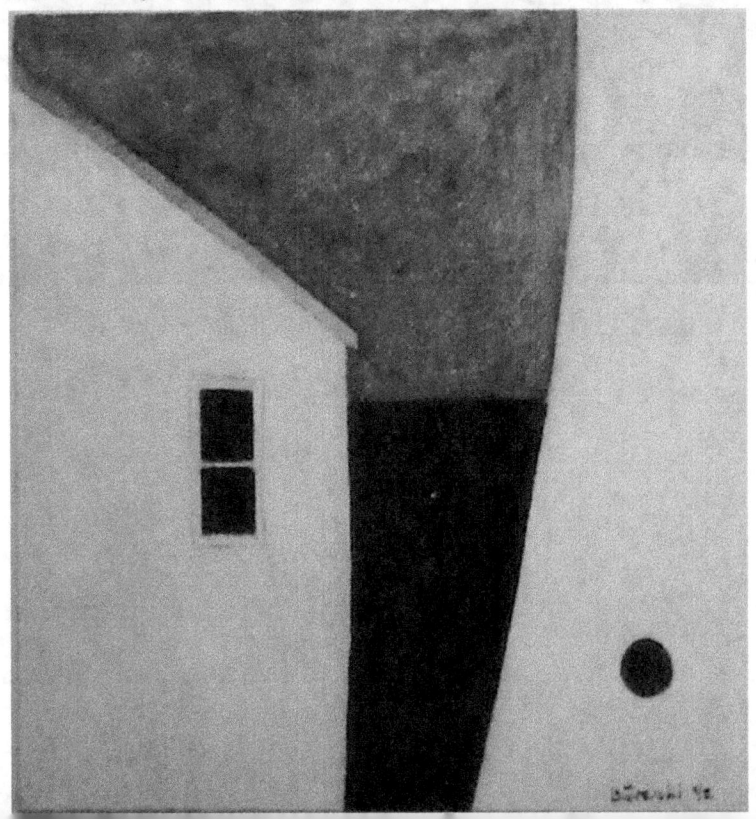

Noel Betowski, *Quay*, 1992, below, and *St Just,* 1982, above (Great Atlantic Map Works)

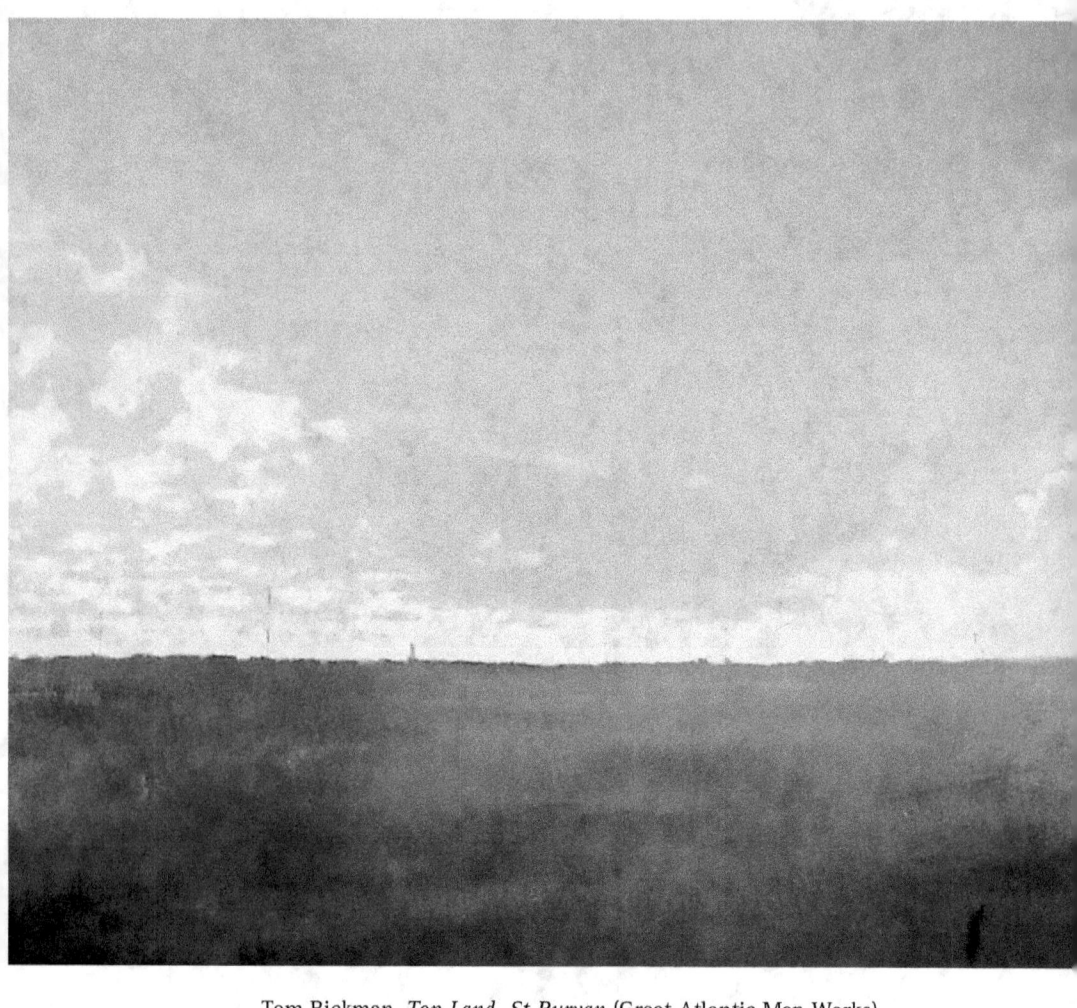

Tom Rickman, *Top Land, St Buryan* (Great Atlantic Map Works)

3

KURT JACKSON'S PAINTING

INFLUENCES

Asked about his artistic influences, Kurt Jackson found the question difficult to answer (it was a question that students liked to ask him).[29] His influences, he said, could include everyone, really. He tended to namecheck all of the people one would expect: British Romantic painters like J.M.W. Turner and John Constable, the French Impressionists, the Neo-romantics of the 1950s, and the St Ives/ Cornish movement of the 1940s and 1950s (Peter Lanyon, Karl Weschke, Sven Berlin, etc). Also Barbara Rae, Anton Tapiès, Joan Eardley and Robert Rauschenberg (Rauschenberg was 'a genius at mixing media... somehow he invents a whole new way of working and starts afresh', Jackson remarked [P, 22]).

---

29 As if, by magically absorbing the same influences, you can transform yourself.

Probably the biggest influence on Kurt Jackson's formative years as an artist was his father, a painter, and his mother, also an artist. Jackson said he watched his father making paintings many times (they were mainly abstract works, but Jackson senior also produced water-colour sketches of landscapes).

Just as vital for Kurt Jackson though, was music or poetry. Jackson said he could be much more inspired by reading a book of poetry by, say, W.S. Graham, than by leafing through a glossy art book. Music is less straightforward to analyze as an influence, but it's worth remembering that Jackson has been artist-in-residence for the Glastonbury Festival for years, and the Glasto experience is clearly nourishing for Jackson (in my humble opinion, Glastonbury is the finest music festival in Britain – along with the Notting Hill Carnival).

KURT JACKSON AND BRITISH ART

The art of Kurt Jackson is in general modernist, and in particular part of High Modernism. It is not postmodern, or Conceptual, or idea art, or Process art, or installation art. However, it does manifest some of the marks of postmodern or Conceptual art (British land artist Chris Drury has remarked that all art is basically conceptual art, because artists are always dealing with concepts).

Kurt Jackson began his painting career in the 1980s, the era of art movements or styles such as 'Neo-Geo', 'Neo Pop' ('New Pop'), the new 'gestural' figuration, or 'Neo-Expressionism' in Germany and America, or the return to figuration in David Salle, Eric Fischl, and others. Going back a little further, to the end of World War Two, among art movements and styles, the following have little connection with Kurt Jackson's art (or vice versa): Superrealism, Pop Art, performance art, Fluxus, Op Art, Body Art, installation art, video and digital art, kinetic art, outsider art, magic realism, Transavantguardia, sound art and internet art.

Kurt Jackson's art tends not to be a part of those trendy art movements of the 1980s and 1990s, but to hark back to earlier forms of (High) Modernism, and further back again, to the 18th and 19th century British landscape tradition.

There are some affinities, though, between Kurt Jackson's art and some 1960s and post-1960s art movements: Arte Povera, post-painterly abstraction, Minimalism, Postminimalism, assemblages, lettrism, and land and environmental art. Taking in all of the art movements of the 20th century and modern times, as well as the ones noted above, there are obvious links between Kurt Jackson's art and Expressionism,[30] Der Blaue Reiter, Impressionism, Postimpressionism, Abstract Expressionism and perhaps Fauvism and Constructivism.

Kurt Jackson's art also has affinities I would suggest with the British 'New Ruralists' or the 'New Romantics' or 'Neo-romantics' – David Inshaw, Graham Sutherland, Peter Blake *et al*, an art which developed from the mid-20th century onwards. It's an art of a romantic, nostalgic, spiritual Britain, a Britain which becomes the Albion of mythology and ancient religion. It was the kind of neo-romanticism championed by art critics such as Peter Fuller, and in the films of Michael Powell, Derek Jarman and Ken Russell (in the films of Powell and Pressburger such as *Gone To Earth* and *A Canterbury Tale* – and of course the mighty *A Matter of Life and Death,* and the incredible documentaries that Russell directed for the Beeb in the Sixties, such as *Dante's Inferno*, about the Pre-Raphaelites, or *The Debussy Film*).

The 'New Ruralists'/ 'New Romantics' painters, though, have a very strong fantasy and religious component in their art, which goes back to visionary artists such as William Blake, Henry Fuseli and John Martin. That fantastical aspect isn't found in Kurt Jackson's art – he isn't painting angels, ancient Roman cities or flying horses yet. Give him time, though, and maybe we'll see angels floating over Sennen or Zennor (it's not too much of a stretch to imagine an angel soaring over Priest's Cove in a painting. I only hope that when the angels come, they don't wind up looking like that plasticky, 'New Age' art).

---

30 Think of the sublime, visionary seascapes of Emil Nolde, for instance, or the landscapes of Ernest Kirchner or Georges Rouault.

❖

Kurt Jackson, then, is definitely *not* part of the 'Young British Artists' group (now, like then, not so 'young'), the *Sensation, Frieze* and ex-Goldsmiths' College crowd who became media darlings in the Nineties: Tracey Emin, Damien Hirst, Sarah Lucas, Gavin Turk, the Chapman brothers and others. To my knowledge, Jackson didn't go to those London parties and openings in the mid-1990s, didn't hang out with Keith Allen, David Bowie, Oasis and Blur. Jackson didn't have his art bought up by Charles Saatchi, and wasn't fashionable or '*avant garde*' enough to be nominated for the Turner Prize. Jackson didn't appear to be one of those awful, schmoozing, middle-class wannabes who pretended to be Cockney lads (dubbed 'Mockneys'), wasn't part of 'lad culture' of *Loaded*, or of mid-Nineties Britpop (Oasis, Pulp, Supergrass, Blur, Spice Girls), or of Tony Blair's New Labour, the 'rebranding' of Britain, and so on.

It's not just the physical distance that Kurt Jackson had (and has) between West Cornwall and London, or perhaps the mistrust in Cornwall of people from 'up country', it's a cultural and social gulf. The London art world is really not the world of many Cornish artists. It's not provincialism, or a British suburban outlook which is wary of big cities or intellectuals or the London media world. Rather, it's a disinterest in much of what goes on in the capital. That simply isn't their world, their life. (However, Jackson admits that he isn't really a 'Cornish' artist. His origins are actually in the South-East of Britain).

There is something, though, in the difference between London and Cornwall as social and physical environments in which to live. There are people who live in small towns and villages in the West Country who find going up to London a trying, exhausting experience. Some people put it off if possible. After the peace and quiet of the moors and lanes of Cornwall, Devon and Dorset, even a medium-sized town, with its noisy roads, pollution and crowds, can appear ugly and tiresome. At that scale in rural Britain, even a small town like Falmouth or Truro can appear a bustling metropolis by comparison with the tiny hamlets in the countryside. Jackson admitted:

I have not so much a phobia as a dislike of urban life. It's just doesn't suit me, I go to London once a year to see a show, but even then I only last about two days before I'm ready to come home. I don't feel comfortable there, to be honest.[31]

ROMANTICISM

It was the American sculptor Carl Andre who noted, quite rightly, that the British landscape is 'one vast earthwork'.[32] Part of Kurt Jackson's painting draws on the British landscape tradition, the tradition of the pastoral, the sublime, the Arcadian. Romanticism in relation to Jackson's art means the tradition of British Romantic poetry (Williams Blake and Wordsworth, John Keats, Percy Bysshe Shelley and Samuel Taylor Coleridge); the British Romantic painters (J.M.W. Turner, John Constable, Thomas Girtin, John Sell Cotman and Richard Wilson); also the Hudson River School (Thomas Cole, Frederic Edwin Church and Albert Bierstadt); and the Romantic attitudes and aspirations of infinity, extremism, nostalgia, mythology, soul, magic, nature and the Gothic.

In contemporary British art, one can detect the continuing influence of the elements of British Romanticism (as well as the Neo-Romant-icism of the 1930s and 1940s): the anarchic idealism of Shelley, the luscious sensuality of Keats, the epic nature poetry of Wordsworth, the angelic visions of Blake and the synæsthetic poesie of Coleridge.

The Romantic ethics noted above – infinity, extremism, nostalgia, mythology, soul, magic, nature and the Gothic – can be found in some of Kurt Jackson's paintings.

(1) The Romantic notion of infinity can be discerned in Kurt Jackson's evocations of the sea, a 'last wilderness'. A place with no barriers – i.e., no limits to dreaming (the 'dreaming sea' as Peter

31 Quoted in C. Rogers.
32 C. Andre, in A. Causey, "Space and Time in British Land Art", *Studio International*, 193, 98, Feb, 1977, 126.

Redgrove put it).

(2) The Romantic ethics of taking things to extremes – of taking one idea and pursuing it until every ounce of juice has been extracted from it (I would say that Jackson has certainly attempted to explore Priest's Cove to an extreme).

(3) Nostalgia: oh, there's plenty of nostalgia in Kurt Jackson's art – and in all art, and it's one of the aspects of his art – and all art – that undoubtedly appeals to art lovers, for all the obvious reasons. A nostalgia for a golden age, an era when people worked off the land, an era of full employment, both mediæval and pre-industrial, *and* of the Industrial Revolution (but pre-computers, pre-digital). A nostalgia for a time when life was simpler, easier, better, fuller, richer, whatever.

It's a wish-fulfilment, of course, because life certainly wasn't like that. But nostalgia – and the utopian desires in art – should never be under-estimated.

(4) The eternal, soul and magic – like conventional or instutional-ized religion – aren't really a part of Kurt Jackson's art – not in the same way as they're central to the art of Leonardo da Vinci, say, or Gustave Moreau.

(5) Kurt Jackson doesn't draw on mythology – there's no Goddess Venus rising from the sea at Priest's Cove, no Perseus battling serpents below Kenidjack cliffs, no crumbling statues of Greek or Roman deities in the ruined temples of the mines of Botallack or Geevor. There is a personal mythology, though – Jackson's conscious biographical allusions.

(6) Nature – that's Kurt Jackson's chief subject.

(7) The Gothic – well, the British Romantic Gothic is thriving in contemporary culture – in *Harry Potter*, *Lord of the Rings*, Charles Dickens TV adaptions – but there ain't much Gothic in Kurt Jackson's art. The *unheimlich* or 'uncanny' in Jackson's art isn't ghosts or *doppelgängers* or cackling witches, it's the natural world. But, of course, the whole point of a poetic sensibility is that the world itself is extraordinary and strange, that even 'ordinary' things like trees or the sea are actually very extraordinary.

So Kurt Jackson's art is romantic with a 'small 'r', rather than

Romantic with a capital 'R', in the technical sense of drawing on historical, literary Romantic tenets of the early 19th century. It uses some of them, but not the religious, mythological, spiritual, Gothic and narrative elements.33

However all of contemporary art can be seen as post-Romantic art – it all draws on Romanticism, as it draws on the Renaissance (contemporary art, including Jackson's art, is still operating very much within a Renaissance sense of space, for instance. Jackson's art, like all contemporary art, hasn't advanced much from Renaissance notions of the pictorial).

THE PAINTER'S PAINTER

Kurt Jackson is something of a painter's painter – in the sense of being devoted to painting, in making painting a central aspect of his life (other 'painter's painters' would include Max Beckmann, Gustave Moreau, J.A.D. Ingres, and Giovanni Bellini). For some people, going out to paint as much as possible, in all weathers and conditions, could be regarded as excessive, or compulsive. Maybe. I think of writers such as André Gide or Rainer Maria Rilke, for whom a day was somehow 'wasted' or unfulfilled if some creative work hadn't been achieved that day.34 There are plenty of artists who operate in bursts of intense activity, then have weeks or months (or even years) when it doesn't happen, doesn't come, won't work. Or they lose interest. Or something else happens which sweeps aside artistic endeavours.

Kurt Jackson seems to be an artist who doesn't find it difficult to make art, doesn't get anxious about it, doesn't suffer from 'painter's block'. The paintings seem to flow fairly easily from his brushes – or,

33 Kurt Jackson has also said that his art isn't romantic – paintings made on the sea in boats are not romantic (P, 18-19). Maybe the manufacture of some of those paintings isn't romantic, and maybe some of the paintings of industries aren't romantic, but Jackson's art as a whole, is deeply, passionately romantic.
34 More recently, writers such as J.K. Rowling have said they get restless when they've been away from writing for too long.

at least, his daily, weekly and monthly output is high enough to suggest that he just gets on with it. He doesn't seem to fret about his paintings in the Vincent van Gogh manner, and isn't self-absorbed in the Ad Reinhardt style (van Gogh fretted, but that didn't stop him producing some 800 paintings in his short life).

Judging from interviews and documents of the artist at work, Kurt Jackson doesn't seem to be the kind of painter to sit around in his studio worrying about why a painting isn't working. He's not like those artists who ponder for ages on some detail. Stories of Leonardo da Vinci recalled that when he was painting *The Last Supper* in Milan he would arrive, paint a very small amount, then leave it for a few days; at other times, he'd simply sit and look at his painting for hours, without doing any work at all.

Leonardo da Vinci was described thus by Matteo Bandello during the painting of *The Last Supper.*

> It was his habit, as I myself have witnessed and observed on several occasions, to come here in the early hours of the morning and mount the scaffolding, for the *Cenacolo* is somewhat high above the ground; he was accustomed (I say) to remain there brush in hand from sunrise to sunset, forgetting to eat or drink, painting continually. Then he might stay away for two, three or four days without setting hand to it, or he would remain in front of it for one or two hours and contemplate it in solitude, examining and criticizing to himself the figures he had created. I have also seen him (as caprice or fancy took hold of him) departing in the middle of the day when the sun was in Leo from the Corte Vecchia, where he was working on his stupendous clay Horse and he would come straight to Delle Grazie; and he would climb the scaffolding, seize a brush, apply a brush stroke or two to one of the figures, and suddenly depart and go elsewhere.[35]

The preference for working on paintings every day is not really compulsive or obsessive in Kurt Jackson's case: it can appear compulsive to those on the outside. For artists, rather, I would guess that it's the enjoyment of simply working, of doing something interesting and creative. Rainer Maria Rilke said that the poet should enjoy what would appear to outsiders to be the dull, repetitive chores of writing poems. The sorting, the editing, the rewriting, the polishing; in short, the *doing* of it all.

35 M. Badello, in Robert Payne: *Leonardo da Vinci,* Robert Hale 1979, 14.

Kurt Jackson works in a similar manner: he's an artist who seems to me to enjoy the act of painting. *'The experience of painting is very important to me,'* remarked Jackson (P, 27, my italics). (Jackson has acknowledged that there *is* an obsessive element to his art – of his series of Priest Cove works, for instance, he spoke of 'my ongoing fascination and exploration (and maybe obsession) with this part of the West Cornish coast'.[36])

THE END OF PAINTING?

Kurt Jackson's art is not particularly trendy (or trend-driven or faddish) – it's not installation art or Conceptual art, or the kind of fashionable art lauded by the international art cogniscenti. It's not likely, I don't think, to be on the cover of *Frieze* or *Flash Art*. Jackson is a 'painter's painter', but perhaps not an intellectual or philosopher-painter (like Piero della Francesca or Wassily Kandinsky). He has tackled political issues, but they are certainly not central to his art as they are to many of the artists that the international art scene exalts. If Jackson took on issues such as diaspora, or the Middle East, or AIDS, some art critics might take to his art more readily (they'd have more to write about than pretty pictures of landscapes, which is how some art critics have seen Jackson's art). I don't agree with that view: as you may have gathered, I like Jackson's art a lot.

Instead, Kurt Jackson's art is more conservative and modest. And it's still traditional easel painting – no different, essentially, from painting of the past four hundred years or more. But that isn't negative, because it's also a very beautiful art. Does art have to be 'new' to be valuable? No.

Jasper Johns said in the film documentary *Painters Painting* (1970)

36 Quoted in *The Painted Etchings*. And he said he was reluctant to learn a musical instrument, in case that turned into an obsession instead of painting. Kurt Jackson chucks away paintings and works, but produces plenty, so there's always enough for exhibitions.

that 'a lot of people have said that painting is dead, but people continue to work' (Emile de Antonio's book of his documentary is a superb introduction to contemporary painting, and highly recommended).[37]

They do. Painters still paint and sculptors still sculpt, even though those forms of art are often regarded as old-fashioned or out-moded. These days, art is often a bunch of TV monitors in a gallery playing some obscure, grainy imagery of God knows what, slowed-down, with a soundtrack of radio noise lost in between stations. And a woman in her fifties (dressed all in black, of course), who has a face like a horse, turns to her companion (who also wears black, and also heroin-thin), and intones haughtily, 'dahling, this is one of the most *sublime* of pieces of a postmodernist deconstruction of the human condition that I've ever seen!' And the man, who has a nasal whine like an ambulance siren, replies, 'Ooooh, yes, Esmerelda, *yes!*'

---

37 E. de Antonio, *Painters Painting*, Abbeville Press, New York, NY, 1984.

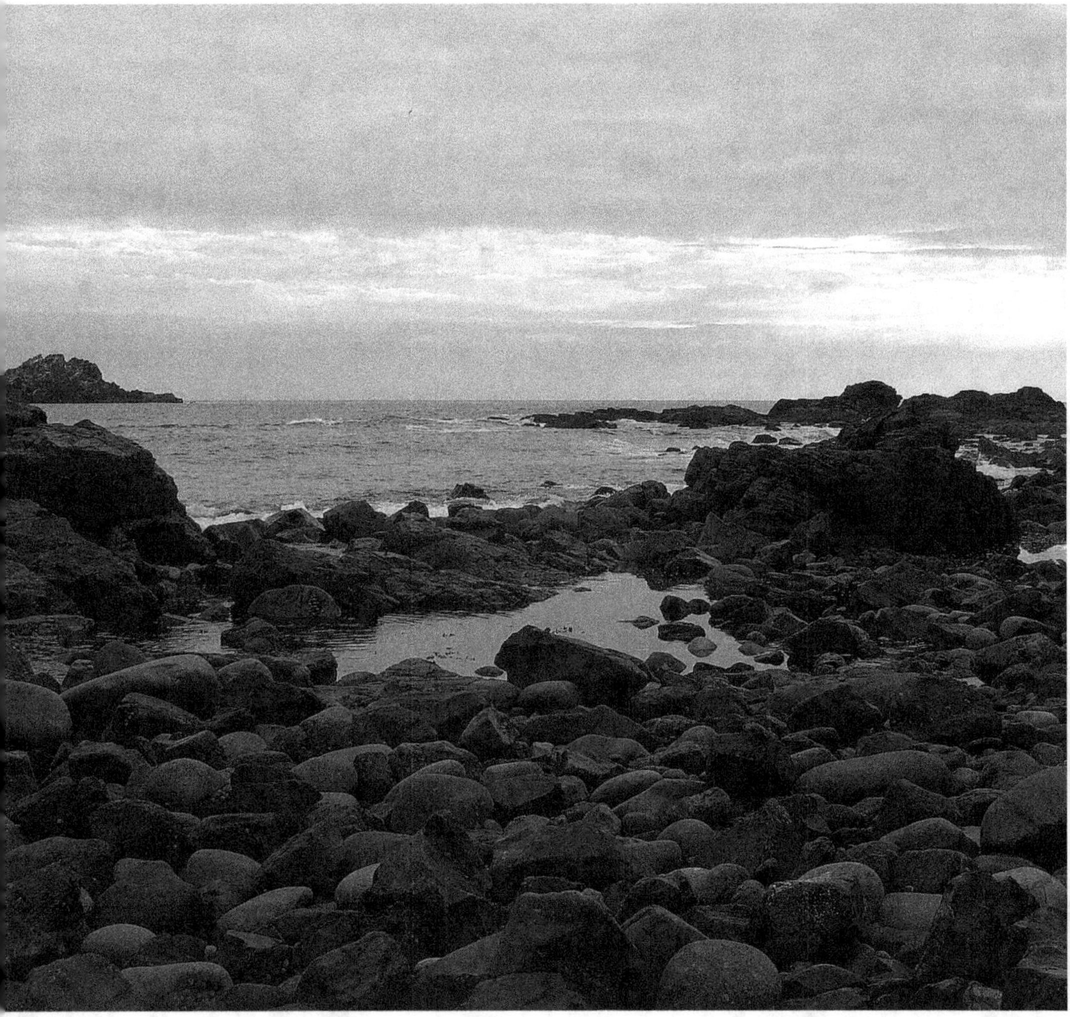

Dusk in Priest's Cove.

Priest's Cove takes its name from the town of St Just and the saint
Just, 'Just' being 'East', and 'Priest' being 'Porth' or 'Per East' (hence the
title of one of Kurt Jackson's exhibitions of Priest's Cove paintings, *Porth*).

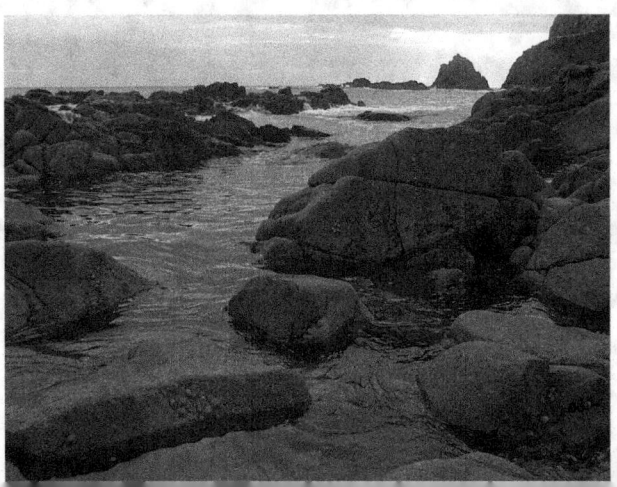

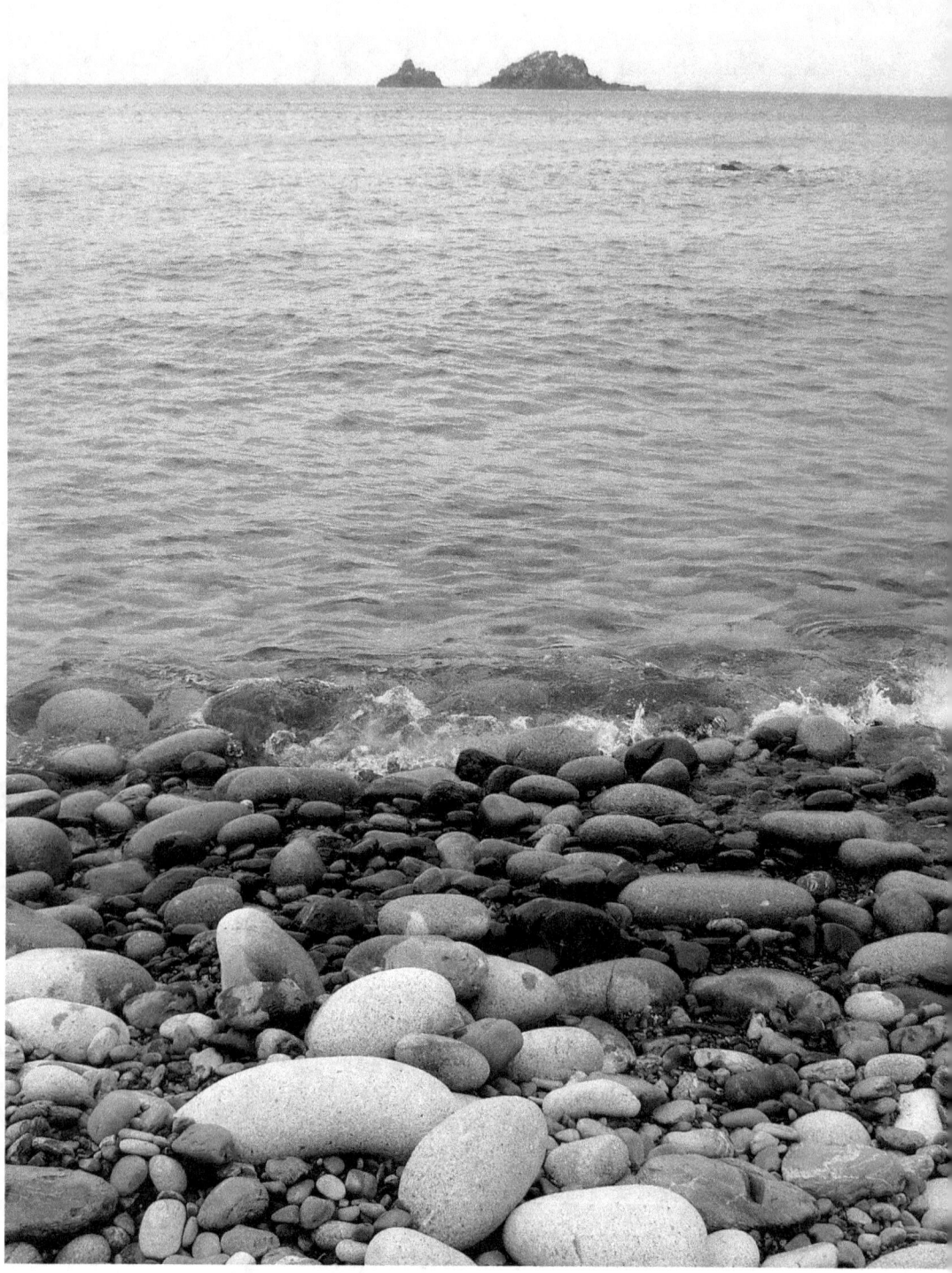

The Brisons from Cot Valley, West Penwith

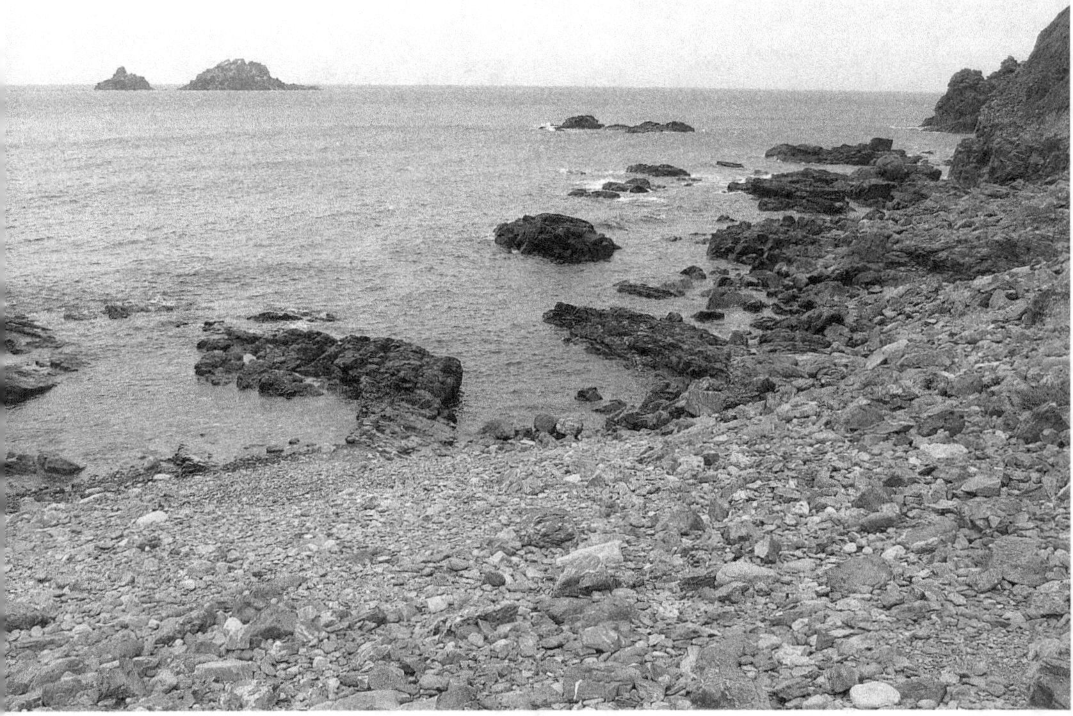

The tide comes in... the tide goes out...
at Priest's Cove

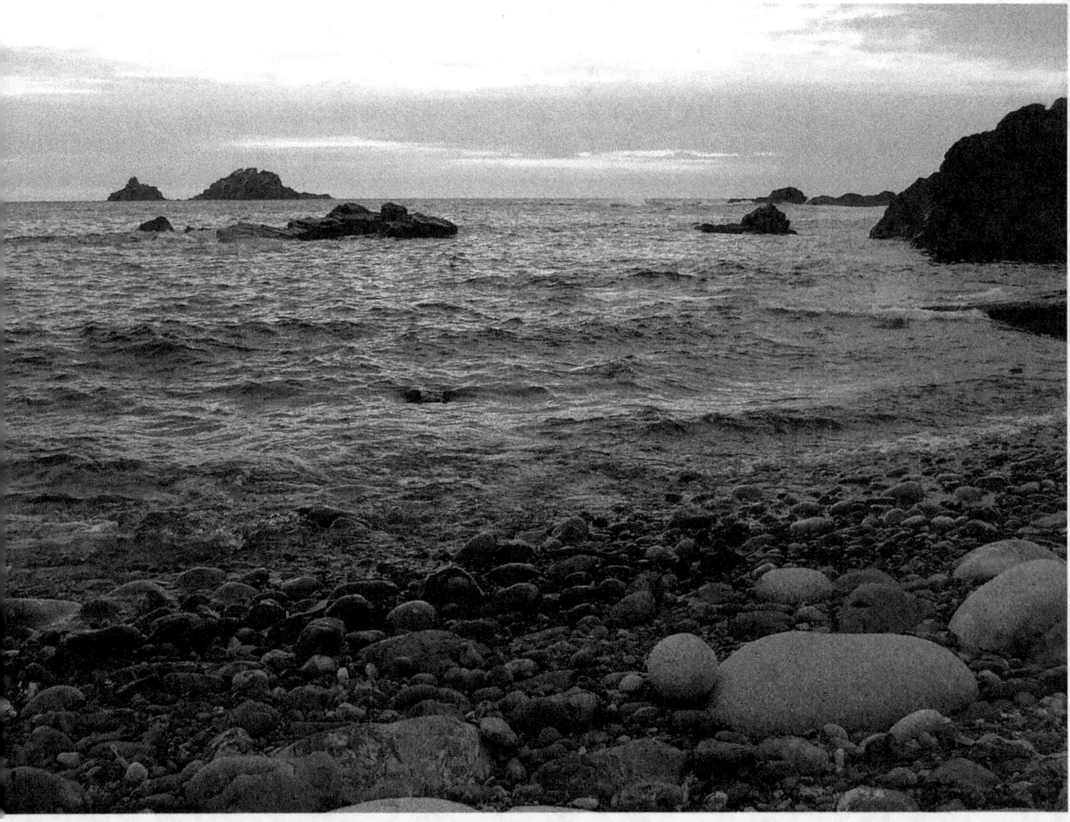

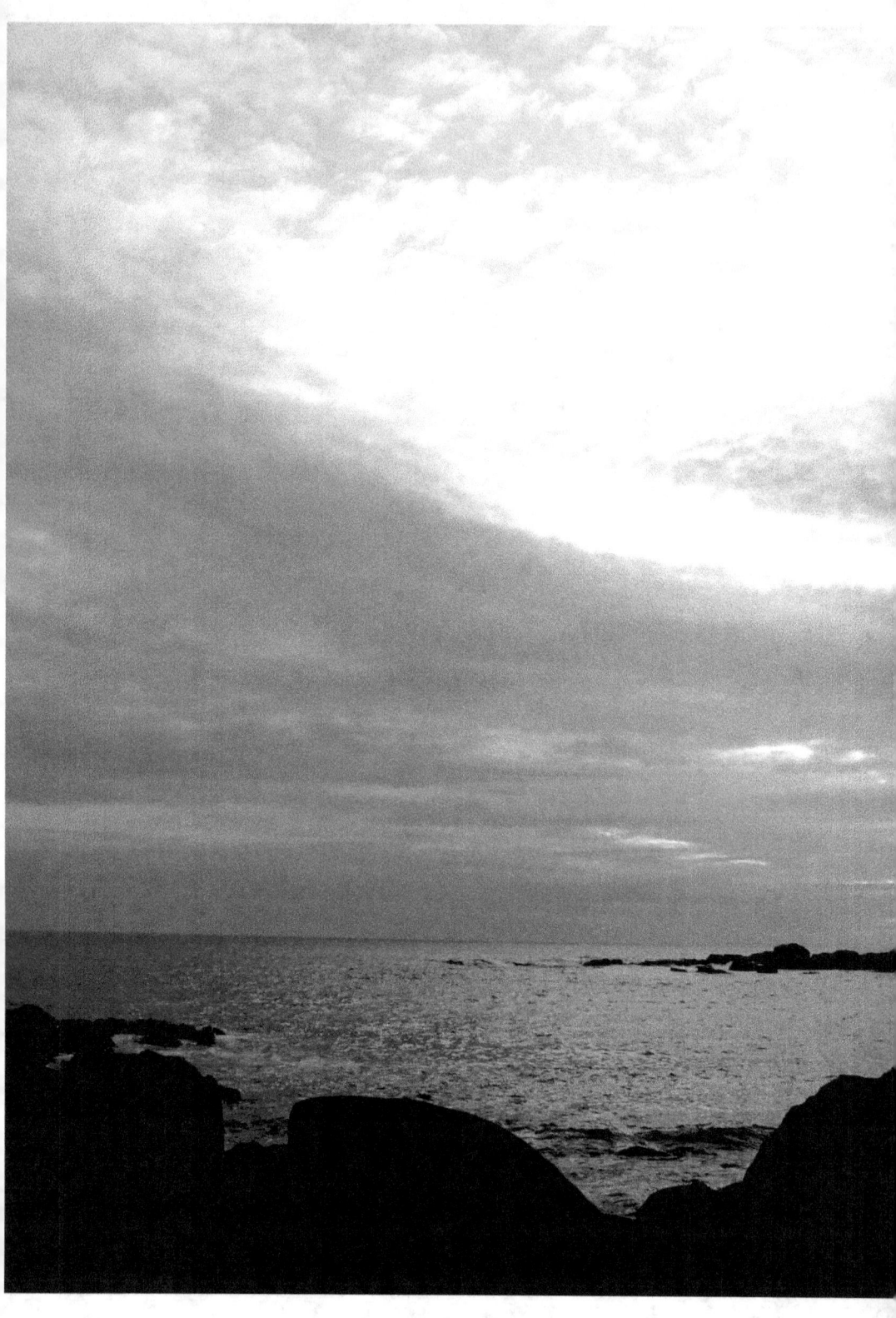

A big sky at Priest's Cove in Cornwall

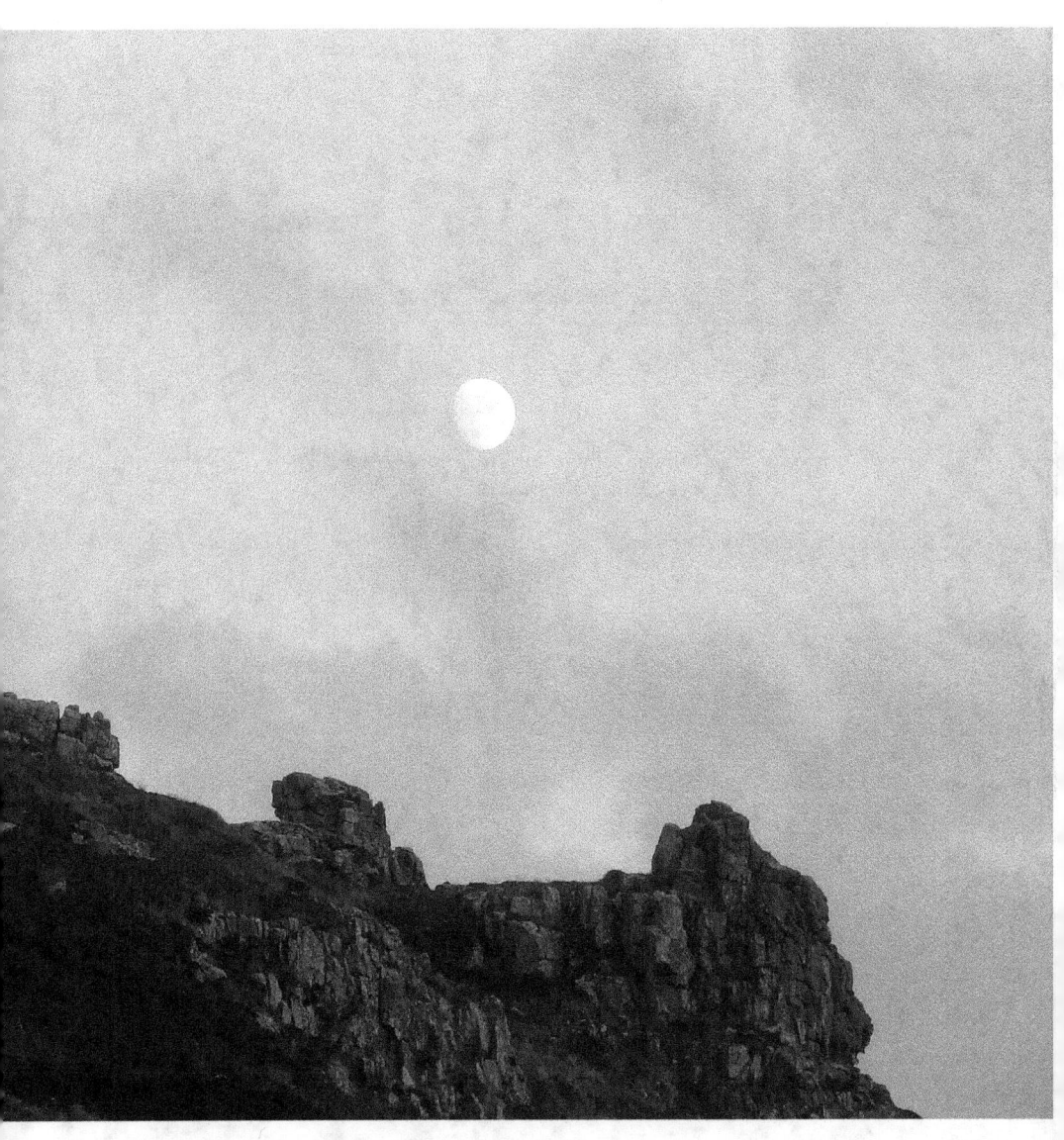

The moon sailing over Priest Cove

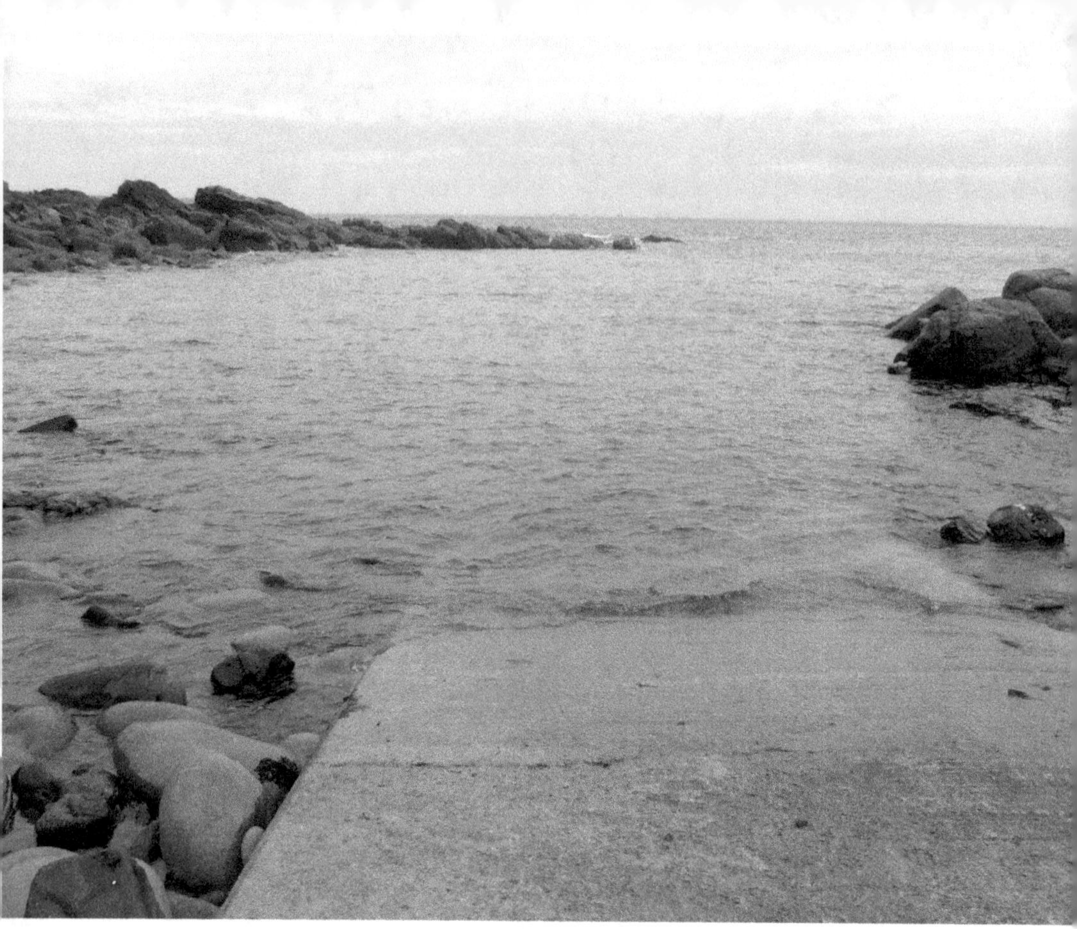

The slipway at Priest Cove (above), and looking back from below the cape (below).

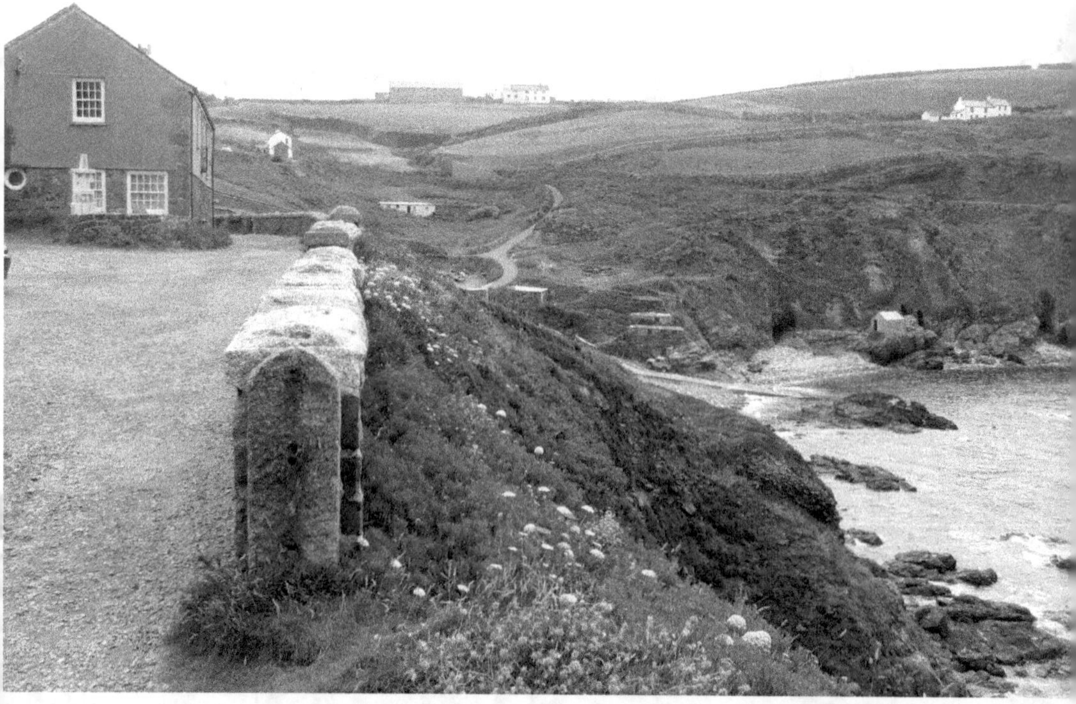

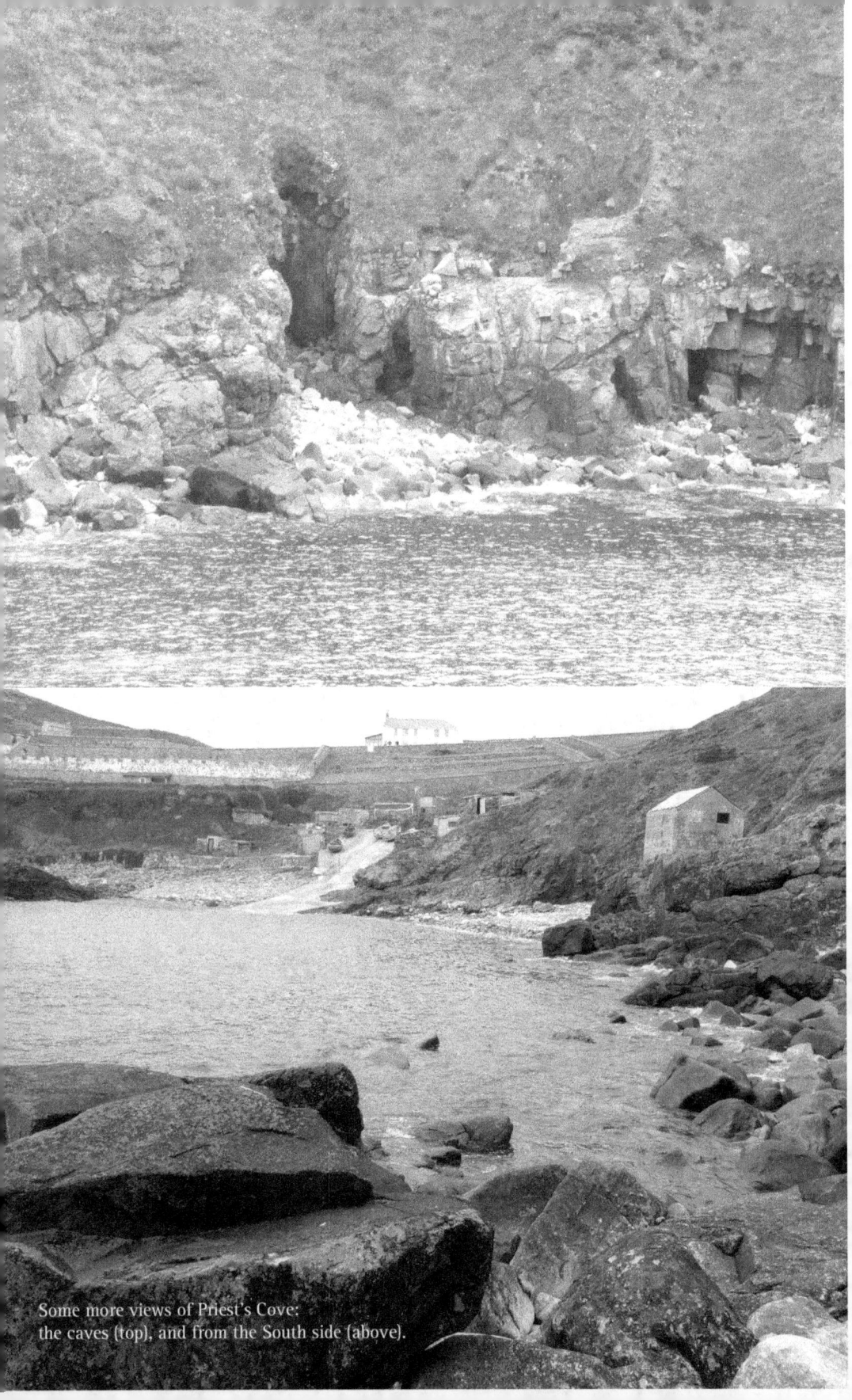
Some more views of Priest's Cove:
the caves (top), and from the South side (above).

The waters reglitterized, as Henry Miller would say,
from above Nanven beach.

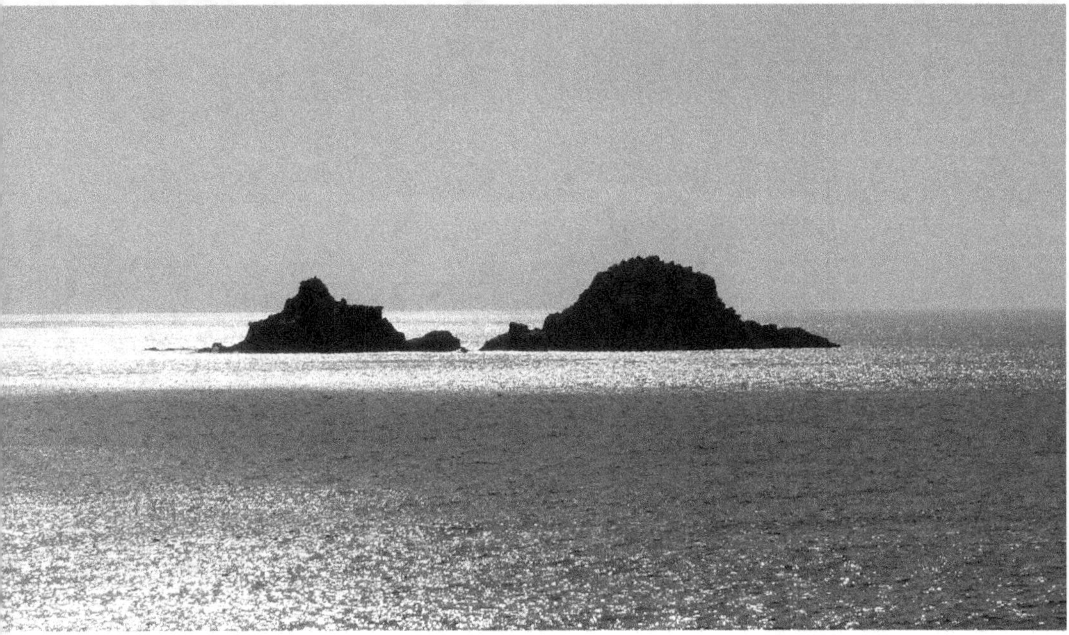

The ever-present Brisons rocks (above), and the tidal pool at Priest Cove (below).

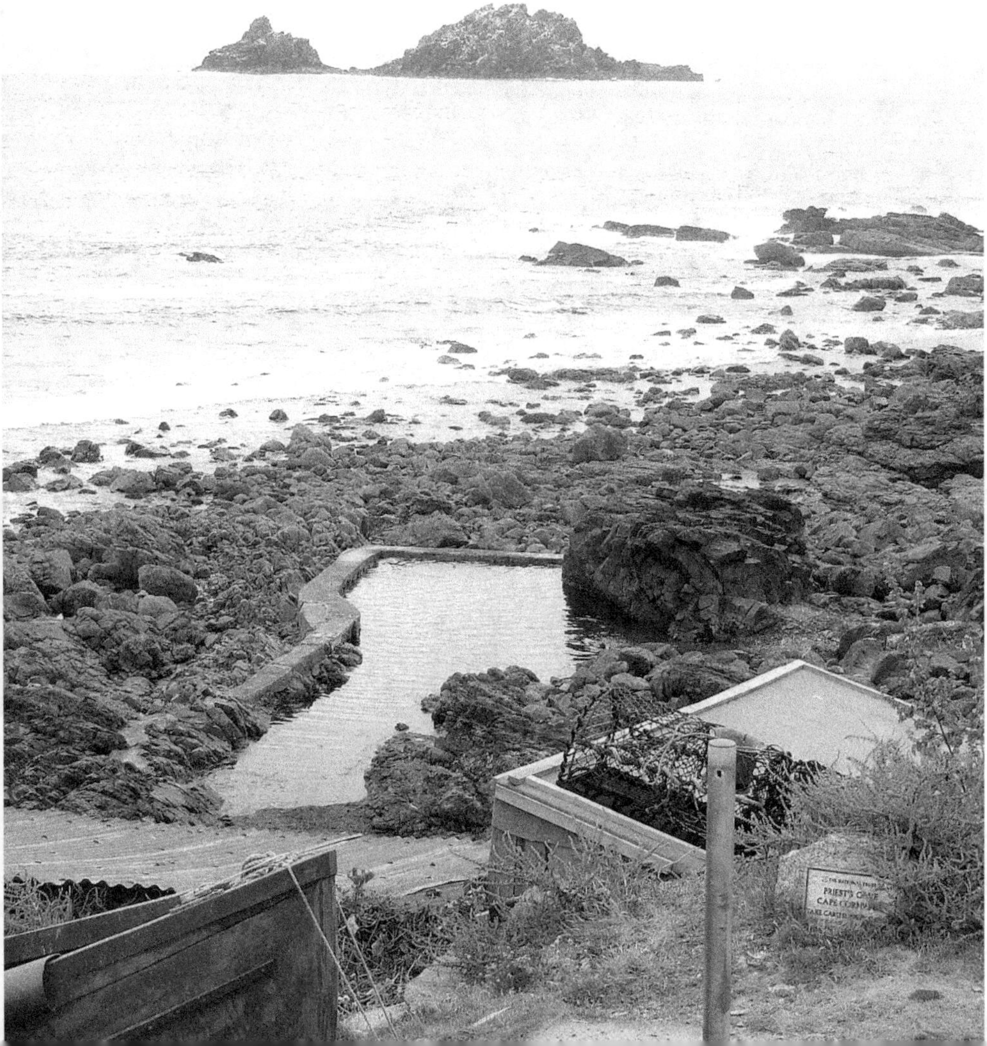

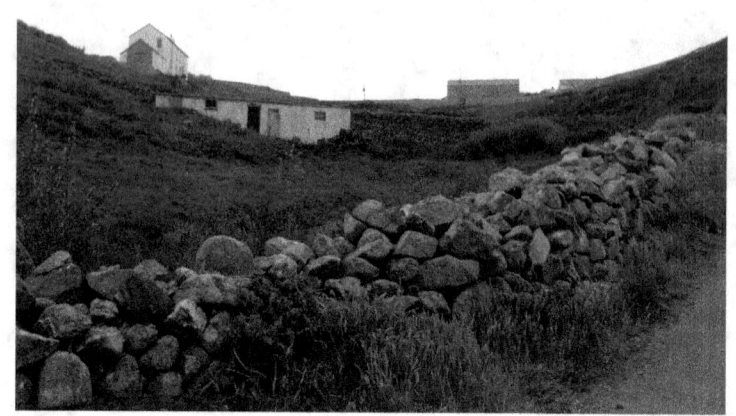

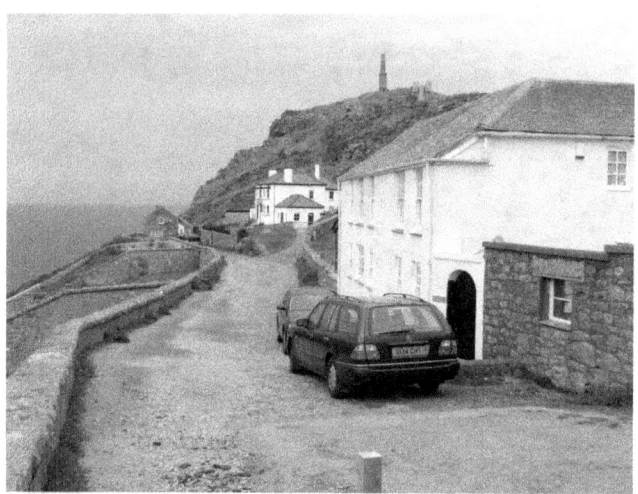

Some other views of Priest Cove: houses, cars, boarded-up buildings, food stalls and restrooms.

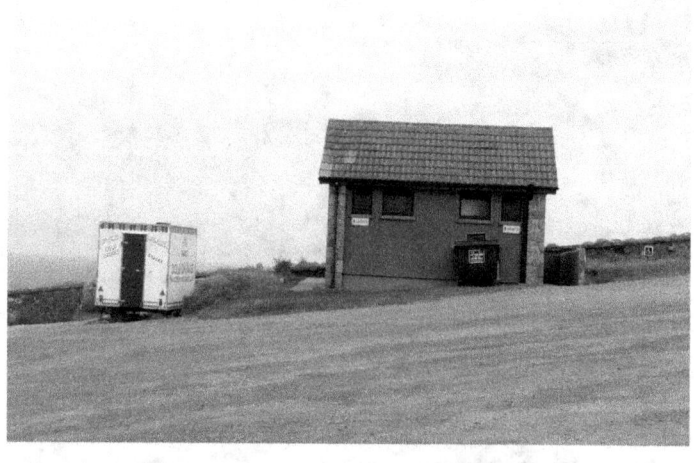

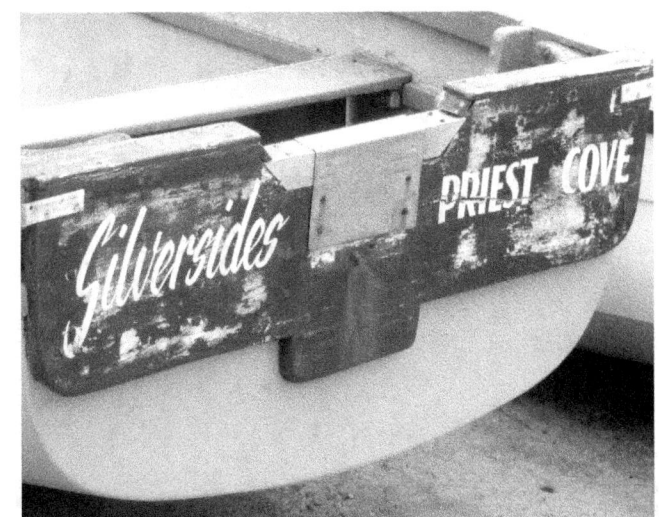

Boats at Priest Cove

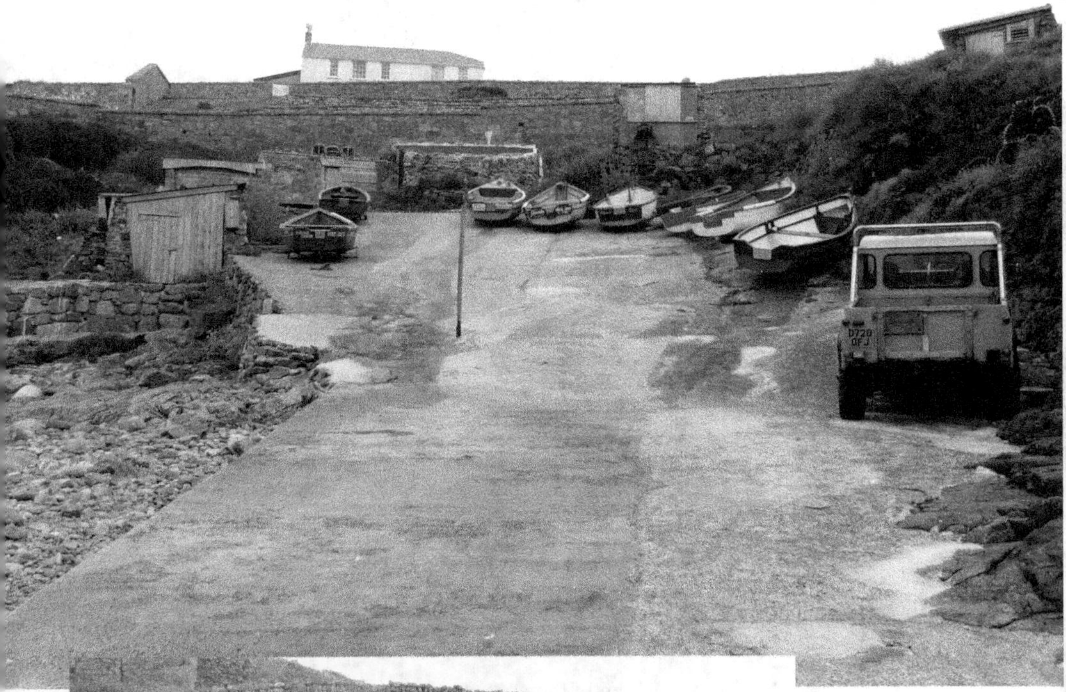

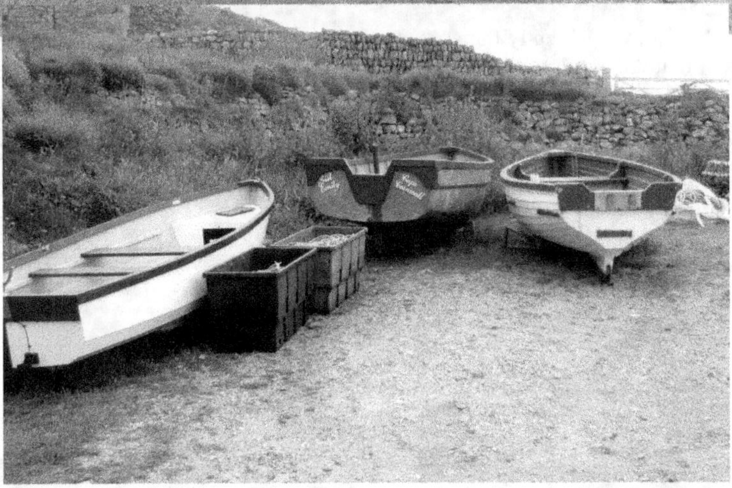

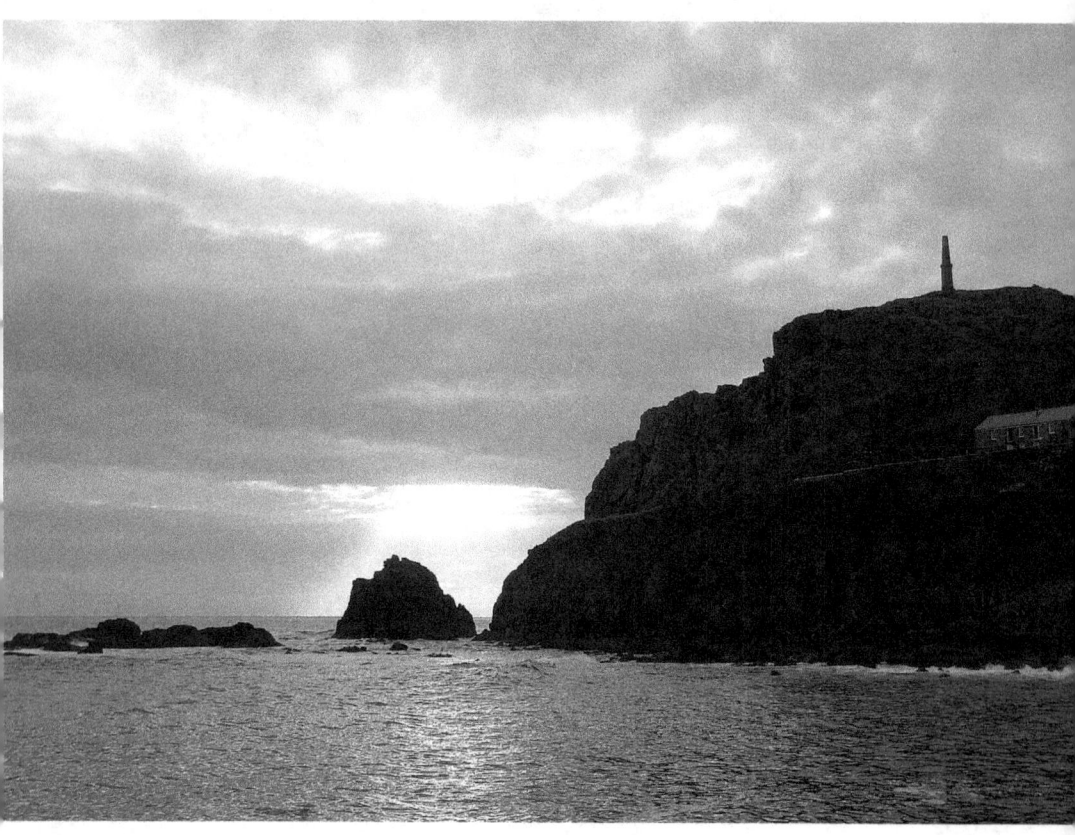

Sunset in Midsummer at Priest's Cove.

Cape Cornwall is apparently the only cape in England. It's a small headland that juts out into the Atlantic Ocean. Like the church atop Glastonbury Tor, Cape Cornwall is 'completed' by the chimney from the Cape Cornwall Mine (there was once a beacon here). Cape Cornwall, now owned by the National Trust, was once fortified in the Bronze or Iron Ages, as was Maen Castle nearby. Stone cists, burials and barrows have been discovered on the Cape.

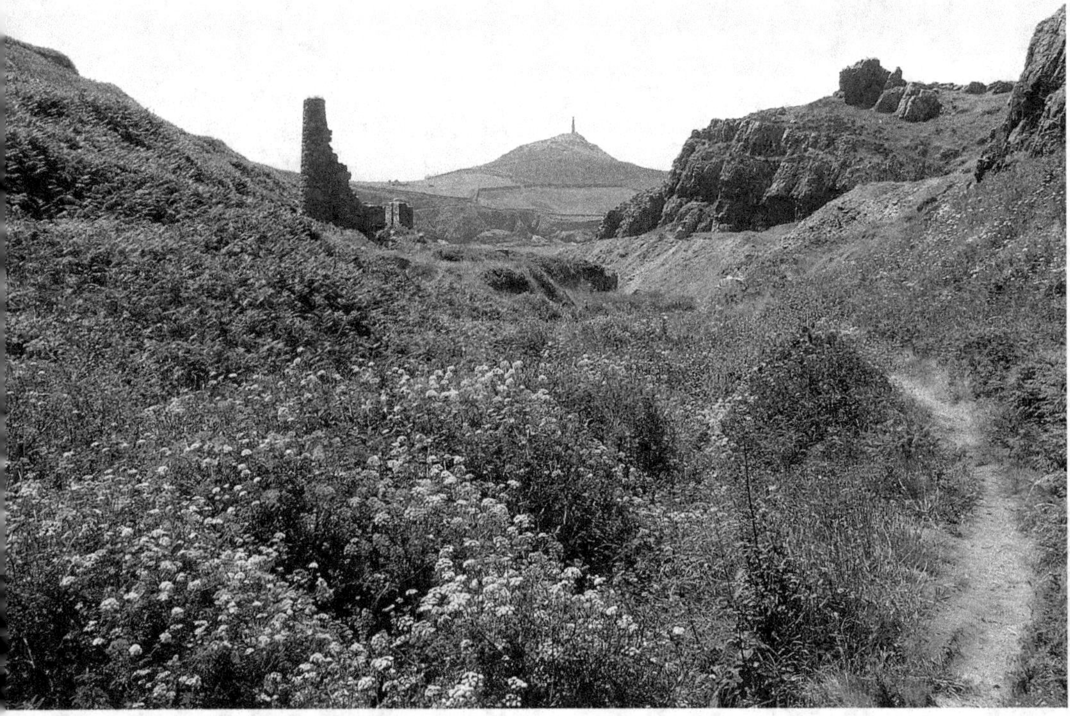

Kenidjack Valley, on the North side of Cape Cornwall

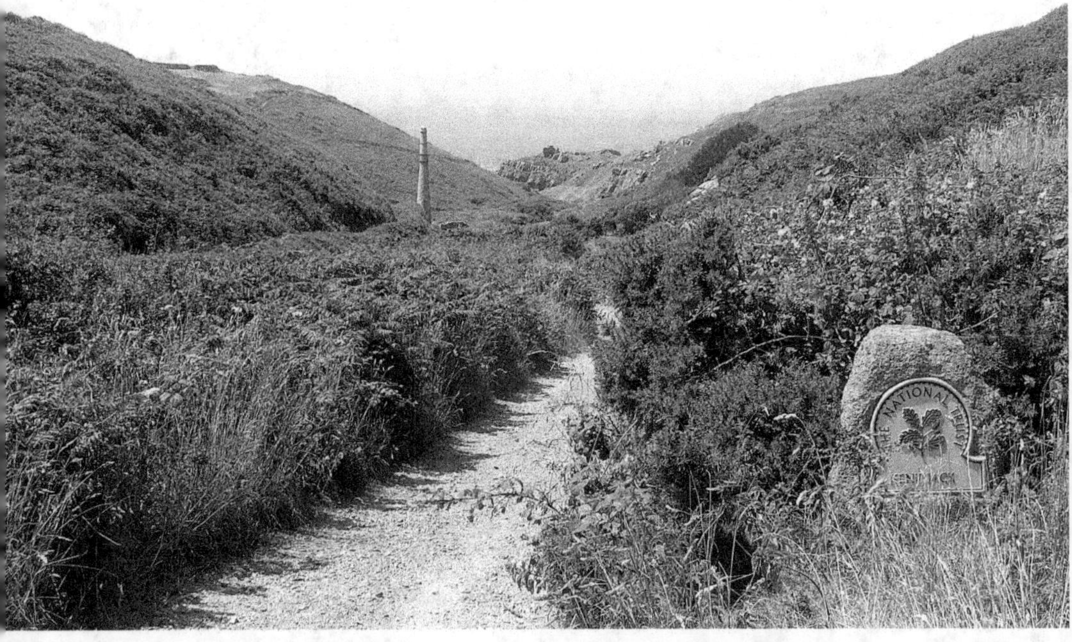

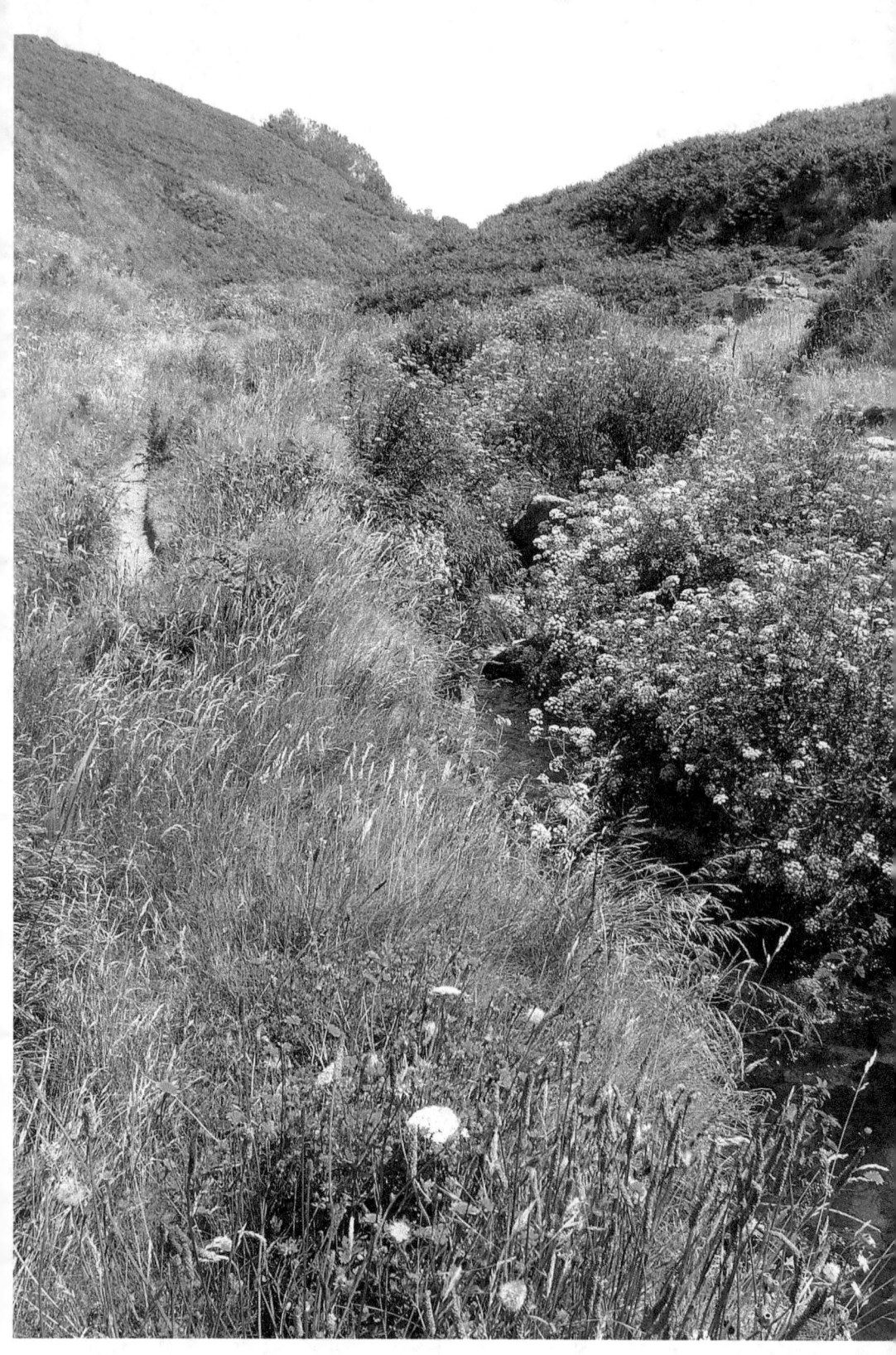

Kenidjack Stream in Midsummer

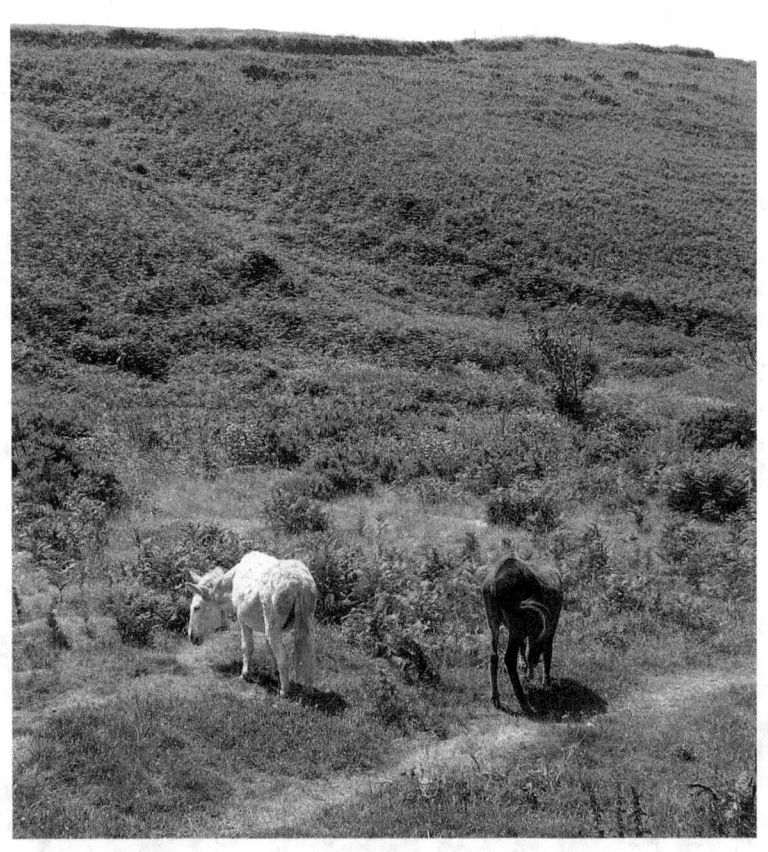

Sleepy Kenidjack Valley in the noon-day Summer sun

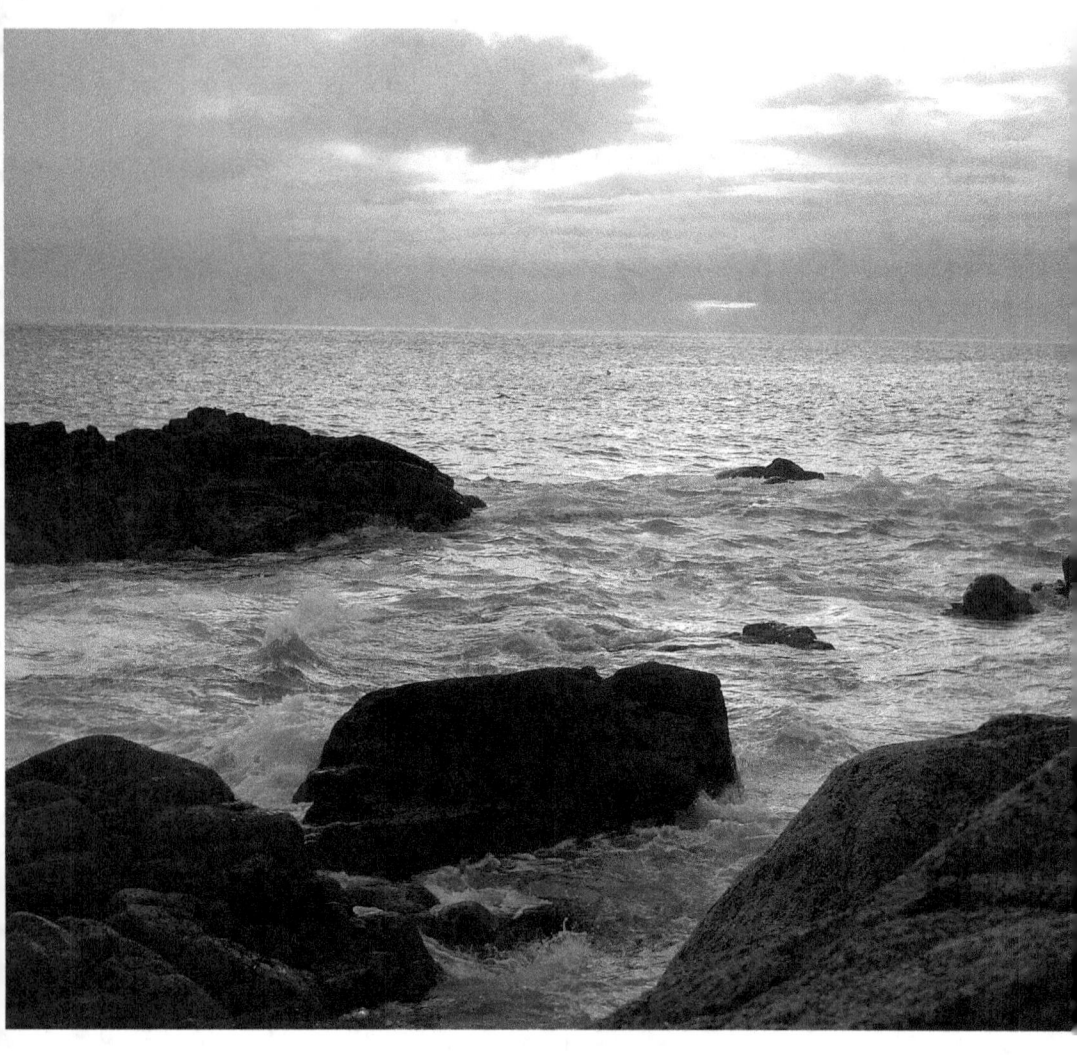

One of the best places in the world to be:
looking West, across the Atlantic Ocean,
into the sun, into the light,
on the far edge of England
(sun-down at Nanven beach)

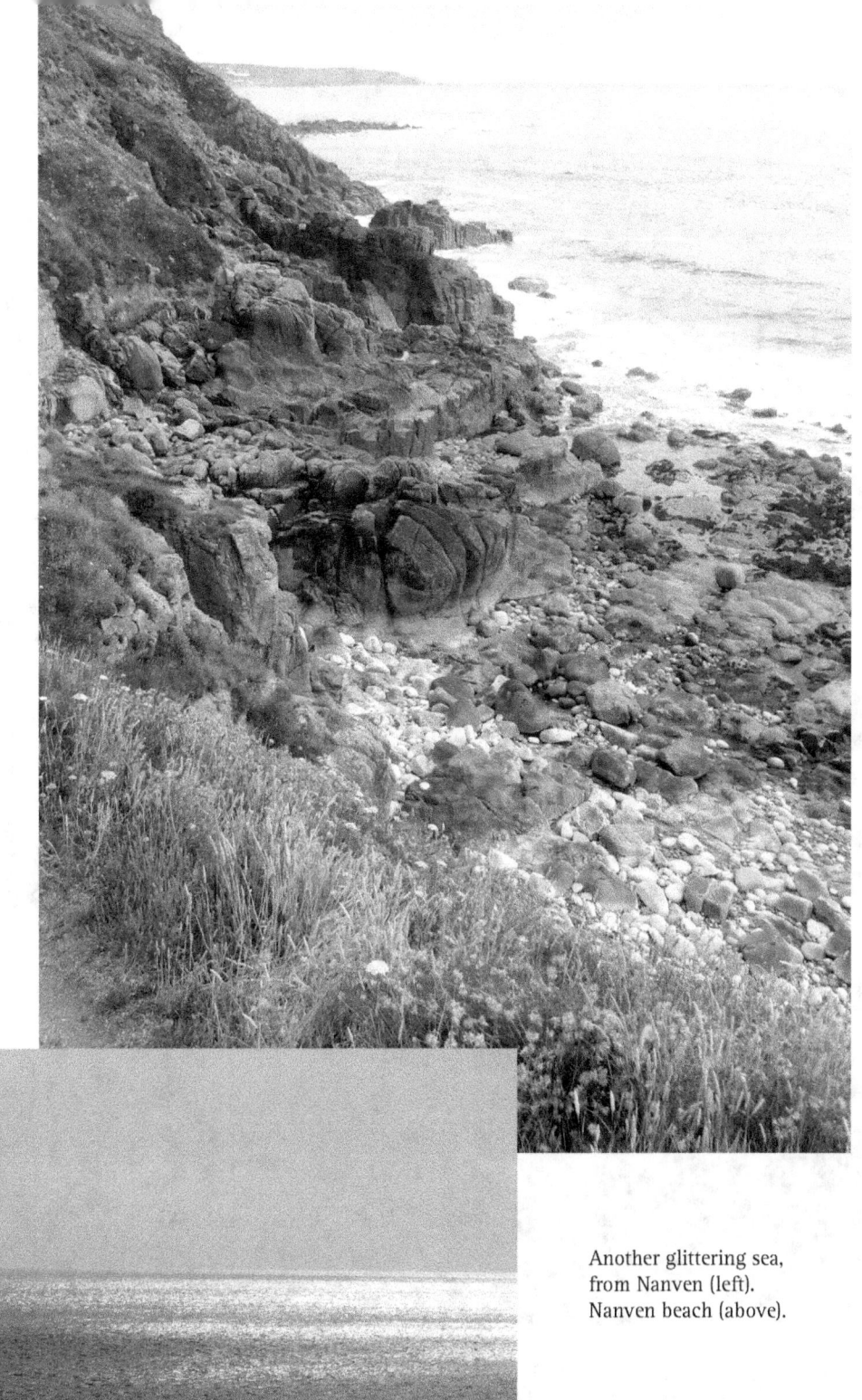

Another glittering sea,
from Nanven (left).
Nanven beach (above).

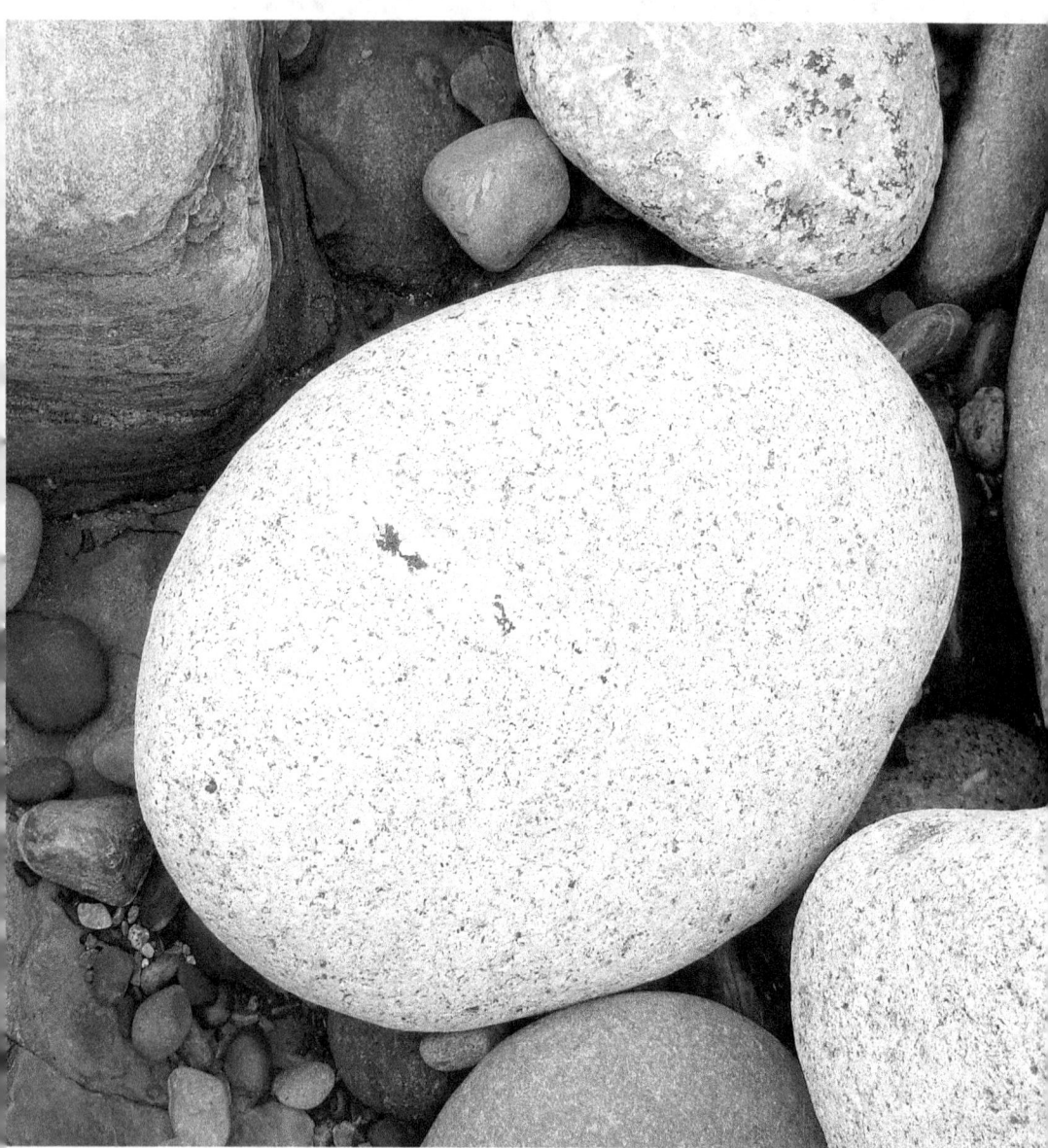

The white granite stones at Nanven beach
are readymade Brancusi sculptures.

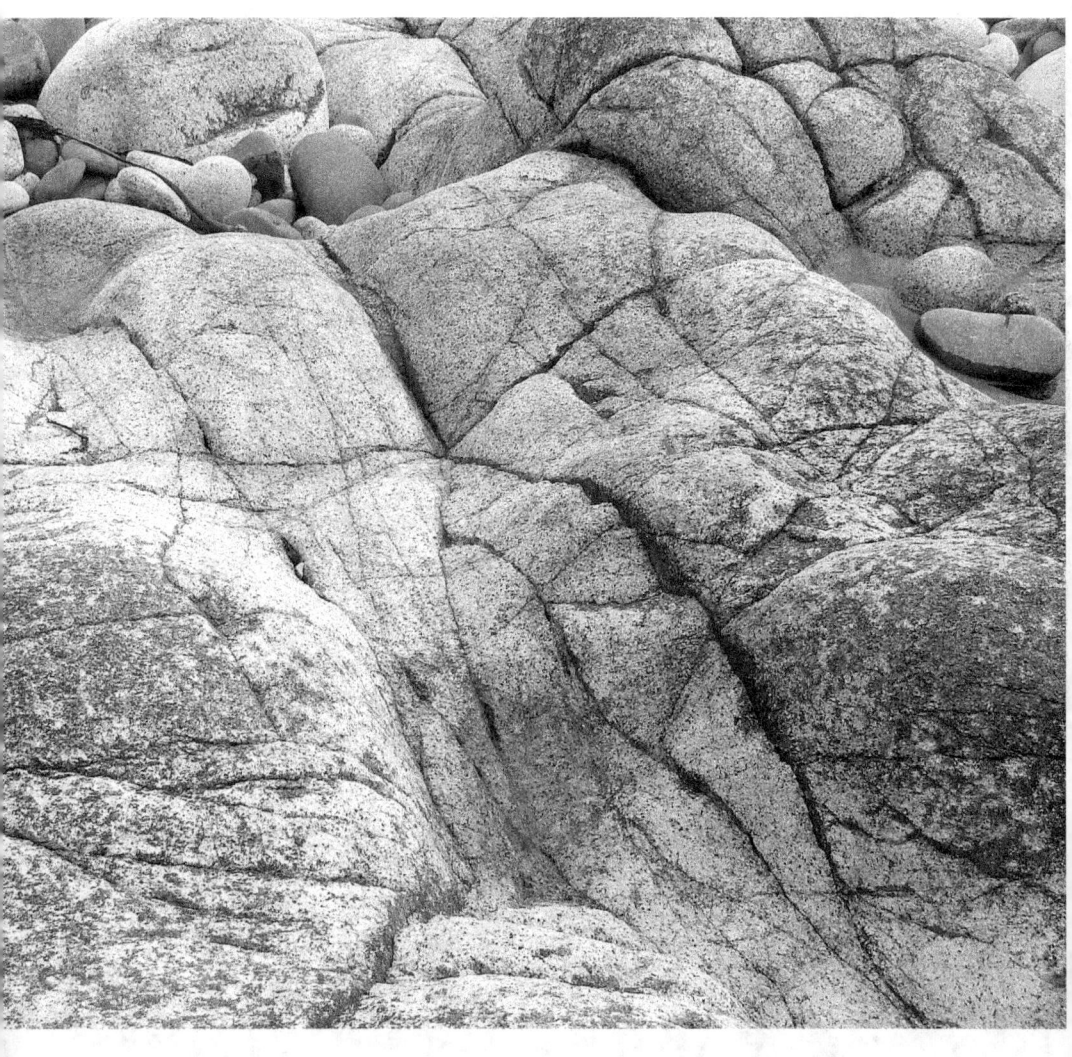

The 'body rocks' at Nanven near St Just, which Jackson has painted,
as in *On the Body Rocks, Nanven*.

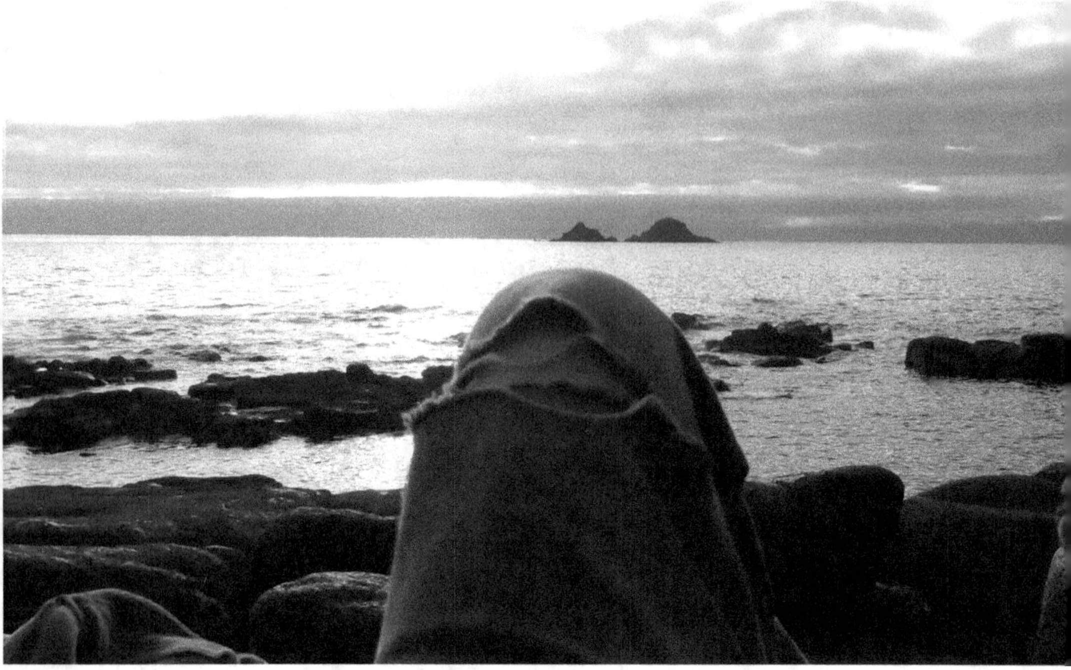

The sea from the end of Cot Valley, Cornwall, in 2013,
with the Brisons rocks impossible to miss.

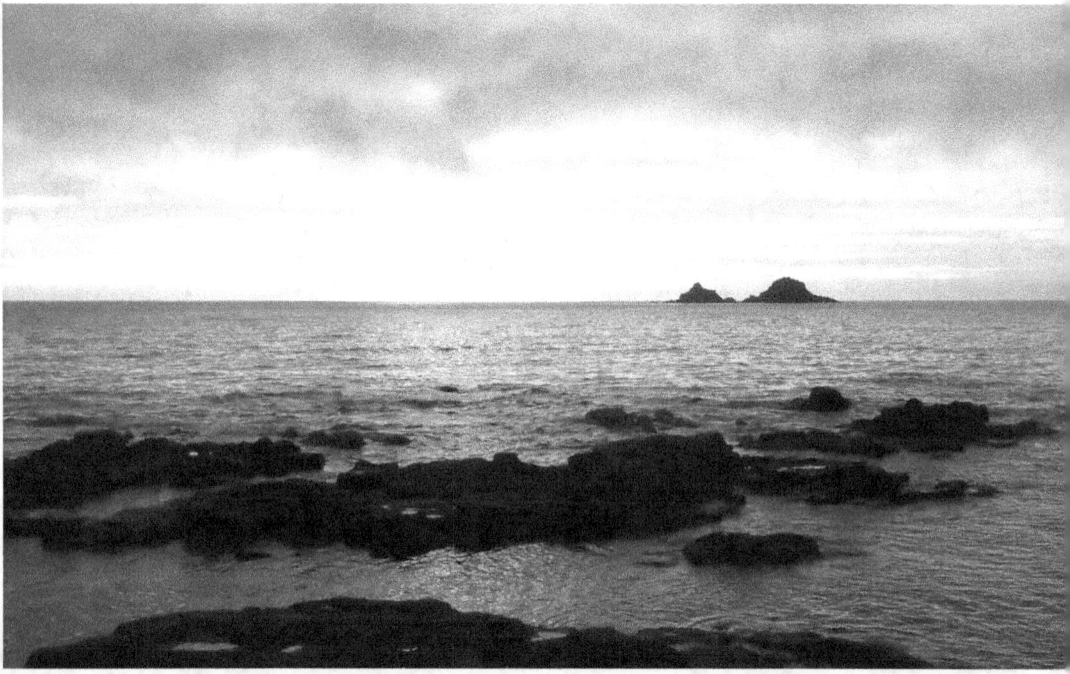

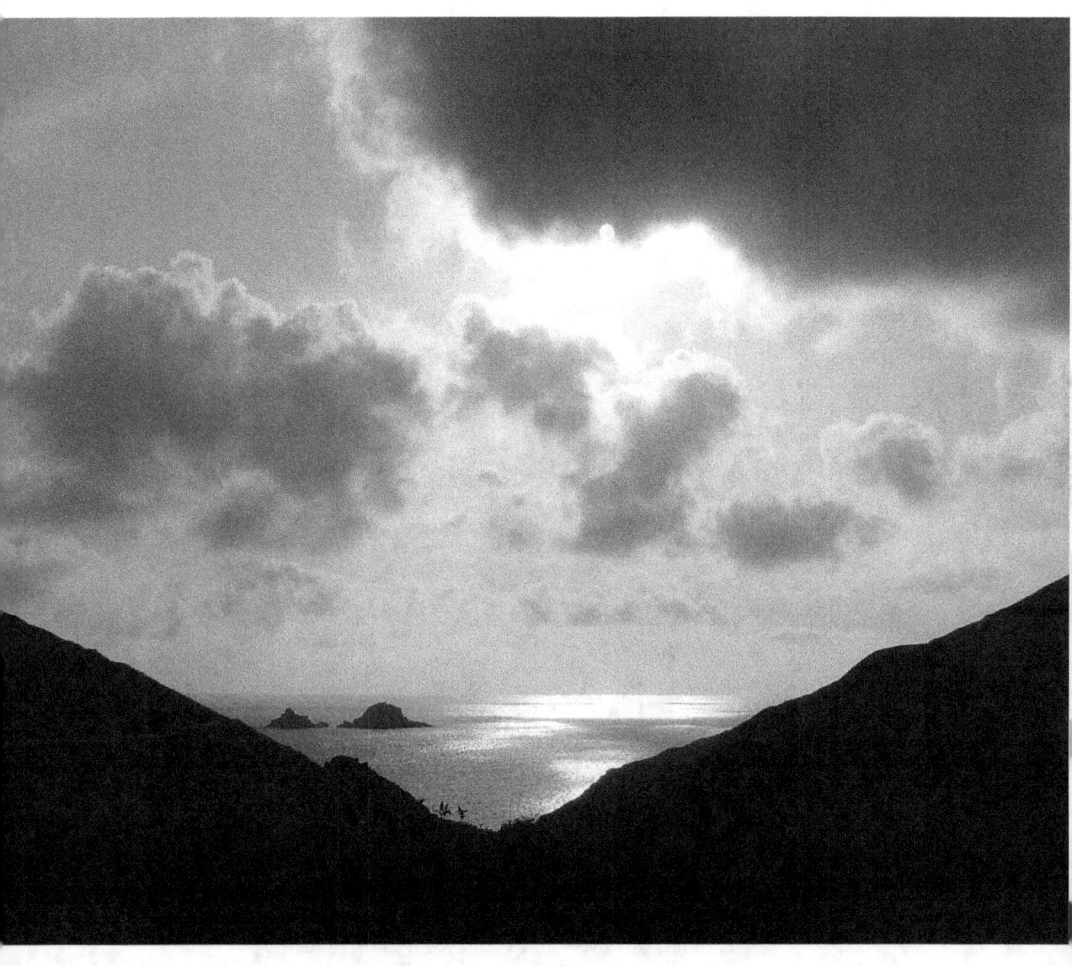

It helps if you start with terrific elements:
here you've got the sea, the light, the sky, the clouds, the sun
Cornwall, the 'V' shape, Summer, and great weather.
In Cot Valley.

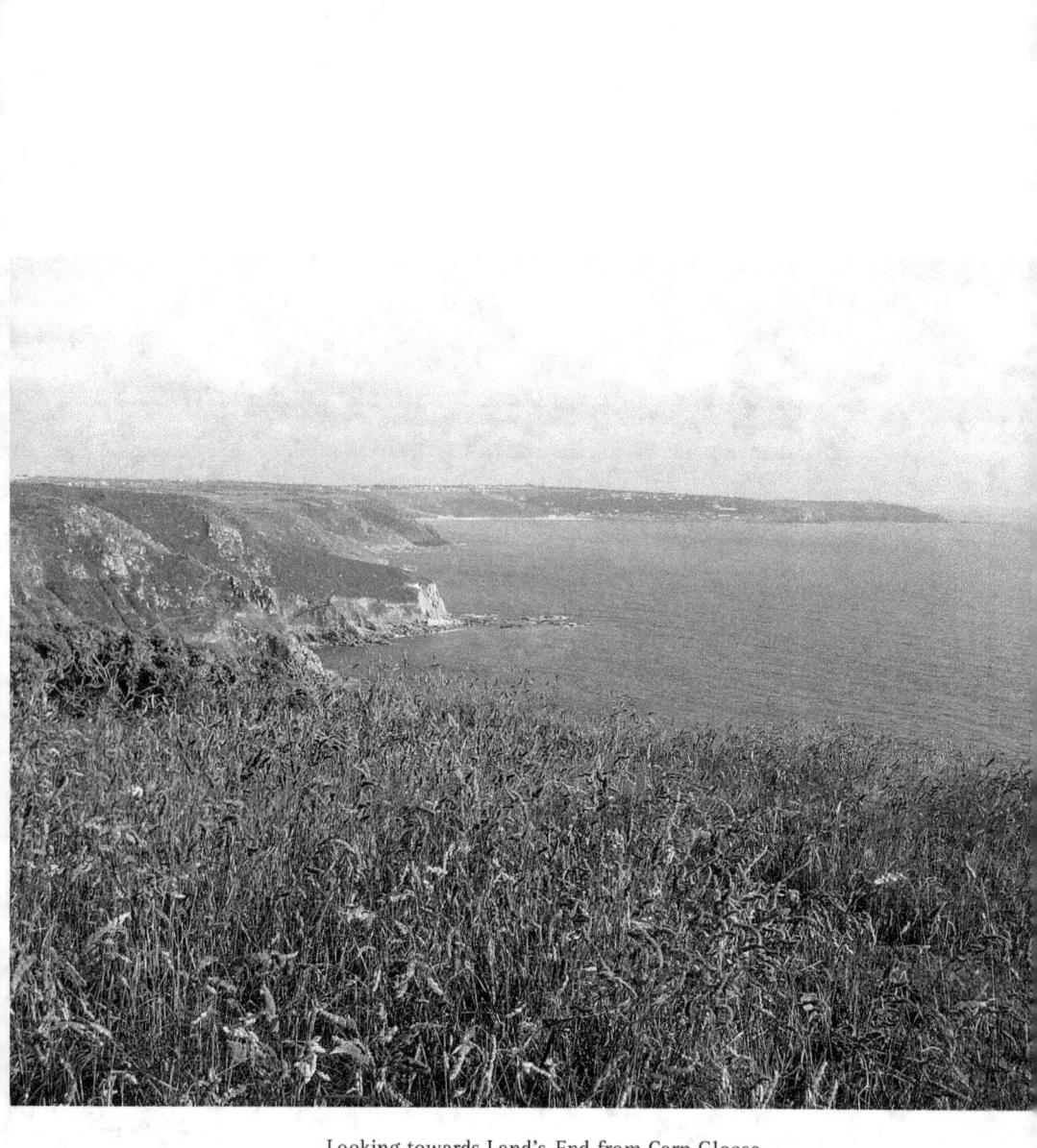

Looking towards Land's-End from Carn Gloose

The sheeted sea coming ashore
And hanging its pictures up in the hedges,
Its unsalted portraits,

The surface of the sea doubling
As it opens into sleep,
A source among white sources, cresting.

(Peter Redgrove, from 'Round Pylons')

The sea seen from Carn Gloose.

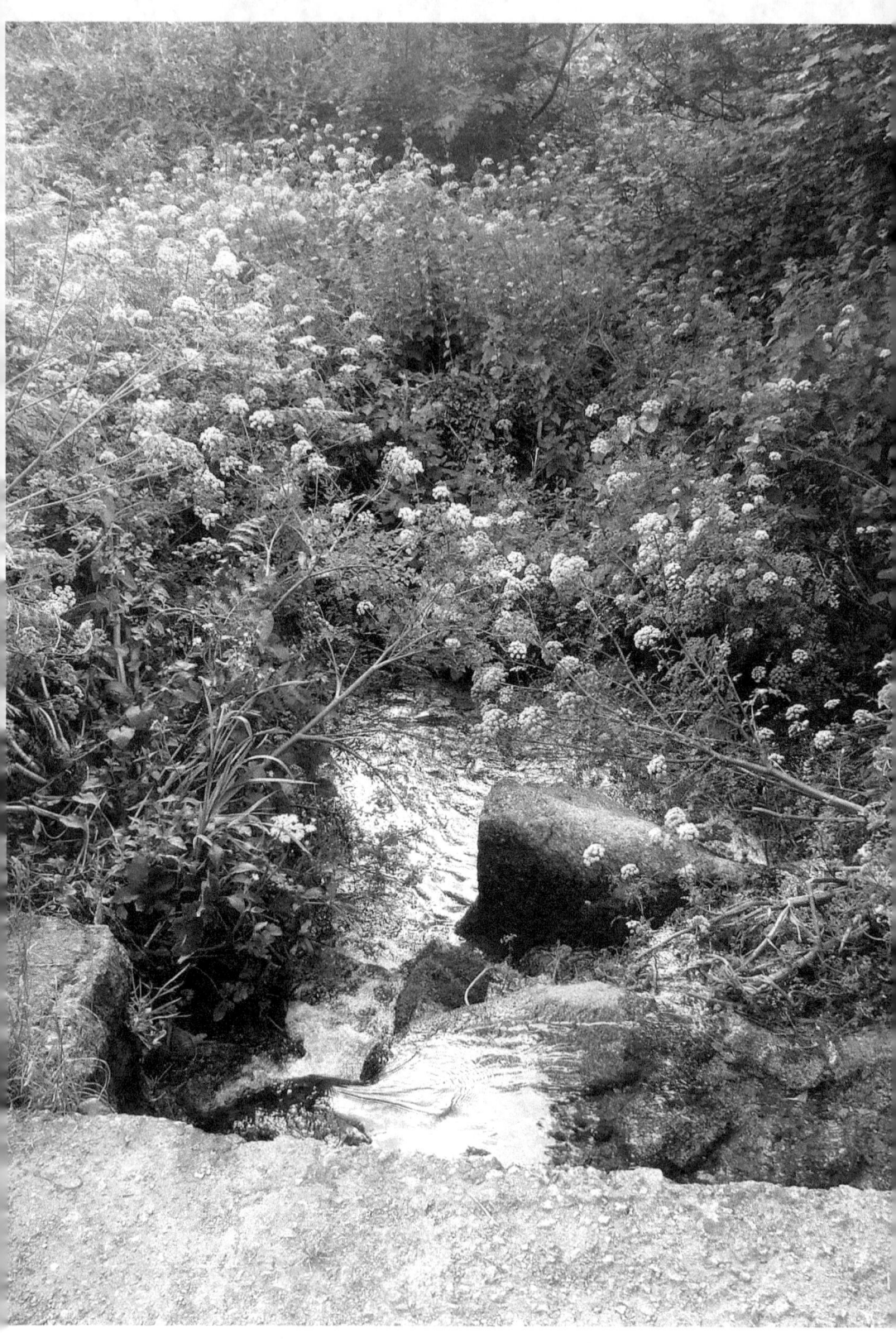

The little Cot Stream from one of the bridges in the valley.

Following Cot Stream down to the shining sea

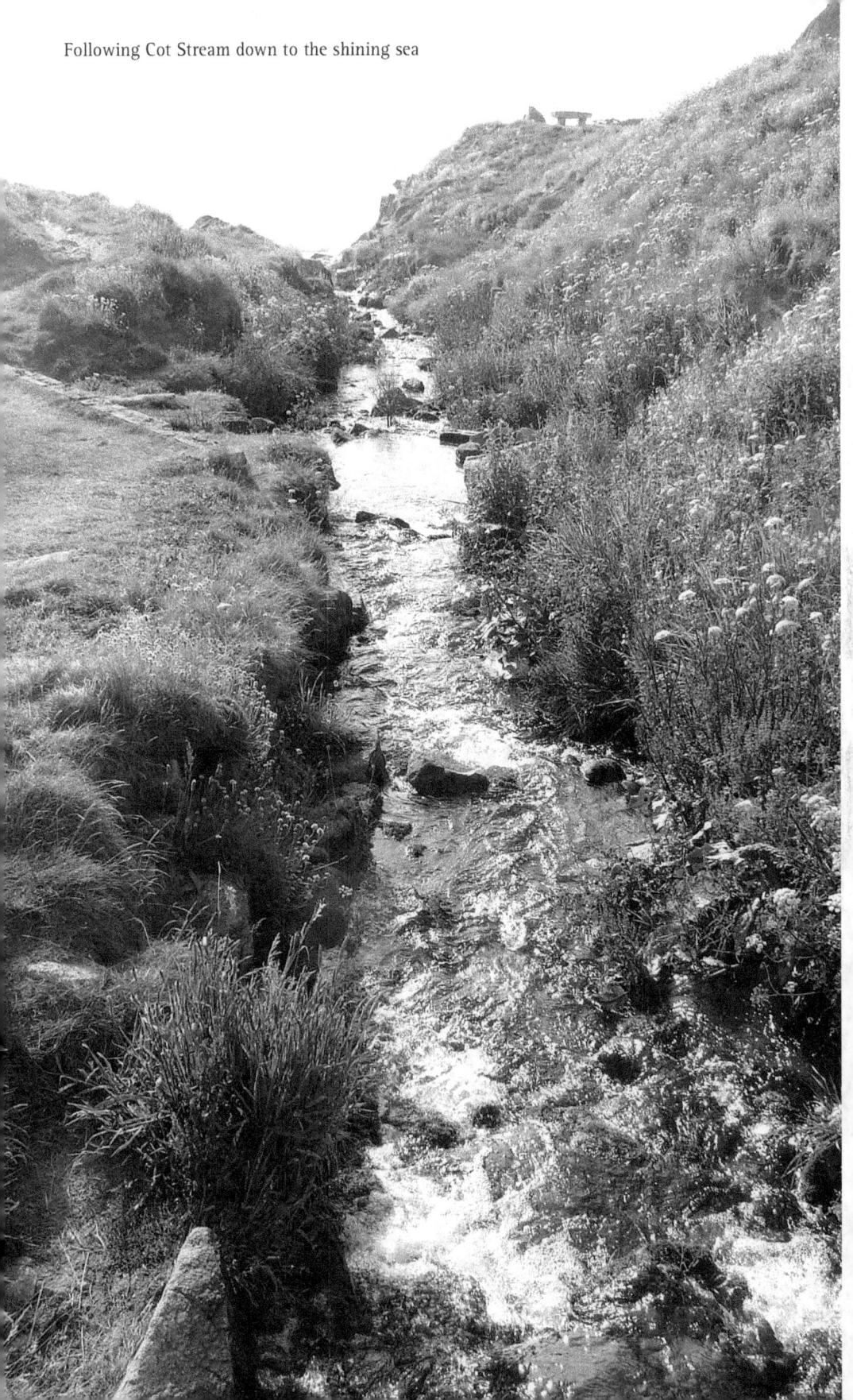

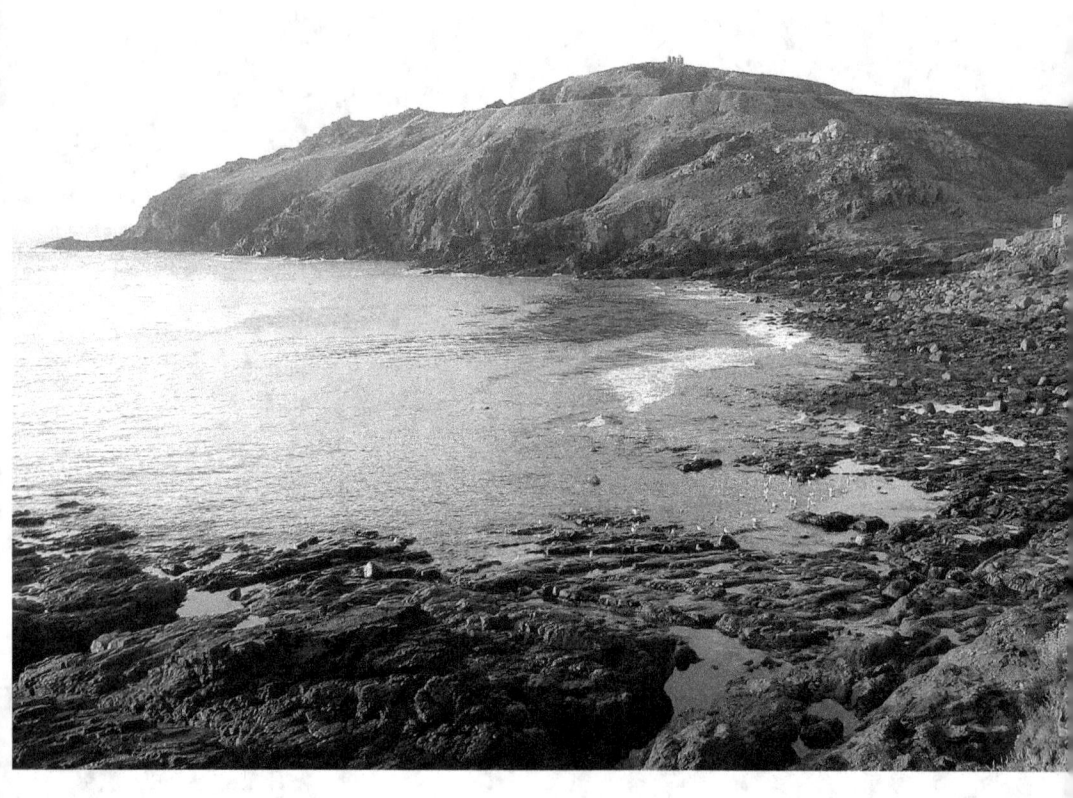

Looking towards Castle Kenidjack from Cape Cornwall

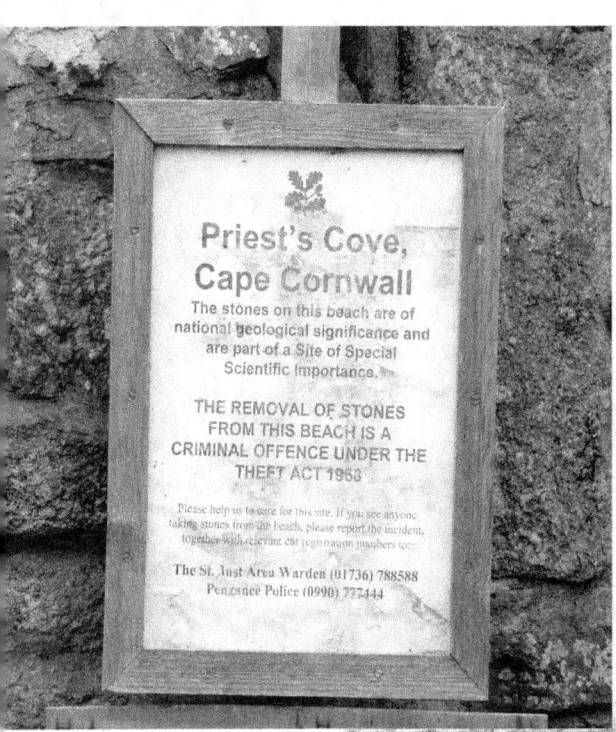

Signs at Priest Cove

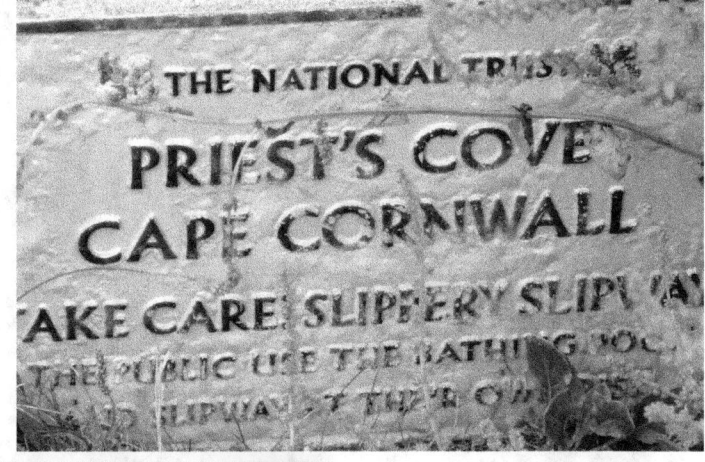

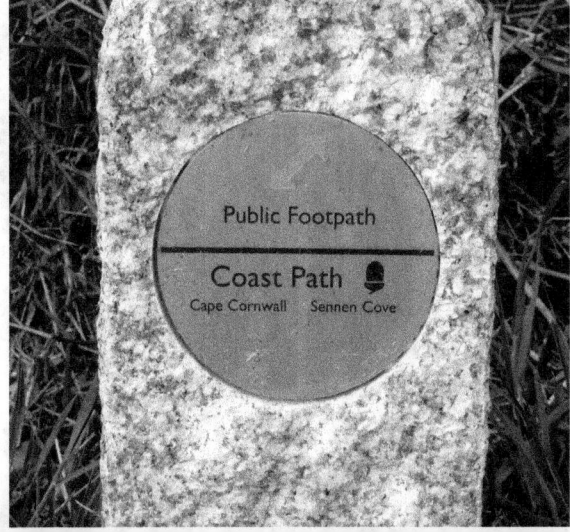

The A3071 road between St Just and Penzance

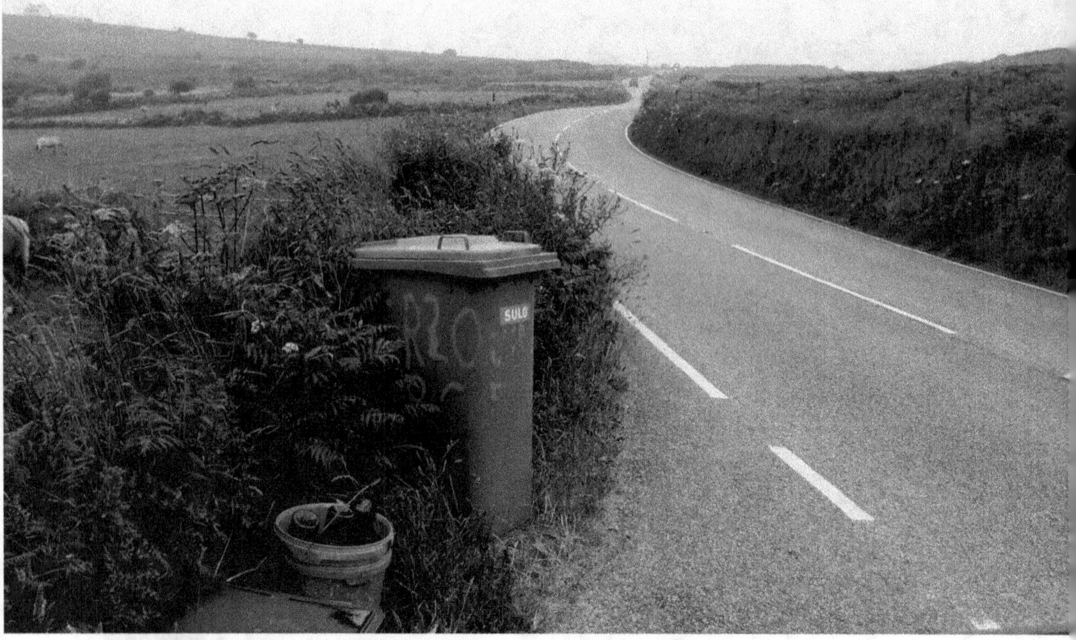

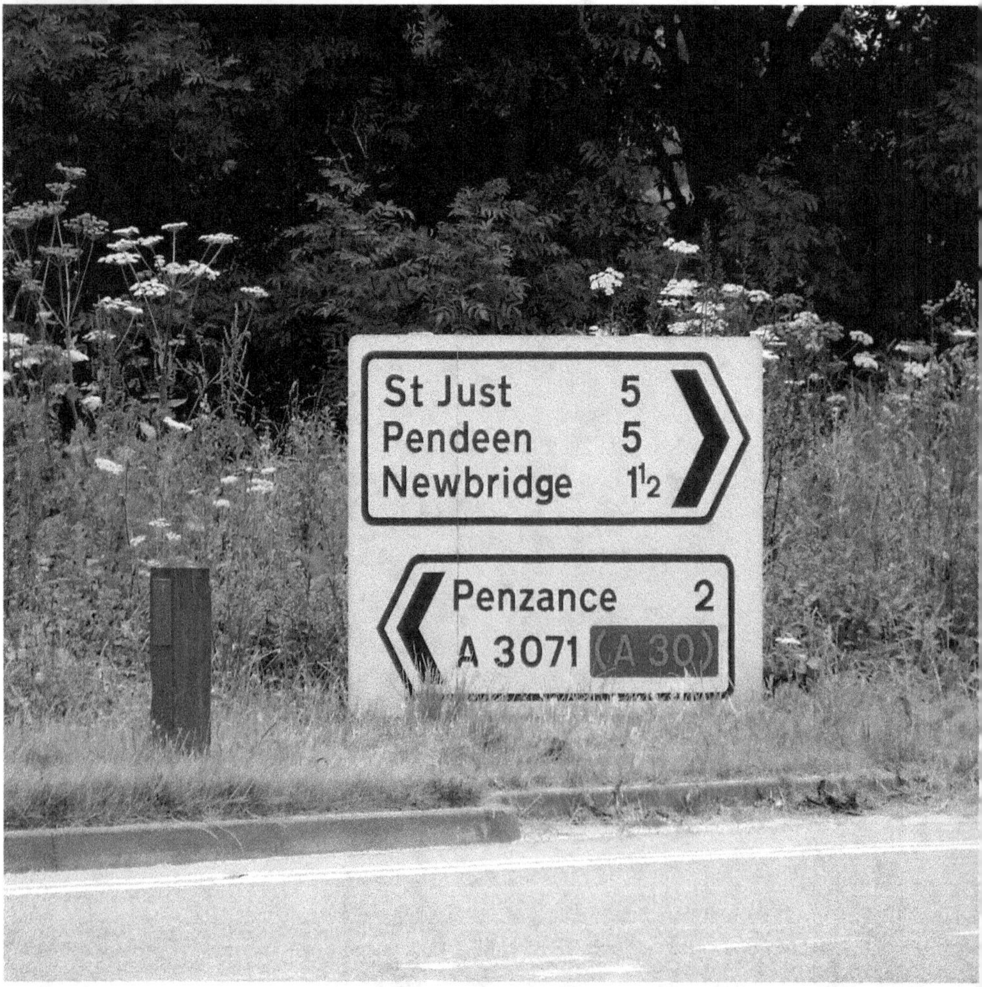

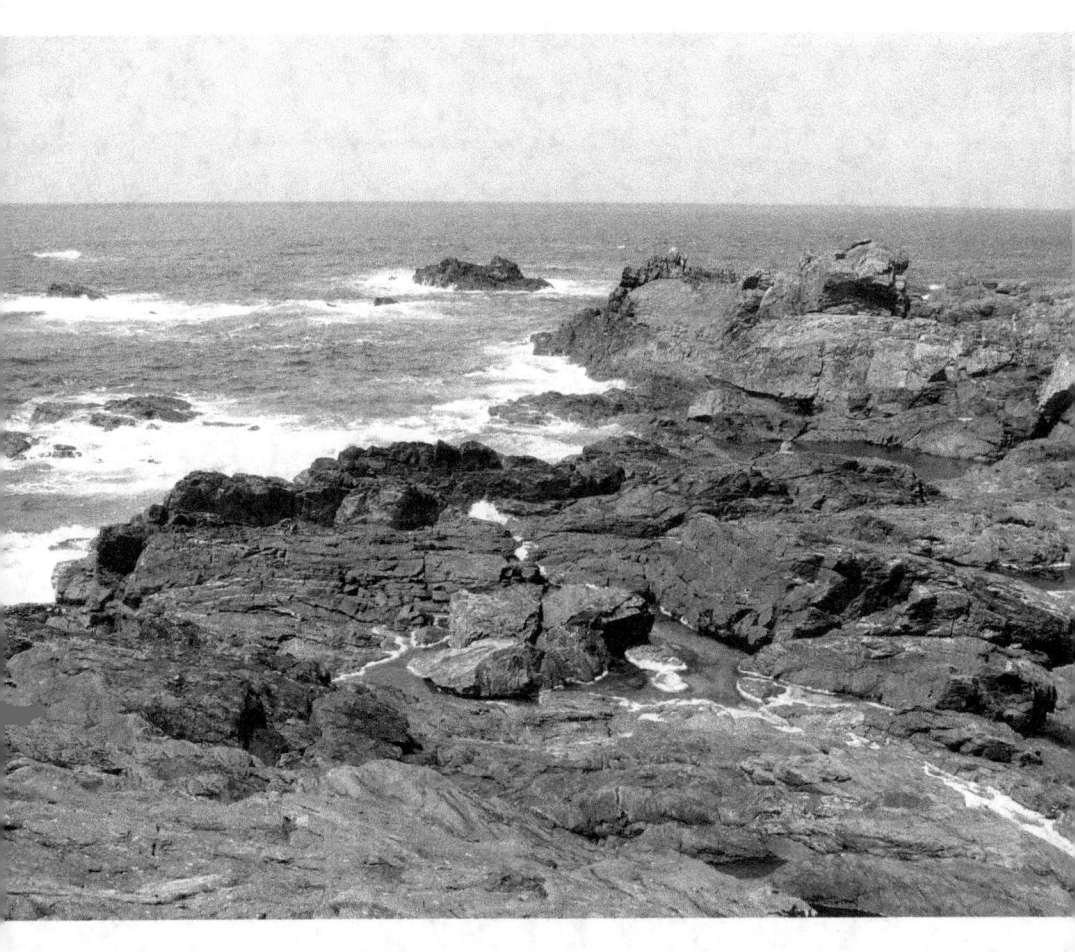

The Avarack, Pendeen

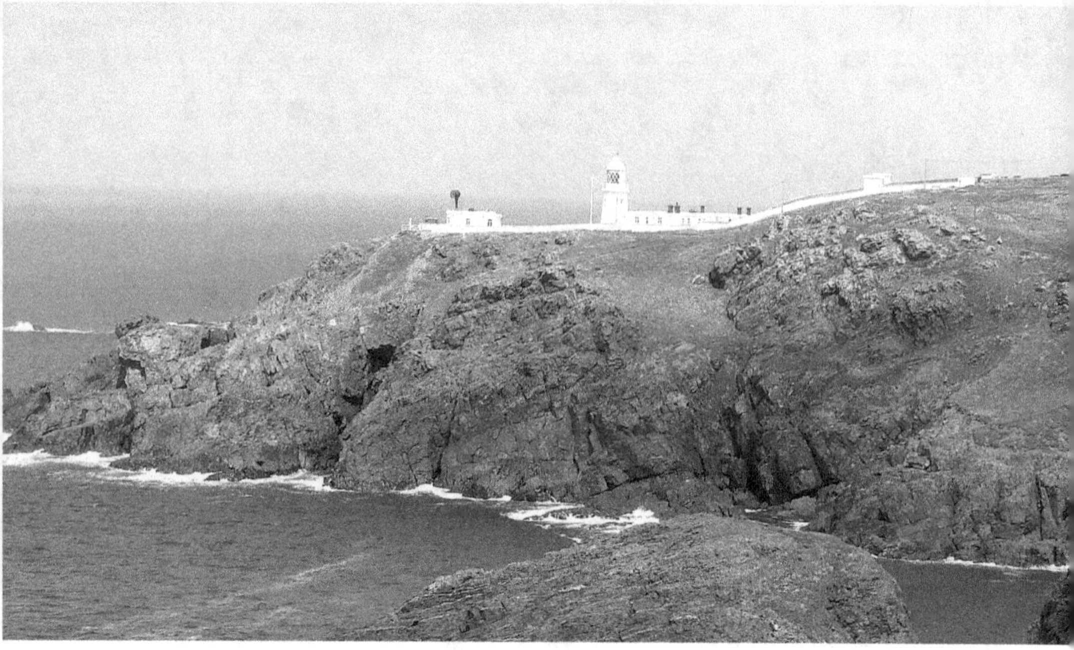

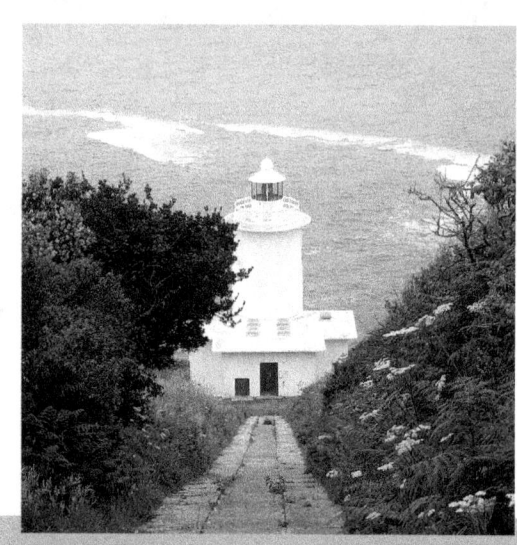

Some Cornish lighthouses:
Pendeen (above),
Tater-du near Lamorna (right),
and the most famous one:
Godrevy, near St Ives (below).

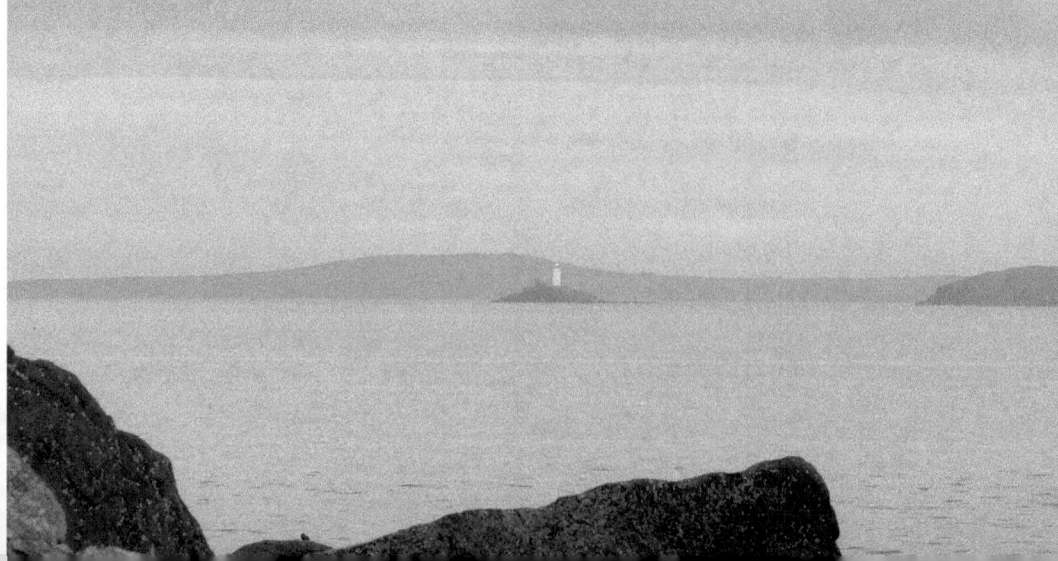

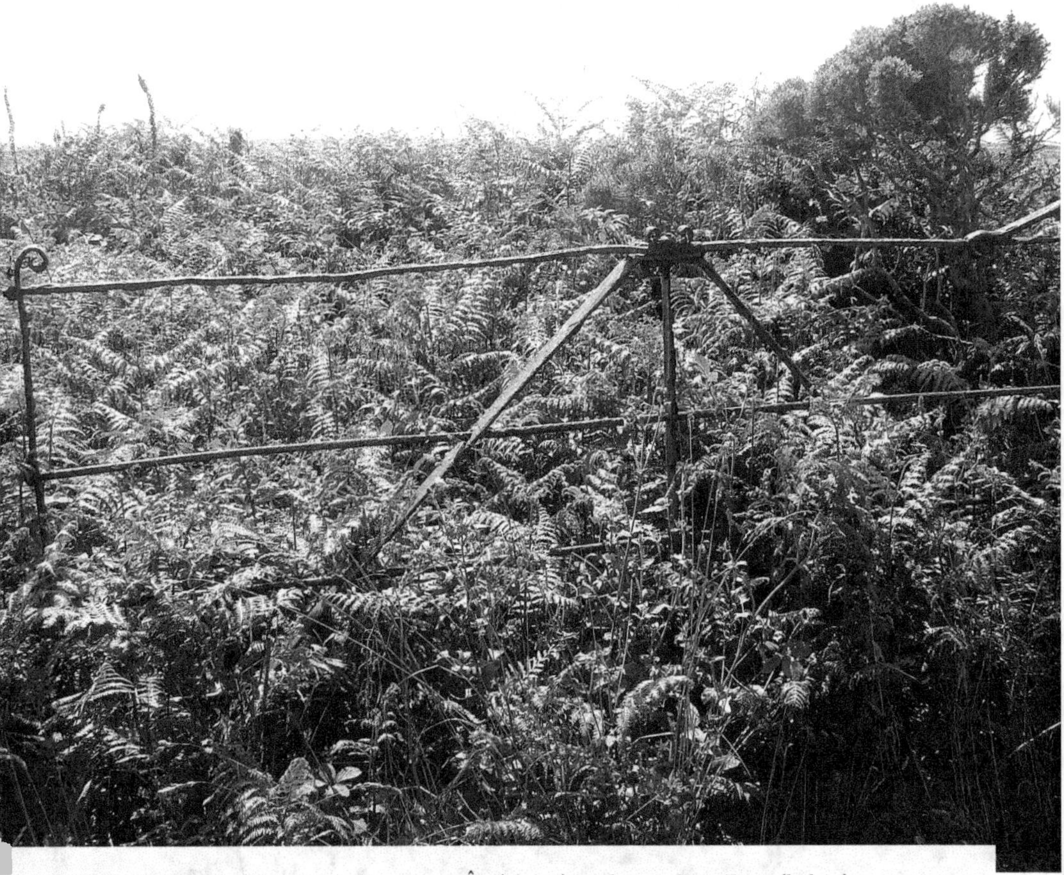

Cornish hedges – near Boscawen-Ûn (above), and near Carn Euny (below).

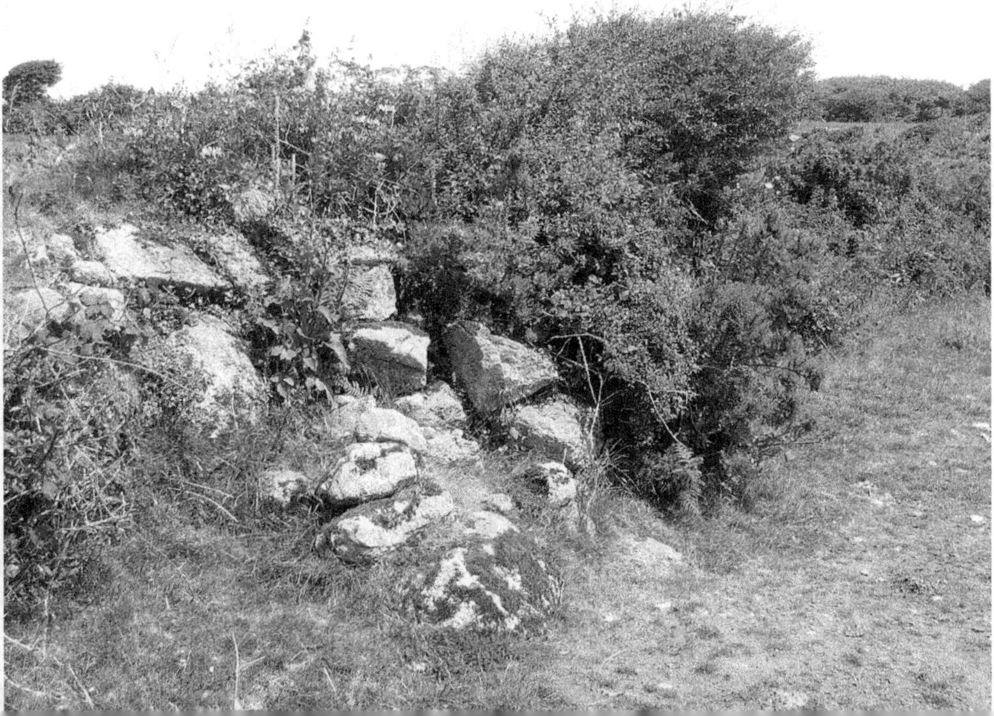

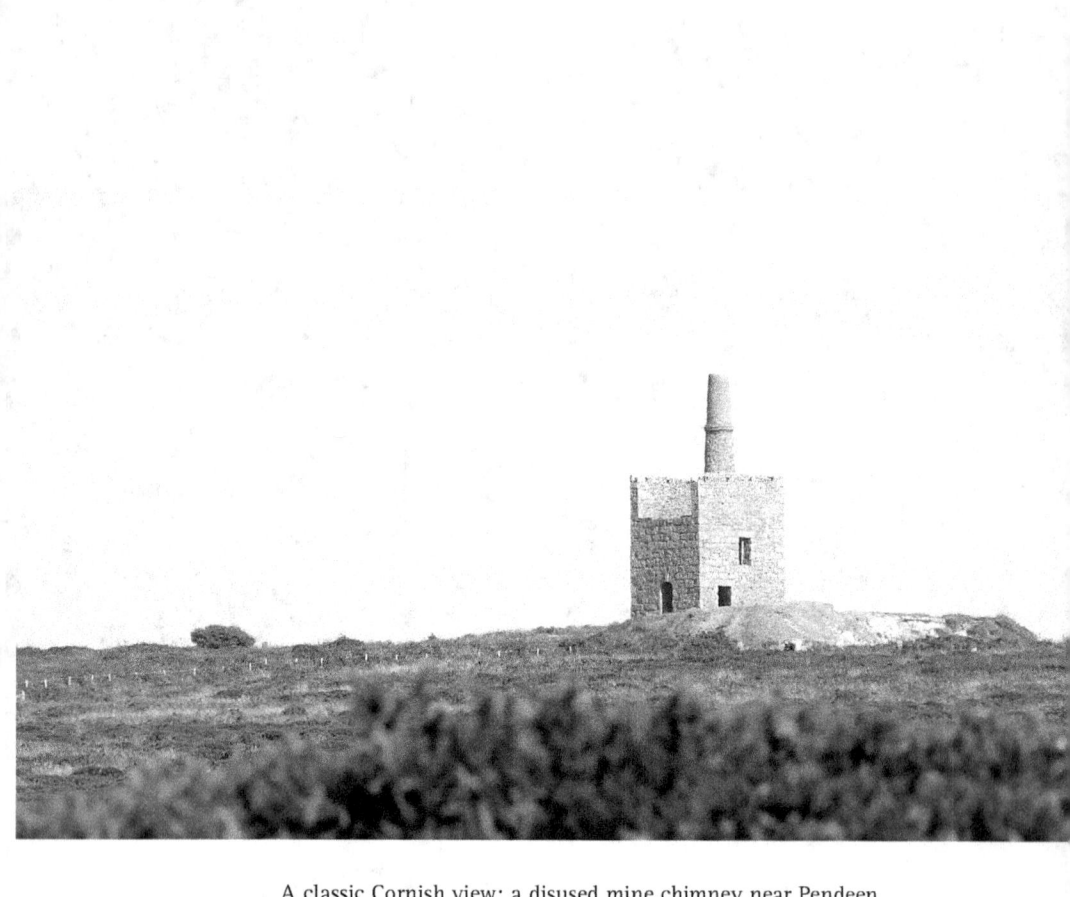

A classic Cornish view: a disused mine chimney near Pendeen.
Jackson remarked that he tried to avoid putting the disused chimneys and mine
workings into his paintings, because they were such a cliché of the area. But then he gave
in, after painting in the mine at South Crofty, accepting that the chimneys and engine
houses were part of Cornwall.

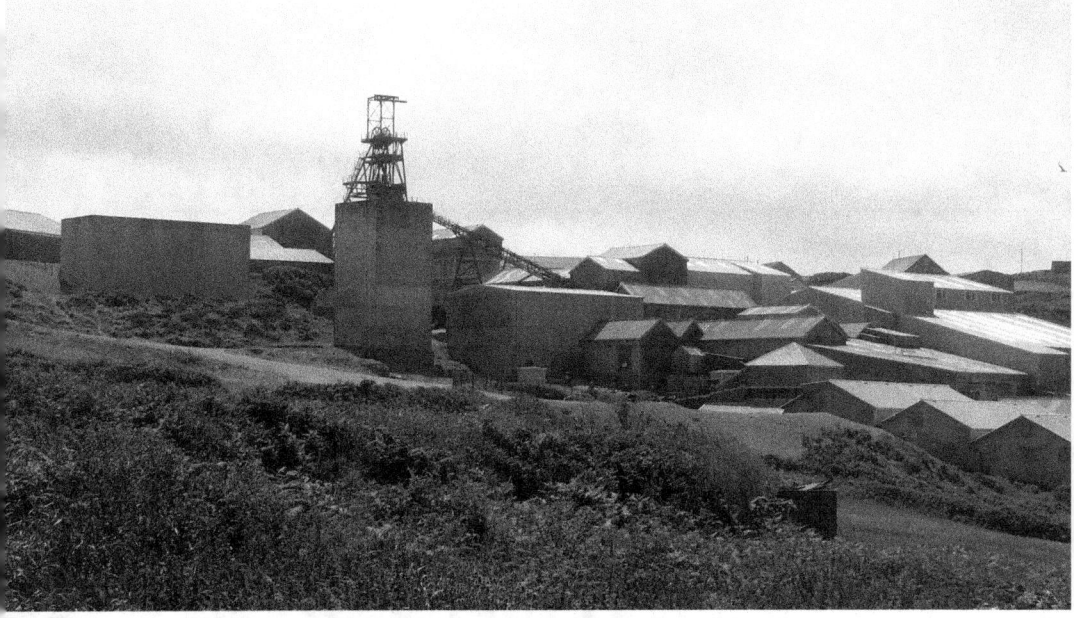

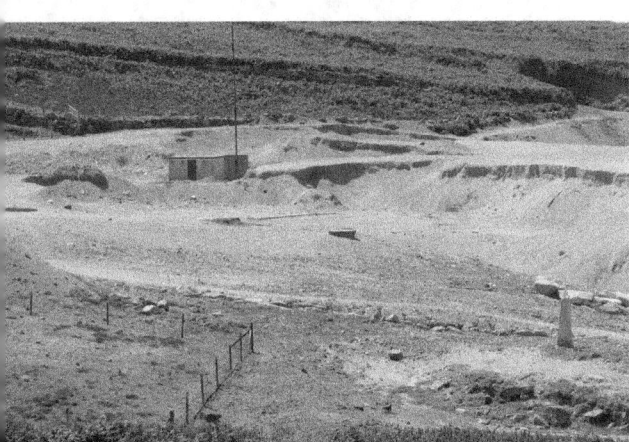

One of the last working mines
in Cornwall: Geevor, near Pendeen
(a working tin mine until 1990).

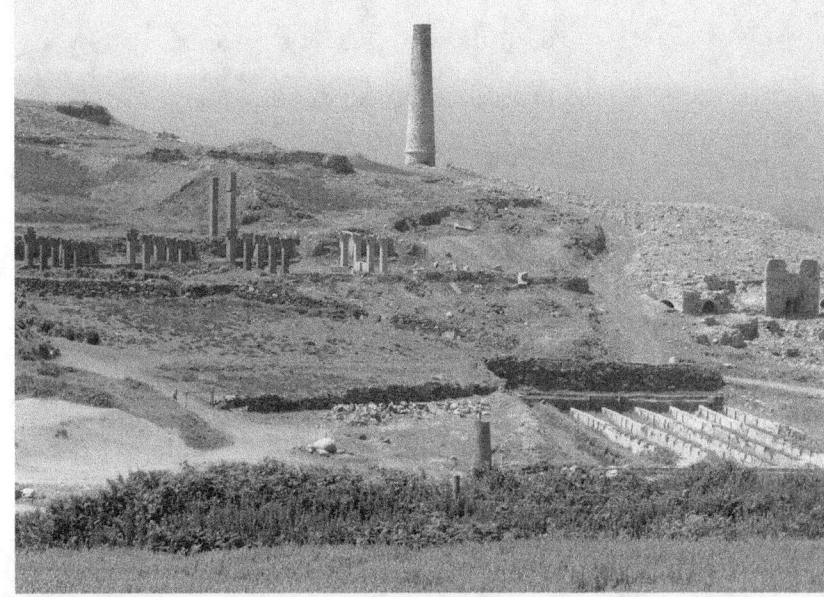

Out of this same light, out of the central mind,
We make a dwelling in the evening air,
In which being there together is enough.

(Wallace Stevens, from 'Final Soliloquy of the Interior Paramour')

The sea from the road up at Carn Brea.

PLACES IN KURT JACKSON'S ART

A litany of Kurt Jackson places would include:

Cornwall
Priest's Cove
Cape Cornwall
Cot and Kenidjack Valleys
The Scilly Isles
Scotland (Jura, Wester Ross)

Kurt Jackson isn't just painting Anything, Anywhere. There is a definite subject to each of his paintings, which is a distinct place (and also time and date). In his art it's not just a general view of a landscape, it's Kenidjack Valley, or Sennen beach, or St Michael's Mount.

And it does matter *to me* exactly where Kurt Jackson made his paintings. Somehow, his art wouldn't have the same resonance for me if it was painted in Slough or Croydon or Basingstoke (for readers who don't know Slough, Croydon or Basingstoke, they're known as dull towns in Southern England. Think Canada or New Jersey if you're in the U.S.A. That's a joke – apologies to anyone who adores Slough, Croydon or Basingstoke!).

But if Kurt Jackson's paintings had titles such as *Cardiff Street, Slough, 18.4.99*, or *Two Kids Skateboarding Outside Burger King, Swindon*, or *Kempshott Housing Estate, Basingstoke*, they wouldn't have the same resonance *for me*. There might be great landscape paintings that could be made in dull places, of course, and a good artist could make interesting art anywhere. Jackson has said: 'I don't like to paint random places, I like there to be a purpose for it' – a commission, or an autobiographical connection.

Maybe French film director Jean-Luc Godard is right when he said in the 1982 film *Passion*, 'partout c'est beau'. Maybe 'everywhere is beautiful'. OK, all I'm saying is that Cornwall and other attractive landscapes in Kurt Jackson's art must play some part in its appeal. Just my opinion.

But it matters that Kurt Jackson's paintings are of beautiful land-scapes and seascapes and skyscapes. It matters also – *to me at least* – that Jackson is not only painting Cornwall, a very special place, but also West Cornwall. And not just West Cornwall, but West Penwith. And also a very particular area of the peninsula: the area around Cape Cornwall and St Just. One aspect of Jackson's art that attracted me to it when I first saw it in Penzance was its depiction of places I knew very well, and revered.

One wonders if Kurt Jackson's art would have the same sort of impact if the viewer didn't know the places he's painting. Knowing Cot Valley, Priest's Cove, Carn Gloose, Tregeseal and Botallack intimately enhances the paintings. Even in the area around St Just, there are views which are not what I would call romantic and poetic: St Just has some housing estates and scruffy streets which don't often appear in Jackson's art. Jackson's art often quietly seems to elide heavily industrial, or post-industrial, or run-down and urban landscapes (he has avoided mine chimneys, for instance). However, he has also painted those sorts of places from time to time – as in *The Thames Project*.

❖

Many of Kurt Jackson's paintings may be about particular places, or have been inspired by particular locations, but the final paintings could depict many places around the world. Jackson's series on Cornish rivers and estuaries, for instance (*The Cornish Estuary*), contains pictures which are recognizably Cornwall – *Hayle Estuary From the Saltings* (2004), *Looking Out From Under the Oaks On the Banks of the Fal* (2004), and *Dusk, Smell of Fish, East Quay, Hayle* (2003) – and can be compared with the real places. But there are many others – such as *Estuary Mouth* (2004), *Little Petherick Creek, Near Padstow* (2004), and *Winter Low Sunlight, Tamar Meander, Halton Quay* (2004) – which don't contain enough readily identifiable landmarks to situate them in Cornwall. They might be rivers in Alaska, or China, or Africa. For the painter, it's important that the paintings were produced in or inspired by these places, but for the viewer it's not the same. The viewer wasn't there. Mark Rothko talked about that – how the painter experienced the subject of the painting directly, but for the viewer is was always at some distance. The observer can never have the same experience as the artist.

And some of Kurt Jackson's *The Cornish Estuary* paintings sink towards abstraction, recalling the Impressionists' meditations on water and reflections (such as those by Claude Monet or Alfred Sisley). In these paintings – *And When I Got Up...* (2004), *Chiffchaffs and Mullet* (2004), *Helford Blizzard* (2004), *Lowe Pool, March, Early Evening* (2004), and *Snow and Sunshine, Gillan Creek* (2004) – the elements of representation and figuration are dissolved in washes of watercolour as the painter explores the ever-fascinating effect of light on water. (And notice how often in the river and estuary pictures Jackson has put the water in between himself and the sun, so the images are backlit yet again).

❖

Does it make any difference if one knows the places an artist is depicting in their art? No, but it does enhance the experience of their art. It does help a little contemplating the art of, say, Gustave Moreau, if one has visited his house and museum in Paris. If you've made the trip to the Musée Moreau, off the beaten track, up rue de la Rochefoucauld, and seen that dark, late 19th century interior (very highly recommended), it definitely adds to your appreciation of Moreau's exotic, dense Symbolist art.

And the San Marco Museum in Florence makes a huge impression, the perfect context for viewing the religious paintings of the Renaissance artist Fra Angelico. You step into those small, whitewashed monks' cells and the murals of scenes from the Christian story make total sense.

Undoubtedly the most impressive artist's house in Cornwall is Barbara Hepworth's place in St Ives. You can't forget that secluded garden and studio tucked away in the back streets of St Ives, with glimpses of the town, the church and the sea. Probably most of the people who enjoy Kurt Jackson's art haven't visited many (or any) of the places he's painting, but it enhances his art knowing sites like Priest's Cove and St Just very well.

BEAUTY SPOTS

Note that, although Kurt Jackson has been painting for most of his career in Cornwall, in the midst of some of the most romantic and beloved of British landscapes, he does not (often) paint the obvious 'beauty spots' or the many prehistoric sites. It might be tempting for a landscape painter working in Cornwall to tackle the big vistas, such as St Michael's Mount, Porthcurno, Land's End, Tintagel, the Eden project, Bodmin Moor, the Tamar estuary and views across the Helford River. Of course, these particular parts of Cornwall have been painted countless times, by the professional and the amateur artist.

Very famous locations, such as St Michael's Mount or Land's End, do crop up in Kurt Jackson's work, but not as often as they might be expected to. Land's End is sometimes glimpsed in the background of Jackson's sea-pieces and views over Tregeseal or Cape Cornwall, but it's off to one side. And St Michael's Mount (which dominates the South side of West Penwith) was at the end of the *St Michael's Way* series (and in *St Michael's Mount*, 1999, a view of the Mount from the beach at Marazion, and in *Waiting For a Cow Jam at Ding Dong*, 1999, there's one of the classic views of St Michael's Mount glimpsed from far away, in a silvery sea, with the low tableland of the Lizard glimpsed beyond).

Note too that Kurt Jackson's art tends to steer clear of the rich history in ancient structures in Cornwall – the stone circles, the standing stones, the Mên-an-Tol, Lanyon Quoit, the burial mounds and prehistoric settlements. And the many mediæval and religious buildings, like churches and castles. They do turn up in his paintings from time to time (for instance, Carn Gloose, Kenidjack Castle, Chûn Quoit, and Tregeseal stone circle). He has painted Carfury standing stone a few times (*Carfury Standing Stone*, 1989), and a holed stone at Kenidjack (2002). But, although Jackson has links with 'New Age' culture, with neo-pagan culture, and has lived near a stone circle for years, he has usually avoided obvious pagan or megalithic art.[38] (A good deal of 'pagan', hippy, 'New Age' and mind, body, spirit art is extremely mediocre, too often recalling gaudy 1970s airbrushed fantasy art.)

Cornwall is a heavily documented county. Like London, Oxford, Stratford-upon-Avon, Bath and Edinburgh, it has been photographed, videoed, painted and sketched thousands of times. There must be probably millions of images of Cornwall by now, existing in Mini-DV tapes, in VHS tapes, in digital camera stills, on DVDs, in computers and tablets, in colour snapshots, in cel phones, in sketchpads, in photo albums, and in canvases. No inch of Cornwall has been left unphotographed or unpainted. Going to Cornwall to paint in the early

---

38 Walking out to a stone ring when he first moved to West Cornwall helped to confirm Kurt Jackson that this part of England was a good place to live (P, 17).

21st century would be like going to Paris or New York City: it's all been used in art many, many times, for many, many years, and, like Paris or New York, has supported all sorts of artists' colonies (from crazy individuals to formal societies). However, anyone is free to paint or photograph Cornwall: you can't copyright a sparkling sea, as Michael Jay told me.

On his website (kurtjackson.com), Kurt Jackson offers one of his dumbest, most arrogant statements.[39] Jackson asserts (*pace* developing his own art gallery in St Just):

> for many people Priest Cove, Cape Cornwall and Kenidjack are now synonymous with my paintings.

It's worth reminding ourselves that Priest's Cove, Cape Cornwall, Cot and Kenidjack Valleys have been around for hundreds of thousands of years, and Jackson's art has had a high profile only since 1998-99 (that is, less than 15 years, and it's past its peak). It's also worth noting that 100s of artists have worked and continue to work in this area. And let's not forget that art features in the minds of only a *tiny* percentage of people who visit the area: go to Priest's Cove on a hot Summer's day and ask the bikini-clad sun-bathers and the wet-suited surfers if they've heard of Kurt Jackson.

Like, *no*.

Anyhoo, if Cornwall (and this part of West Cornwall), is associated with any painter, it is Britain's greatest artist, J.M.W Turner. It is *Turner – more than any other artist –* who has fixed the image of Cornwall in the cultural consciousness of Albion.

---

39 Some of Jackson's statements and interviews, including the texts he includes in every exhibition catalogue, are sometimes pretentious and over-wrought.

PRIEST'S COVE AND CAPE CORNWALL

The heart of Kurt Jackson's art, the very centre of all of the landscapes he has been painting all these years, is undoubtedly Cape Cornwall. And one part of Cape Cornwall in particular: Priest's Cove (sometimes known as Priest Cove; on the Ordinance Survey maps, it's Priest's Cove). It's a spectacular piece of Cornish coastline, once thought to be the furthest point West, before it was superseded by Land's End.

Cape Cornwall is apparently the only cape in England.[40] It's a small headland that juts out into the Atlantic. Like Glastonbury Tor, Cape Cornwall is 'completed' by the chimney from the Cape Cornwall Mine (there was once a beacon here).[41] Cape Cornwall is now owned by the National Trust.[42] Cape Cornwall was once fortified in the Bronze or Iron Ages, as was Maen Castle nearby. Stone cists, burials and barrows have been discovered on the Cape.

What else is there at Cape Cornwall? Stone walls (plenty of these). Fields (everywhere). A few houses (some very prominent and white). A golf course nearby, back towards St Just (Cape Cornwall Golf and Country Club).[43] A hotel. A small car park. Toilets. A refreshment stall in Summer. The South-West Coast Path passes by, from Land's End to Pendeen, following the clifftops. A narrow lane winds down from St Just (though the best way to approach Cape Cornwall is on foot along the coastal path or across the fields).

Priest's Cove itself, once a mediæval landing stage, is now a rocky beach with a stone jetty and a few fisherman's huts and a few boats pulled up the concrete slipway. Out to sea are the rocky outcrops of the Brisons, very distinctive rocks, so prominent you can't miss them anywhere you look (you can see the Brisons in many other artists' work). At one time, Kurt Jackson said he excised the Brisons from his Priest's Cove paintings because a friend told him they looked like a silhouette of Charles de Gaulle in the bath, and he couldn't get that

40 A rather pointless piece of information that's always trotted out in tourist brochures.
41 Am I the only one who reckons that Glastonbury Tor would be much less intriguing without the church tower at its summit? Rounded hills are appealing, but that tower gives the Tor a distinctive silhouette.
42 And the National Trust, bless 'em, are now charging for the car park (£3 = $4.50).
43 The golf course, which I loathe, takes up a huge slice of land around Priest's Cover, where white, middle-aged men hit balls around the grass.

image out of his head (P, 21). But the Brisons appear in works such as the *Porth* series. The cliffs run down to Sennen and Land's End to the South, with the lighthouse at Longships clearly visible a mile of so beyond the headland. Along the cliffs to the South are the wonderfully named Carn Gloose (sometimes 'Gluze'), and Ballowall Barrow, a large prehistoric burial mound that you can climb into, right next to the road.

On either side of Cape Cornwall are two valleys, Cot and Kenidjack. From Cape Cornwall looking North the remains of Kenidjack Castle can be seen, and mine shafts and mine workings towards Botallack. The Scilly Isles can be clearly spotted from the cliffs around Cape Cornwall, with the lighthouse beam there lingering long after the islands have disappeared into the twilight.

Priest's Cove takes its name from the town of St Just and the saint Just, 'Just' being 'East', and 'Priest' being 'Porth' or 'Per East' (hence the title of one of Kurt Jackson's exhibitions of Priest's Cove paintings, *Porth*). It's not a great place for swimming, being rocky and often rough (the crowds tend to head for Sennen or Porthcurno, especially those into surfing and body boarding). However, I have been at Priest's Cove in Summer when it's jammed with sun-bathers in bikinis, and guys in wetsuits riding the surf beyond the rocky shoreline, and kids horsing around in the small tidal pool just below the Cape.

There may be more amazing landscapes in Cornwall or England or Europe or wherever, but there is something about Cape Cornwall that is very special. Some landscapes just chime with you. It's a combination of elements: sky, sea, rocks, cliffs, light, clouds. The sea and the sky dominate everything here, a gigantic heavenly bowl or dome. The sea, the sky and the light are always changing. Or maybe it's special because you have the whole of England/ Britain behind you, and nothing in front. Nothing, that is, for thousands of miles of ocean. Or it could be the lure of the West, of looking Westwards – the idea of 'the West' and 'Westness'.

The sea is everywhere.

And this sea is so spectacular, so enormous, so full of energy, it really feels like the *Atlantic Ocean*, not the *English Channel*. Something

Atlantic and *very big* and wild and a real ocean, rather than some bit of water separating England from France. And there really is nothing out from Cape Cornwall until North America. It's not like looking out from the coast in Wales, where Ireland is across Cardigan Bay and the Irish Sea.

Setting out West from Cape Cornwall one might reach North America, or perhaps magical kingdoms like Atlantis or lost Lyonnesse. If you spend a lot of time up on the cliffs or on the granite boulders just above the surf you can begin to believe that sunken realms such as Lyonnesse or Westernesse or Atlantis could just possibly have existed (and if they didn't, they should have).

British authors such as Thomas Hardy and J.R.R. Tolkien were fascinated by a land West of England that had sunk beneath the waves. Tolkien, for instance, created his own version of the Atlantis myth in his book *The Silmarillion*, calling the island Númenor, which the gods (or Valar) overwhelm with a tidal wave when the Númenóreans (encouraged by Sauron) sail for Valinor, the Blessed Realm, in a bid for immortality. You can dream of such magical realms in this part of Cornwall – it seems to encourage it.

John Ronald Reuel Tolkien, by the way, liked Cornwall a lot, and wrote of a visit to Kynance Cove on the Lizard:

> Nothing I could say in a dull old letter would describe it to you. The sun beats down on you and a huge Atlantic swell smashes and spouts over the snags and reefs. The sea has carved weird wind-holes and spouts into the cliffs which blow with trumpety noises or spout foam like a whale, and everywhere you see black and red rock and white foam against violet and transparent seagreen.[3]

J.R.R. Tolkien here evokes the immense power of the ocean in this part of Cornwall – it's an aspect of the environment it's impossible to ignore. The number of shipwrecks around the coast, for instance, runs into thousands and thousands. And Kurt Jackson from time to time mentions in his art the thunderous waves which sometimes get a little too close. There's an elemental power to this part of England – when that tide is coming in at Priest's Cove, there's nothing on Earth that can stop it (nothing on *Earth* – after all, the tide itself doesn't have an

Earthly engine – it's driven by the moon. That's a startling fact, if you think about it: the water is rushing towards your feet, but it's not the wind that's propelling it, but the moon, a quarter of a million miles away!).

For a painter, the appeal of Priest's Cove and Cape Cornwall is a combination of inspirations: the ever-changing nature of the sea, the sky, the light and the colour for a start. That's plenty to be going on with, and could keep an artist occupied for a long time. What else? It's a quiet spot (out of season, and on mizzly (rainy) days). Access is good (it's easy to reach from St Just). The fact that it faces West and South is important too, for a painter like Kurt Jackson, who, like William Turner, likes to paint into the sun, who likes to have the sun (and the clouds) reflected off the sea in front of him.

While we're talking about Priest's Cove, other artists of recent times have painted there. One of my favourites is Paul Evans, who has often painted Cornwall, as well as Sussex and Suffolk.[44]

❖

One of the things that Kurt Jackson's Priest's Cove paintings and drawings do is to remind viewers that everything changes but nothing seems to change. Anyone who's visited the sea or looked at the sky will know that the ocean and the heavens are continually changing – the light, the colour, the tone, the shapes, the clarity, the movement, etc. Yet the sky and the sea also seem to be much the same, over days and months and years and decades and centuries and millennia.

We will all die – but the sea will still be surging around Cape Cornwall in a hundred years... in 200 years... in 300,000 years.

Every time Kurt Jackson visits Priest's Cove he seems to paint pretty much the same view: always facing out to sea (almost never with his back to the sea, almost never painting the boats and walls and cliffs and houses and steps and concrete ramps and car park), and nearly always with the horizon line cutting through the composition (usually halfway, or in the golden proportion, lower or higher). The viewpoint is usually close to the level of the water, and usually at the base of the cliffs (Jackson worked in a cave sometimes, and sometimes in an old

---

44 We used his wonderful painting of *Priest Cove* (2006) as the cover for our book *The Best of Peter Redgrove's Poetry.*

fisherman's hut).[45] Sometimes the view is wide, and includes the Brisons, and Land's End. Sometimes it's zoomed right in, and selects just a section of the ocean.

In *Paintings of Cornwall and the Scillies*, Jackson identified three aspects of his art that were important for him:

(1) 'the experience of *being there'* in that particular place and time;

(2) producing something that resembles the place;

(3) the pleasure of painting itself, using the materials, and making marks (quotations from *Paintings of Cornwall and the Scillies* are hereafter cited as [P]: P, 27).

Very occasionally Kurt Jackson has included human figures in his Priest Cove paintings. In *Self-Portrait On Priest Cove* (1995) there's a rare self-portrait in Jackson's favourite place. A dusk painting, a painting of gloom and shadows and a brooding grey sky... the figure's just discernible in the darkness of the foreground, staring at the viewer in a mystery and obscurity that Rembrandt van Rijn was so skillful at evoking.

Thus, over the years, Kurt Jackson has collected a large group of artworks which respond to the ever-changing yet ever *un*changing seascape at Priest Cove. It's the fascination with something that appears to be constantly in flux yet the fundamental elements remain constant: the sea is always in that place there, the cliffs are always there, the rocks and stones are always there... That's a mystery, part of the mystery of the world.

It's partly a fascination, even an obsession. As Kurt Jackson put it, 'all of the seascapes are an ongoing study of a subject that constantly fascinates me', and Jackson admitted: 'I think I will always choose it as a subject' (P, 27).

---

45 Some of Kurt Jackson's Priest's Cove paintings are entitled *Sheltering In an Old Fishing Hut On Priest Cove* (1998) and *Looking Out of the Cave, Priest Cove* (1998).

Kurt Jackson has painted the sea hundreds maybe thousands of times in his career, but it's always a very particular kind of depiction of the ocean. It's impressionistic, vague, with broken colour and loosely worked surfaces. Jackson does not attempt a 'realistic' or photoreal depiction of the sea. I think he's after the effects of light on water, and an impression of movement and energy. But he doesn't usually try to depict a wave or waves in detail, in a photorealistic fashion, or like the landscapists of the 19th century did.

When you look at the sea at Priest's Cove or Sennen Beach or Treen or wherever, you can't help noticing the individual waves. At Priest's Cove and all along that West-facing coast, the waves are slamming into the cliffs and rocks and beaches with a never-ending force and movement. They are waves each weighing hundreds of tons, crashing against the rocks with tremendous power. And when the sun is westering, it often shines behind the waves, making them partially transparent, which's an extraordinary effect (and that translucent effect is a *major* challenge to a painter!).

Priest's Cove, Tide Coming In Fast (1994) was an important early painting by Kurt Jackson that attempted to portray a wave in detail – a big, blue wave topped with surf and spray. The viewpoint is low down on the beach, so the incoming waves break the horizon (if you want to make a wave look impressive, a low viewpoint is often best).

Priest's Cove, Tide Coming In Fast is relatively rare in Kurt Jackson's art, which usually depicts the sea from a distance, so the waves are bunched together and are usually represented by jagged lines of white, as in *On the Body Rocks, Nanven, Big Silver Sea From Carn Gloose, Strong Offshore Wind, Low Sun,* and *Tide Coming Up Fast, the Cove, Cape Cornwall.*

Another rough sea is portrayed in a watercolour, *Priest Cove* (1997), a painting composed entirely of a variety of blues (cobalt, ultramarine, prussian), with the paint drips left showing across the bottom section of the painting (retaining the paint drips was the signature motif of Brice Marden's early paintings. Leaving in the drips is a recurring device in Jackson's art).[46] One half of *The Tide Is Roaring In* (1999) consists of splashes and drips of white pigment, to represent the foam spraying over the rocks at Priest's Cove.

In *Priest Cove* (1998), another angry sea at Priest's Cove is captured with broad washes of watercolour or gouache and layers of white in the foreground, with the spray over a black rock indicated with spatters of white pigment. *Late Afternoon, Big Sea Pounding Into the Cove* (2001) has a similarly loose handling of pigment.

PAINTING PRIEST'S COVE

Among Kurt Jackson's other Priest's Cove paintings are:

The Fog Lifts, a mixed media painting of 1996, in which Kurt Jackson chooses to portray the ever-mobile sea with a single wave cresting in the middle ground, with the base of the composition dissolving into foam and black rocks. One of the more 'realistic' depictions of waves close to the shore occurs in 1998's *Priest Cove, Cape Cornwall*: still very impressionistic and expressive, but the heavy, shadowy look of the waves just before they crest can be discerned clearly.

Below Black Carn (1996) is an unusual Priest's Cove picture, because it's a wide horizontal format (most of the Priest's Cove paintings are squarish). The familiar line of cliffs[47] extending out towards Land's End is the focal point, with the sunlight breaking over the ocean below them. *Below Black Carn* is a picture of all the blues – cobalt, ultramarine, prussian – giving a brooding, greenish cast to the image. *Foreshore, Priest Cove* (2000) is unusual amongst the *Priest's Cove* series in having the rocky shore taking up half of the composition.

Another moody, broody picture is *Rain On Its Way*, a painting made

---

46 The sketchbooks contain images of Priest Cove in gales, rain, storms, wind and heavy seas.
47 Familiar if you've spent any time in the area, that is.

in December, 1998, with a gun metal calm sea and a cloudy sky suggesting the low pressure weather which can produce sudden changes, like rain showers. *Rain On Its Way* is more abstract than usual, with only a suggestion of rocks in the lower righthand corner. The sea's reduced to bands of dark cobalt, while the foam comprises spattered pigment in the foreground.

In 2001's *One of Those Days You'd Never Forget*, a lilac and purple sky looms over a boisterous, foamy sea at the Cove. A similarly noisy sea forms the lower half of *What's Changed?* (2001), a picture 48-inch square with a dense steel grey sky done in watercolour. In *Big Wet Sea* (2000) a bank of sombre grey clouds are backed to the horizon above a sea running thick with foam. In *Big Sea, Priest Cove* (1999), Kurt Jackson concentrates on the layers of foam and spray created by the waves rushing towards the shore below Cape Cornwall.

1998's *Winter Solstice* reveals a busy ocean with foam sprays all over the place. The palette comprises pale blues and whites, but the white acrylic has been flicked all over the surface of the picture, suggesting white spray lifted by the wind. 'Cape Cornwall' is rubbed into the lower righthand corner, as in so many of the Priest's Cove paintings. 1998's *Priest Cove* is one of the signature *Priest's Cove* images, depicting a clamorous ocean and a woman looking for driftwood on the shore below.

Bottom of Carn Gloose (1996) is just along the coast from Priest's Cove, and depicts a calm sea with a pale lilac and blue watercolour sky made distinctive by thick oval splodges which resemble thumbprints. *Hazy Land's End From Below Carn Gloose* (2000) is similarly peaceful.

An unusual image, apparently made at night, *Nighttime; Very Mild and Still* (1998), is a loose, abstract painting with only rough areas of black hinting at the horizon line of the ocean.

Some of the calmer images of Priest Cove are the most abstract: without the waves to suggest depth, the pictures sometimes turn out flattened, with the horizon as close as the foreshore. In these pictures – *Priest Cove, 16.11.98* (1998), *Five and a Half Miles To Land's End* (2000), *Sky, Sea, Earth, Kernow* (2001), *Calm Before the Storm* (2000), and *It Was Sunny All Day* (1998) – the flattened spaces and monochrome effects (primarily blues and greys) suggest the art of James Whistler, or Chinese landscape painting (the link to Oriental art is commonplace in modern art discourse, particularly with the Abstract Expressionists and Minimalists, of course. But here it pays off: some of Jackson's images at Priest Cove do have that flattened, semi-abstract quality of Chinese landscape art, an art which's all about rendering the lyricism of the natural world, and not least the effects of light on water).

COT VALLEY AND KENIDJACK VALLEY

One aspect of Kurt Jackson's landscapes that you'll notice immediately is the preponderance of the colours red, brown and orange. While landscape art in Britain might typically comprise greys, blacks, blues and greens (the clichéd view of Blighty as a gloomy, rainy, foggy country of little towns and muddy fields – a view unchanged since the Roman times), Jackson's art often leans towards the warm end of the spectrum – but not for sunsets, but the landscape itself. Very often the hot colours of orange and red and light brown are ranged across the lower third of a Kurt Jackson picture. It's as if the ground is on fire, or smouldering, or turned to a lava flow.

Many of the paintings of the Cot and Kenidjack valleys in West Cornwall are like this: *Cold Wind, Warm Sun, Kenidjack Valley* (1998), *Cot Valley* (1998), *Late Afternoon Cot Valley* (1998), *Cape Cornwall From Kenidjack Valley* (1994), *Kenidjack Stream, Hot & Breezy* (1995), *Cot Stream* (1995), *Cot Valley, Sunshine On a Rainy Day* (1995), *Hailglower, Kenidjack Stream* (1997), *Kenidjack Valley, Warm Spring Afternoon* (2000), and *Kenidjack* (1994).

Often the streams in the Cot and Kenidjack valleys runs through the lower middle of the composition, offering blue-grey-white reflections of the sky.[48] Paintings such as *Cot* (1997) depict the bowl-shaped outline of the valley where it meets the sea. More recently, Kurt Jackson has produced a series entitled *The Kenidjack Oils*, which contains paintings such as *Dark Valley* (2006).

It's a curious way of seeing the land around the Cot and Kenidjack valleys. I can see where Kurt Jackson possibly takes that orange and red from – the bracken, the heather, the gorse, the knotweed, and in particular the late afternoon light, which casts a golden glow over everything. The light is of primary importance here: the Cot and Kenidjack valleys seem to be crucibles of light, laboratories of light, where light is created and hurled around the slopes. And notice took that in the Cot and Kenidjack valley paintings Jackson has set up his viewpoint looking down the valleys, towards the sea and towards the light. These valleys run East to West, with the distant ocean framed by shallow V-shaped slopes.

But Cot and Kenidjack valleys are not orange and red all of the year (I have seen them on fire from time to time, which's interesting), so this colour is more visionary or interpretive than 'realistic'. What this hot colour does is to remind the viewer that Kurt Jackson is not producing a documentary of a place, but an interpretation, a response. It's *art*, folks! Not documentary or record keeping. (Landscapes across Britain are seldom the bright red that Jackson includes in some paintings: red of poppies, yes, reddish bracken or ferns, yes (though bracken's more usually brown), and sometimes the dark purple of heather, but not bright red). Jackson acknowledges in interviews that he is not sticking slavishly to reality, but exaggerates colours. Of course – who wants 'realism'? You're in the middle of 'real life' all the time anyway!

Other paintings of Kurt Jackson's which take red and orange as the centrepiece included *Hawthorn, Autumn-Winter* (1999), a yard-square acrylic canvas, *Croak of a Raven Above Me* (2004), *Catchers Pool, Kenidjack* (2006), *Sitting In an Old China Clay Quarry, Below Carn Euny, A Red Kite Over the Red Roofs of Henley* (2005) and *On the*

---

48 Linked to the paintings of the streams of Cot and Kenidjack valleys are pictures such as *Nancherrow Stream* (1996), *Meg's Stream* (1997), *Late Afternoon Stream in Lower Porthmeor Valley* (1998), and *Drift Stream* (1996).

Gump Up To Chûn Quoit (1997).[49] *Trencrom, Cold Toes* shows a bright red world. *Cove* (1996), part of *The Cape* series, depicts the Cornish cliffs as bright yellow and orange. Another *Cape* picture mixes yellow and oranges with the azure of bluebells (*Early Evening*, 1997).

And the groups of paintings that Kurt Jackson has produced in Scotland also contain plenty of vivid reds and oranges (not colours one immediately associates with Scotland – the Scotland of mountains and glens and overcast skies and rain and midges and endless greenery and rocks): *Skye Is In the Distance* (2005), *Allt Na Biabaig, Under the Umbrella* (2005), *Maol Nam Damh, 24 Degrees C, Midday Sun* (2004), and *The Paps From Cnoc Ruairidh At Dusk* (2004).[50]

It's striking just how hot Kurt Jackson has rendered the landscape in paintings such as *Loch, Bog, Moor, Mountain, Rock, Sheep, Frog-spawn* (2005), *The Sun's Gone In, Skye Is Hidden In the Sky* (2005), *Above the Loch, Diabaig, Dusk* (2006), and *Beinn Alligin, Tom Na Grungalch* (2005). It's as if the earth is on fire, or the surface of the earth is switched with the surface of the sun for a moment. And that makes the contrast with the cool blues of the sea and sky so much stronger in these pictures.[51]

The *Kenidjack/ Tregeseal* paintings, made in 1994, comprised 110 paintings which followed the Kenidjack stream from up on the moor down to the sea. Every twenty paces Kurt Jackson painted the stream (it's a tiny brook which runs East to West near St Just, through Tregeseal and Nancherrow). In the *Kenidjack/ Tregeseal* paintings, the stream is in the centre of the compositions, with the slopes of the

---

49 The Gump, for those who want to know, is a piece of land near Chûn castle and quoit. 'They say you should walk across it with your coat turned inside out, so the spriggans – the local pixies – who live here in large numbers can't get the money out of your pockets. It is stunning in summer, covered with cotton grass, heather and gorse and wandering cattle', explained Kurt Jackson.
50 Most of the images in the *Neil's Place* series comprise a patch of land in the fore-ground, an expanse of ocean, distant hills, and the heavens. The impression is that Kurt Jackson is always looking out – out towards something in the distance – a look from the tamed land into the untamed wilderness.
51 Not all of the *Neil's Place* images are painted with warm hues, though: some capture that cold grey light associated with the Celtic fringe – such as *Salmon Farm Loch Diabaig* (2005), *7.30 p.m., Loch Diabaig, Gulls Screeching, Sun Sinking* (2005), and *A Woman Walks By Shouting At Her Sheepdog As It Rounds Up the Sheep On the Hillside* (2005). Images with a brooding stillness – you can almost hear the wind in the grass and the distant splash of waves.

Kenidjack valley rising on each side.[52] And bridges. Houses. Disused mines and chimneys (they're everywhere around Kenidjack). Linked to the *Kenidjack* series is a series of small paintings of a hawthorn tree at Morvah, just along the coast from St Just: *Hawthorn Tree* (1993). A painter and a tree.

In some landscape paintings by Kurt Jackson, the colours veer off into abstraction. Some of the key works of *The Cornish Hedge*, for example, contain colours which might have some relation to the real world, but more seem to be more about the artist's response to a place and an experience. In *Every Hedge Has an Eye, Every Ditch Has an Ear* (2004), for instance, a bright blue area of pigment doesn't seem to relate to the natural world. These paintings are clearly more about putting pigment onto a canvas or piece of paper, than interpreting the world. In these paintings, Jackson allows the wet paint to run down the paper or support in lengthy drips (and the drops of paint spattered around the painting aren't cleaned-up either). *The Hedge That Gave Me Shelter From the Storm* (2004), *From Witches and Weasels* (2004), *Hayle Estuary, Low Water* (2002) and *End of a Hot Day, Lussa River, Jura* (2003) are paintings about drips and splattered paint, paintings which draw attention to their making, paintings which don't tidy up the application of the media. And if you reframed these paintings, cutting off the sky and the horizon, you'd have something much more abstract, recalling Gerhard Richter's dazzling canvases of smeared pigment.[53]

52 A well-known landmark in the area, Carn Kenidjack, kind of spooky-looking, has appeared in some Kurt Jackson paintings, such as *Rain Pouring On a Burnt Moor, Carn Kenidjack* (2001).
53 For instance, 1980s paintings by Gerhard Richter such as *Untitled (531-4)* and *Group of Trees (628-1)* are near-abstract pieces, consisting of thick brushstrokes, in the Willem de Kooning or Howard Hodgkin manner. See Richter's superb website: www.gerhard-richter.com.

> I visit the islands regularly; they have a milder climate and the light is particularly intense – ideal for painting. There's a great diversity of birds, plant life and marine eco-systems. Best of all, the islands are even more tranquil than West Penwith. I can spend the whole day on a deserted stretch of beach with my family, painting in complete peace and isolation.

Kurt Jackson (P, 31)

Mr Jackson has been visiting the Isles of Scilly for many years. Nearly all of Jackson's Scilly paintings are seascapes and skyscapes of one sort or another. The smaller, less touristy island of Bryher is a favourite for him: *Scilly, Submerged Hedges* (2004), *Sheltering From the 70 mph Winds and Horizontal Rain Behind Hedges of Granite and Bracken* (2004), *Scilly Hedge* (2004), *Bryher Dusk* (2004), *Calm Before the Storm, Bryher Evening* (2004), *Eastern Isles From St Martin's, Scilly* (1998), *White Island, Scilly* (1997), and *Scilly Dance* (1997).

The Scillies paintings are typically composed in a format that Kurt Jackson had used throughout his career: the horizon through the middle of the picture, land at the bottom, and the sky above, with distant hills or islands breaking up the composition. It's a pictorial format that appears at every stage of Jackson's career, from the early Cornish paintings, to *The Paps of Jura, The Thames Project* and *Neil's Place* images. You see it in the paintings along the River Thames, such as *Infant Thames In Spate Near Castle Eaton* (2005), Scottish images such as *A Scottish Summer With No Midges* (2004) and *Shepherd and Dog Above the Loch* (2005), and Cornish pictures such as *Creek of the Camel, Tide Dropping* (2004), *Linseed/ Flax Field Above Mount's Bay* (1998), and *Eastern Isles From St Martin's, Scilly* (1998).

Kurt Jackson as an artist is in love with broad expanses of water, with the ground below and masses of land in the distance. The water might be lakes, rivers or the sea, and the distant land masses might be islands, or hills, or the far shore of a river. It doesn't really matter *what* the landscape is: what counts is the arrangement of water, land, hills and sky. And what really counts is the combination of *land* and *water* and *sky*. Or just *water* and *sky*.

Nornour From St Martin's, Scilly (1997) is that kind of watercolour painting: an open expanse of water, distant low islands, and the sunlight creating wide areas of silver on the sea. In *Glas* (2006), a medium-sized oil painting, the ocean stretches to the horizon in smooth hues of pale blue, all in the same tone, with the horizon and clouds floating in the air far away.

It seems that if Kurt Jackson found himself in front of any expanse of water outdoors he'd be happy: in some respects, Jackson is more of a *water* painter than a *land* painter, a waterscapist rather than a landscapist. Or maybe water and sky: a waterscapist and skyscapist. In a group of pictures such as *The Cornish Hedge*, for instance, which one might imagine would be confined to images of hedges and walls and fields and paths, Jackson manages to cram in plenty of images of water (in particular, the ocean surrounding Cornwall).

Some of *The Cornish Hedge* images, for example, are really sea-pieces: *Prehistoric Clifftop Hedge* (2005), *Morning Behind a Hedge of Granite and Lichen On Bryher* (2004), and *The Shade From the Hedge Leaves Some of the Frost Unmelted* (2005). And all of those pictures of 'submerged hedges' on the Isles of Scilly are really stone walls. Though the titles may refer to 'hedges' of stones or plants, the subject is really the sea and the sky.

5

THE SKY, THE SEA,
THE LIGHT, THE SOUND

A ship, an isle, a sickle moon –
With few but with how splendid stars
The mirrors of the sea are strewn
Between their silver bars.

J.E. Flecker, 'A Ship, an Isle, a Sickle Moon'

THE SKY

It's not only the ocean in the coastal areas around Cape Cornwall and
St Just that's endlessly changing, that inspires Kurt Jackson's art, it's
also the sky. The sky absolutely dominates this part of Cornwall. One
could say that West Penwith is England's version of the 'Big Sky
Country' of America's West (it's a great phrase, 'Big Sky Country', but
it really describes the immensity of the elements here). Jackson can be

seen, then, as an artist who's 'working with' the sky (Andy Golds-worthy's phrase – Goldsworthy spoke of 'working with the sky', and with light – in his sculptures of sticks mounted in lakes in the Lake District, for example).

Another attraction of painting by the sea is the uninterrupted horizon it can offer, the sense of enormous space. Kurt Jackson's paintings draw attention to the horizon and to wide-open spaces. That's one of the appealing aspects of his art, and this kind of landscape art.

Although Kurt Jackson is categorized as a landscape painter, he has probably painted just as many seascapes as conventional landscapes. I'd go further: he's not only a seascape painter, he's also a skyscape painter. The sky dominates his art, as the sun and sky dominated J.M.W. Turner's art. A glance at a bunch of Jackson paintings reveals not only a large proportion of seas, but also skies. Perhaps it's easier to consider Jackson as a painter of landscapes or seascapes (there are long-established traditions in painting both subjects). But a 'skyscape painter' is an odd way of describing an artist.

One recalls other artists who have worked with the sky. For instance, U.S. artist James Turrell, with his 'skyspaces' and rooms of light (enclosed spaces open to the sky above). Turrell chose the Roden Crater volcano in Arizona to make his land and light art because he wanted to explore the relationship between the low mound of the volcano and the curvature of the Earth, the vaulting of the sky, and the viewer's experience of celestial events such as sunrises, moonsets, clouds and stars.

Dennis Oppenheim's *Whirlpool Eye of Storm* (1973) was a jet trail made in the sky above the Californian desert. Hans Haacke sent balloons floating over Central Park (*Sky Line*, 1967). He wrote of an artwork which would be as majestic and as transient as birds gathering in the sky: 'I would like to lure 1000 seagulls to a certain spot (in the air) by some delicious food so as to construct an air sculpture from this combined mass.'[54] Nancy Holt's *Sun Tunnels* (1973-76) and *Hydra's Head* (1975) were about the relationship between the

54 In W. Malpas, *The Art of Richard Long*, Crescent Moon, 2006.

heavens and earth. Robert Smithson's *Mirror Displacements* (1968) explored the reflections of the sky in a lengthy series of works.

Many artists have created observatories, large structures for the contemplation of the cosmos: Robert Morris, Nancy Holt, Charles Ross, Michael Dan Archer and Julia Barton. And in movies skies often play a key role: I don't just mean the obvious cases, like the thundery skies in *The Ten Commandments* when Moses receives the tablets from God, or *Close Encounters of the Third Kind,* when the UFOs burst out of the clouds (one of the great sky movies, *Close Encounters* has been hugely influential on subsequent depictions of skies in cinema), but also lesser-known examples, like the time-lapse photography of speeding clouds in *Koyaanisqatsi* and *Rumble Fish,* or the later movies of Jean-Luc Godard, where the camera pans around the sky for many minutes in jerky movements handled by the director himself.

The Romanian historian of religions, Mircea Eliade, remarked that the sky was the first manifestation of divinity and the sacred for early peoples. Eliade is absolutely right to suggest that the contemplation of the sky is a primary and very ancient form of religious experience. In short, the sky is the embodiment of transcendence, of spirituality, flight, ascension and revelation. The sky is heaven, where the gods live.

> I believe, personally, that it is through consideration of the sky's immensity that man is led to a revelation of transcendence, of the sacred [Eliade wrote].[55]

I'm not suggesting that Kurt Jackson is a religious painter, or is conscious of dealing with the sacred or spirituality. But those elements are present in his art if one wants to see them. If there is spirituality in Jackson's art, it is of a nebulous, vague nature, and might be applicable to any religion or belief. You could talk about the Tibetan Clear Light of the Void, for instance, or the emptiness at the heart of Buddhism, but it wouldn't really be what Jackson's painting is primarily about. Talking about Buddhism or Zen or Taoism is much more relevant when discussing, say, American earthworks artists like James Turrell or Robert Smithson or Nancy Holt – partly because those artists have

---

55 M. Eliade, *Ordeal By Labyrinth*, University of Chicago Press, Chicago, 1984, 162.

consciously drawn on or referred to religious concepts (with Eastern religions being a favourite).

If the sky is mentioned in Kurt Jackson art criticism, it tends to be in connection with John Constable studies of clouds, or J.M.W. Turner's watercolour sketches (the 'Colour Beginnings'). Even now, in the 21st century, it's unusual to see a painting just of the sky, without any reference to the Earth or the ocean or people or buildings or plants. Jackson is no exception: his paintings tend to have either the land or the sea in the lower half of the composition.

LIGHT AND CLOUDS

One of the most important elements for a painter working out of doors is of course the light. That's stating the obvious, but in a small area like West Penwith, with the sea on three sides, the light is particularly intense, reflecting off the water. On this granite tableland, the views are 360° – there aren't any mountains or skyscrapers or forests to block out sections of the sky. So the artist working outdoors in this part of Cornwall is always very exposed to the light and to the sky.[56] Which's changing all of the time, of course. It's impossible to be out of doors in parts of Cornwall and not be aware of the physical reality of the light, how it envelops everything, how it charges everything with energy, how it never keeps still. When poets talk about the 'light' inside a stone, it can seem an abstract concept, if you're reading a poem on a bus in a city, say. But when one spends some time on the granite cliffs and rocks of Cornwall, it's easy to grasp.

And if we're talking about the light and the sky, we must also mention clouds. Again, this's something obvious and everyday which one might normally ignore. An artist working in the fields, clifftops,

---

56 But Kurt Jackson prefers to find a spot that's hidden if possible. 'When I'm painting I often try to get myself in a place where I'm totally surrounded by rocks on a beach or cocooned by gorse', he says (P, 12).

country lanes and beaches of West Cornwall is going to be acutely conscious of clouds, though. Sure, West Penwith has its fair share of clean, cloudless skies, but days with clouds are far more common (as across the whole of the British Isles). And Kurt Jackson, like any landscape painter, has to be able to render clouds convincingly (even if he's moving into abstraction, and the precise shapes and appearances of the clouds are difficult to ascertain).

Clouds offer a sense of perspective, distance, scale, depth, contour, colour and tone to the sky and the landscape. For the artist taking the sea, rivers, lakes or other bodies of water as their subject, clouds are a key visual component of any composition. If you look at Kurt Jackson's sea paintings, for instance, you'll often see bands of light and dark over the water which're commonly created by clouds, as in *A Roll of Thunder Makes the Pheasants Cough With Alarm In the Sun, Carrick Roads* (2004), *A Seal Bottles In Front of Me* (2001), *Paps of Jura and Knap Point* (2004), or *Priest Cove* (1998).

Clouds, to put it simply, make the world much more interesting. Like trees. If this planet had monochrome grey skies everywhere, it wouldn't have nearly the same fascination for a painter (every landscape painter would become a Minimalist, with landscapes of nothing but grey-on-grey, like the Sixties paintings of Agnes Martin or Brice Marden).

It's no surprise that one of the big expenditures in the visual effects industry in cinema is sky replacement. Films shot in California or Australia often have pure blue skies with one or two wispy white clouds, and that's just no good for dramatic stories, which need moody, cloudy skies. So the blue skies beloved of the tourist industry (look at holiday brochures for vacations in Greece or Miami or Cornwall) are replaced with brooding thunderous grey clouds so that Frodo Baggins, Harry Potter, Spider-man, King Arthur or whoever can appear like they're in some life-or-death, epic story.

Another possible reason for the appeal of Kurt Jackson's art is not just the sea itself, but the curious British pastime of staring out to sea for hours. Every day in Britain, no matter what the weather (and even in the jaws of darkest Winter), there will be people lined along clifftops, beside walls and fences, staring out at the North Sea, the English Channel, the Irish Sea, and the Atlantic Ocean. The big briny seems to hold a peculiar hypnotic attraction for the people who live on this sceptred isle.

The essentials required are a car parked in the prime spot (right up against the fence or wall), and extras such as: a thermos flask of tea, a cheese sandwich, a red checked rug over the knees, the Sunday papers, and the radio warbling golden oldies (the Everly Brothers maybe, or Nat King Cole, or Max Bygraves). (There are a couple of places where this British occupation with the sea has been hilariously immortalized. One is Ken Russell's crazy rock opera *Tommy* (1975), which has a wonderful sequence where the camera tracks past rows of cars with people staring out (shot at Southsea on the South coast), and Paul Theroux's book of travelling the coast of Britain in 1982, *The Kingdom By the Sea*).[57]

So hanging a picture of the sea on the wall at home enables the viewer to stare at the ocean from the comfort of their armchair. And Brits love anything they can do from the comfort of their own armchair (eating, watching TV, talking, sleeping, having sex, doing the crossword, sorting thru their postage stamp collection).

The sea is of course intimately bound up with the history of Britain – a barrier that has stopped only a few of many invaders (it didn't block the Romans, Celts, Saxons, Vikings, Danes and Normans). It's the sea of William Shakespeare, the sea of this green, sceptred island:

---

[57] Paul Theroux writes of 'cars parked and piled up, and people in them, always very old people... They sat in their cars and stared out at the sea. They were on every beach road... I saw them everywhere, eating sandwiches, drinking tea out of plastic cups, reading the paper, looking fuddled. They always faced the water. They were old couples mostly, but they never seemed to be holding conversations' (*The Kingdom By the Sea*, Penguin, London, 1984, 43.) Theroux wonders if it's the sea as solace, but also the grave, and death; the sea as nothingness, and the sea as an escape from life.

This royal throne of kings, this sceptred isle,
This earth of majesty, this seat of Mars,
This other Eden, demi-paradise,
This fortress built by Nature for herself
Against infection and the hand of war,
This happy breed of men, this little world,
This precious stone set in the silver sea,
Which serves it in the office of a wall,
Or as a moat defensive to a house,
Against the envy of less happier lands.
This blessed realm, this earth, this realm, this England...
(*Richard II*, 22. 1. 40)

SOUND

What about the *sound* of Kurt Jackson's paintings? They certainly have a sound. The sound of the wind, above all, but also the sea, and birds, and animals, the odd aeroplane and helicopter, distant cars, distant boats, sirens, and people. The sound of the wind in West Penwith is pretty much a year-round constant. There are very few completely soundless, windless days on the peninsula. The prevailing winds in this part of Cornwall – from the South-West – shift around continuously (and drive the waves onshore).

Then the sea, always the sea: some of Kurt Jackson's paintings of the sea are very noisy: you can hear the sounds in the images of crashing, foaming waves (as in *Priest Cove, 5.11.98, Late Afternoon, Very High Tide, Noisy Sea*, 1998, or *Priest Cove*, 1997, or *Priest Cove*, 1998, or *Winter Solstice*, 1998).

It's the same with most artists who paint the ocean – like J.M.W. Turner's pictures of storms. Turner loved a violent sea, and is the undisputed king of sea painting in British art (as well Britain's greatest artist). At one time he had himself roped to a mast so he could observe a storm firsthand. For the *still* extraordinary, *still* ahead of its time painting *Snowstorm – Steam-boat Off a Habour's Mouth Making Signals In Shallow Water and Going By the Lead* (1842, National Gallery, London), Turner recalled, in one of my favourite Turner stories:

> I got the sailors to lash me to the mast to observe it; I was lashed for four hours, and I did not expect to escape, but I felt bound to record it, if I did.

Paintings like *Nanven, Force 9* (1994), *Wet and Windy* (1999) or *Looking Out of the Cave, Priest Cove* (1998) depict rough seas with boiling waves; *Nanven, Force 9*, a tiny painting – 4 by 7 inches – is one of Kurt Jackson's loosest sea paintings, with abstract splodges of white, grey and pale blue suggesting waves stacked up to the horizon. *Priest Cove, Figures* (1994) is another loose, semi-abstract painting (on drift-wood), but with human figures vaguely discernible against the restless ocean. A watercolour sketch depicts the sea in a force 9 gale. There's a rough sea in *Above the Swimming Pool, Avarack, Flowing Tide* (2006) and *Sunshine On Pendeen Watch, Huge Seas, Deafening* (2006), part of the North coast of Cornwall I know very well.

In *Looking Out of the Cave, Priest Cove* (the 'cave' is a sheltered place in the rocks below Cape Cornwall), the artist employs one of his distinctive devices: allowing the bottom of the picture to be a playground for spattered and dripped pigment which is meant to evoke the foaming, boiling sea.

Some of Kurt Jackson's Priest's Cove and Cape Cornwall paintings are bound to be very noisy: the sea comes in to Priest's Cove straight out of the Atlantic Ocean and breaks upon a rock-strewn beach and granite cliffs. Each wave is very heavy, so it's not going to be peaceful and quiet (especially around high tide, or on a windy or stormy day).

At other times, the sound of the sea can vary from a constant high-pitched hiss to a deep boom that you feel in your belly. But it's always there. The sea around West Cornwall isn't usually a quiet, calm sea of gently lapping waves in tourist brochures. These are difficult waters for ships, of course, with so many shipwrecks on these shores.

I remember sitting next to Loe Pool near Porthleven, one of Cornwall's two freshwater lakes, and listening to the amazing sound of the waves hitting the shore. Down behind Loe Bar you can't see the waves, but you could hear (and feel) the incredible, slightly muffled sounds of the waves, travelling from right to left.

❖

So the *sounds* in Kurt Jackson's sea paintings are present pretty much all of the time, as is the wind. The sounds of the ocean and the wind are of course invisible, and require a different way of thinking and working to render them in a visual medium like painting. But I'm emphasizing the sounds because they are such a concrete and constant reality in this landscape. And sounds are not confined to waves or boats or the wind in coastal spots: they are as plentiful in the forests or the fields or the hills that Jackson paints.

Note that Kurt Jackson often writes down some of the sounds he hears as he's fashioning a painting – the sound of the birds in *A Barn Owl Flies By Silently, a Heron Flies High Overhead Honking Noisily* (2005), or *Cuckoo Call, Bee Buzz, June Evening* (2005), or animals in *Priest Cove, Very Still, the Dolphins Pass, the Tide Comes In* (1998).

Sound is, in fact, a big part of the overall experience of painting out of doors. I'd suggest that one of the reasons that people enjoy Kurt Jackson's art is that it reminds them of being out in the landscape, including by the sea. And the *sound* of the ocean is part of the hypnotic effect of the sea, not just the other senses. (Jackson sometimes refers to the sound of the ocean in his paintings, as in *Still, Only the Sound of the Waves, Low Tide, Priest Cove,* 1998).

It's worth noting that it's just about impossible to capture the quality of a sound – in a painting, in visual form, or in words, and even a mechanical or electronic or digital recording often doesn't get close (those are all *reproductions,* anyway, of something else that's somewhere else). So when Kurt Jackson writes on his paintings about the buzz of insects or the trills of birds, it's in note form only, perhaps as a way of reminding the painter about the experience of making the picture. It's a means of aiding the artist to recover the actuality of the painting's facture (which only the artist has access to – the viewer wasn't there, could never be there). 'The *experience* of painting is very important to me,' says Jackson, 'and hopefully that will show through in the finished work' (P, 27). But the words don't describe the sound, because even the best writers can only offer the hint of a suggestion of the quality of a sound.

The other senses, too, are critical. One might mention, in discussing coastal zones: the taste and smell of salt on the lips, or sea spray on the face, or the feel of granite underfoot, or the heat of the sun on the neck, and so on. There are potentially hundreds of other sensual experiences one could list. In any painting, an artist can only capture and render a few of them.

THE WEATHER

To state that an outdoor artist taking contemporary landscape as their primary subject matter is going to be very aware of the weather is again stating the obvious. But the weather is always prime factor. For those looking at an artist at work in the landscape from outside, something like rain might seem to be the worst daily occurrence. Actually, the wind can be far more trying. Artists such as Andy Goldsworthy have explained how even the slightest breeze can ruin a delicate sculpture of leaves or grass stalks. If you're an artist who makes art out of walking, like Richard Long and Hamish Fulton, the wind is a huge factor.[58]

Of course, rain can hamper an artwork, but so can intense sunlight, or too much heat. Remember, an artist is *working*, s/he's not sitting about sunning themselves. Artists are not on vacation, or on the beach, or lounging about in the back yard; they're *working*. Thus, the cold can be a problem, but often an artist is very physically involved with their piece, so they keep warm. (You'll notice that Kurt Jackson paints year-round, so cold and inclement weather – and not just in Winter – doesn't seem to bother him too much, although sometimes it gets too cold to work. Notice, also, that Jackson often mentions the weather in the titles of his works, as well the places: *Snow and Sunshine, Gillan Creek*, 2004, or *It Was Sunny All Day and the Clouds Started To Come*

---

58 You can see Andy Goldsworthy struggling to stop a sculpture falling apart in the wind in the TV documentary *Rivers and Tides.*

Over and the Sun Got Weaker, 1998).[59]

If an artist is used to getting on with making a work in the Great Outdoors, then the weather isn't usually going to stop them. They'll be prepared for it. The weather might persuade them to alter their plans, of course. But artists are quite accomplished at responding to circumstances, at changing direction when necessary. Indeed, many artists *need* the unpredictability of being outside to make art the first place. A land artist like Andy Goldsworthy says he starts to run out of reasons for being in an art gallery, for instance, and requires the unknown, untameable landscape outside to inspire him to make work. Kurt Jackson says that sometimes he'll bring a painting back into the studio and work on it, then take it outside again, and the process might continue until the painting is deemed finished.

---

59 Snow doesn't appear as much in Kurt Jackson's art as in the art of, say, Andy Goldsworthy or Dennis Oppenheim, but there are snowy pictures, such as *Snow and Sunshine, Gillan Creek* (2004), or the snow falling over Kenidjack stream, or the snowfields in *Across To St Just From Kenython* (2001).

6

KURT JACKSON'S PROJECTS (WORKING IN SERIES)

Kurt Jackson has remarked that it has been important for him to work in series, to have themes or concepts as the basis for groups of work. Otherwise, he's travelling around, seeing a nice landscape and painting it. That is too arbitrary, too haphazard.[60] So Jackson tends to work in series: a series of the South Crofty mines, for instance, or on the Tinners' Way, or on Cornish hedges.

Kurt Jackson's works in series include

＊ a series on mines (*South Crofty*, 1995-97);

＊ works on New Age travellers and their homes – tents and benders (*Travellers*);

＊ the *Kenidjack/ Tregeseal* paintings, made in 1994;

---

60 It's much better to have all of the paintings relating to each other in a show, Kurt Jackson said (P, 21).

∗ a series of paintings on top of Cornish postcards (the tourist postcards sold all over Cornwall which always look like they were made in the Sixties or Fifties);

∗ *The Long Field* (2002), a series of paintings based on a field near his home;

∗ *The Cornish Hedge* (2005), again centred around the area of Kurt Jackson's home;

∗ the rivers of Cornwall in *The Cornish Estuary* (2004);

∗ the *Avon Project* (on-going);

∗ a group of reworkings of a single etching of the sea in *The Painted Etchings* (2004);

∗ a series about quarries (*Delabole Slate Quarry*, 2001-02, and *Carnsew*, 1998-99, at Mabe Burnthouse near Falmouth);[61]

∗ works based around the main road (highways are called A roads in Britain) between Penzance and St Just (*A3071: The Road To St Just*, 2000);

∗ a series about the Tinner's Way, which runs across West Penwith, like the A-3071 (*Tinner's Way*, 2001);

∗ another route-based series in West Penwith (*St Michael's Way*, 2003), a track which runs to St Michael's Mount;

∗ a group of paintings made in some Scottish islands (*The Paps of Jura*, 2004);

∗ a series about the solar eclipse of 1999, where Cornwall was one of the best places on the British mainland to see totality (*Painting the Path of the Sun*, 1998 and *Crossing the Peninsula: The Path of Totality*, 1999);

∗ groups of works about forests (*Two Woods*, 2003, *Three Woods*, 2005), which have personal associations for the artist;

∗ a series about the lighthouses of Cornwall, in *The Lights of West Cornwall* (2008);

∗ *A One-Mile Walk* (2013, Gloucestershire);

∗ *The Dart* (2010), about Dartmoor;

∗ *Kurt Jackson and St Just* (2012, Royal Cornwall Museum);

∗ *This Place: St Just in Penwith* (2012, Truro);

---

61 I've always liked that name – Mabe Burnthouse.

✳ *The Blackberries* (2012-13, London);

✳ the on-going artist-in-residence works at the Glastonbury Festival;

✳ and the on-going group of works made at and about Priest's Cove (*Porth*).

A number of comments can be made about Kurt Jackson's work in series: first, most of them consist of works made in and around St Just-in-Penwith. Water features prominently in Jackson's series: in works about the sea (*Porth*), or islands (*The Paps of Jura*), or rivers (*The Cornish Estuary*). Some of the series focus on small, more modest aspects of the landscape, rather than sea-pieces or skies: there are series on hedges, on fields, and on woods. Most of the series are based around paintings, with a few additional watercolours, etchings, and sculptures.[62] Some of the groups of works were travelling shows – like *Porth*, which travelled to Worcester, Newlyn, King's Lynn and Canterbury.

Many of the subjects of Kurt Jackson's series seem to have personal links: the forests in *Two Woods* and *Three Woods* (the New Forest, Ashcombe), for instance, have autobiographical associations. The Isles of Scilly Jackson has visited many times. The Glastonbury Festival, like Live 8 at the Eden Project (in 2005), are part of pop music culture, which Jackson is very fond of. And the area around Jackson's home in St Just – Jackson's landscape of the soul – are loaded with personal resonances.

One wonders if Kurt Jackson is running out of things he can use for series of paintings: he's done hedges, rivers, crows, Priest Cove, paths, quarries, travellers, forests, Scilly, Scotland, pools, etchings, and lighthouses. What's next? Maybe *The Clouds of Cornwall*, or *Cornish Seagulls*? But don't expect *Cornish Housing Estates* or *The Job Centres of West Penwith* any time soon.

---

62 Jackson's sculptures are entirely minor, rather pointless works, in a post-Constructivist manner *à la* David Smith, Jean Tinguely or Mark di Suvero (tho' mentioning those great artists is to elevate Jackson's 3-D works way too high).

THE CORNISH HEDGE.

Kurt Jackson manages to work seascapes and water into his series of works which are based inland, such as *The Cornish Hedge* and *The Long Field*. Twenty-six of the paintings in the show *The Cornish Hedge* have the sea in them, for instance. And some of the paintings in that show, such as *Above Tregardock* (2005) or *Submerged Hedges and Pouring Rain* (2004), are much more oceanscapes than depictions of Cornish hedges.

One of the two signature canvases in *The Cornish Hedge* series, *The Submerged Hedges Are Exposed Again At Low Water* (2005), painted on the Isles of Scilly, is really a seascape, the walls mere narrow black shapes amongst the whites, greys and pale blues of the Atlantic Ocean.

Some of *The Cornish Hedge* paintings are among Kurt Jackson's less successful images, of his later works. Some of the paintings of gorse or bushes or fields can become a little repetitive, and lack the grandeur and richness of Jackson's best pieces. It's like, yeah, another picture of a gorse bush... so what?

Gorse is one of the common plants in the West Penwith area (it's the bane of walkers, a horrible thing to clamber through), and Kurt Jackson has produced many images of gorse (many can be found in *The Cornish Hedge*): *When the Gorse Is In Blossom* (2004), *Gorse and Whatnot* (2004), *Cornish Gorse In the Sun* (2004), *Fuzzy Bush* (2005), *Whitethroat Singing, Gorse On the Hedge* (2004), *Derelict Croft In the Gorse, Islay* (2004), *May Furze* (2001), and *Amongst the Gorse Above Great Bay, St Martin's Scilly* (1997). The splotches of yellow of gorse are Jackson's version of Vincent van Gogh's sunflowers.

THE CORNISH ESTUARY.

In *The Cornish Estuary* series (2004) there are plenty of seascapes in amongst the riverscapes. The nearest river to St Just is the River Hayle, which kind of turns West Penwith into an island. The Hayle river is more a wide, muddy estuary than a long and winding river. Hayle itself is a rather dull and ugly town – and it's overshadowed by nearby St Ives (and the new out-of-town stores at Hayle which further turn Cornwall into a drab, American suburb). The remnants of industrial and engineering buildings and structures are a reminder of its more prosperous past. Tourists seem to hurry on through Hayle without stopping, making for Penzance or St Ives. You could ask a hundred visitors what they think of the Hayle river and its environs and many wouldn't have a lot to say about it. Hayle seems to be one of those places where it's always dark and rainy, with leaden skies, a town of dirty concrete, railway arches, and endless acres of grey mudflats, but Kurt Jackson turns it into a vista of breezy skies, wide-open spaces, and light glittering on the sea (as in *At Low Tide, the Estuary Becomes a Small River Again*, 2004, *Hit By a Hailstorm After a Sunny Morning*, 2002, and *Sunshine and Fast Moving Clouds Across the Estuary Mouth*, 2004). In Jackson's vision, the Hayle estuary is fitted out with the fluffy white clouds John Constable liked to paint, and a sea so blue and turquoise it could be Greece. So Jackson's art, like all good art, can change the way you see places: Hayle shifts from being featureless and grey to a place offering striking visions of water and skies.

In *The Cornish Estuary*, Kurt Jackson took on many of the famous rivers of Cornwall: Looe, Fal, Helford, Camel, Fowey, and Tamar. None of the rivers of Cornwall are big or spectacular on a global scale, like the Amazon, Nile, Mississippi or Ganges (hell, Cornwall is only 80 miles long and about 40 miles at its widest). But they have their own special appeal – and some, like the Tamar and the Fal – have played an important role in Cornish history (and still flourish).

Two of the loveliest Cornish rivers – the Helford and the Fal – are well-represented in Kurt Jackson's *The Cornish Estuary.* Paintings such as *Down To Frenchman's Creek* (2003), *Gweek Hulk* (2004), *Low Tide, Helford* (2002), *Low Tide and Sun, Helford River Creek* (2002), *Mawgan Creek High Tide* (2002), and *Hot Mylor, Summer Solstice* (2003), capture the solitude, the silence and the serenity of the heavily-wooded banks, the expanses of glistening, oozing mud, and the tucked-away creeks of these lesser-known areas of the Duchy.

Peter Redgrove has written evocatively of the tidal mud reaches of the Helford River, and the practice of bathing in the mud. This is from Redgrove's 'The Jesus Apparition':

Here's the path through the wood to the bathing-place with the ruined boathouse, and the tide's down over the mud, with the sunset on fire in it. All the blacks and heavy frowns have gone, its flanks are purple and blue like electricity, with emerald clefts in chilly satin channels, like silks and velours spun out of earth, laid down by the water. The smell! It's thriving yeast, and ploughed earth. (2007, 36)

You might think, judging from a typical Kurt Jackson painting, that he only paints in High Summer, in beautiful weather. Actually, he seems to work year-round, painting outdoors in all weathers (as well as in the studio). Even in a show like *The Cornish Estuary*, which has plenty of summery pictures, there are darker, bleaker images. The most successful is *Helford Blizzard* (2004), a yard-and-a-half square canvas of pale greys and whites which evokes American Minimal painters like Agnes Martin and Brice Marden (and the semi-abstract Post-impressionist nocturnes of James Whistler are an obvious reference point).

THE THAMES PROJECT.

The Thames Project (2005) was another series of works based around rivers. The series took in Britain's most famous waterway, as well as other rivers (but only in Britain). Jackson painted the River Thames across its length, from beyond Oxford, down to London. *The Thames Project* featured paintings made in or about Whitchurch (Reading), Oxford, Hurley, Henley, Kelmscott, Castle Eaton, London of course, and the Thames estuary.

The London paintings in *The Thames Project* had Kurt Jackson painting in the heart of the capital (at King's Reach, for instance) – not the usual rural or wilderness landscape associated with Jackson. One or two of the big city pictures were views taken from the Savoy Hotel, one of London's posh hotels, which overlooks the Thames.

In taking on central London, Kurt Jackson was operating in the same landscape as the classic images of the London riverscape that featured in the art of Claude Monet, J.M.W. Turner, John Sell Cotman or James Whistler. While Jackson wasn't consciously evoking Monet or Turner or Whistler in his *Thames Project*, it was clear that his paintings were part of that art historical tradition of painting London and its river.

Another aspect of *The Thames Project*, like the works of 2004 through 2006, such as *Neil's Place* or *The Cornish Estuary*, was a return to the more conventional painterly style of Kurt Jackson's earlier works. But that more traditional approach to painting was occurring alongside the more 'experimental' approach Jackson was exploring – in the *Porth* series and the sculptural pieces, for instance.

Pale blues and light greys predominate in *The Thames Project* paintings, and there are a good deal of broody skies. There are large expanses of water, with the viewpoint often tilted down, to look at the water, making the horizon quite high in the composition. And some of *The Thames Project* images are seascapes – of the estuary and the mouth of the River Thames. There are a few pictures of the Henley Festival (but distant, general views, not close-ups of people). And Jackson manages to squeeze in some of his reddened landscapes into the *Thames Project* series – of red roofs at Henley (2005), and Southend (2005). *The Solent Project* (2008), the *Young Liffey* (2008) and the *Avon Project* (on-going) were more river series.

The opening page of *Heart of Darkness*, Joseph Conrad's extraordinary 1902 novella, nails the atmosphere of this part of the planet, with its brooding, monochrome expanses of water and sky:

> The sea-reach of the Thames stretched before us like the beginning of an interminable waterway. In the offing the sea and sky were welded together without a joint, and in the luminous space the tanned sails of the barges drifting up with the tide seemed to stand still in red clusters of canvas sharply peaked, with gleams of varnished spirit. A haze rested on the low shores than ran out to sea in vanishing flatness. The air was dark above Gravesend, and farther back still seemed condensed into a mournful gloom, brooding motionless over the biggest, and the greatest, town on earth.[63]

T.S. Eliot took up this imagery in *The Waste Land* (weaving in ironic snipes at Edmund Spenser – 'sweet Thames, run softly 'til I end my song'), but it's Joseph Conrad who defines in exquisitely economic prose the river and the estuary.

---

63 J. Conrad, *Heart of Darkness*, Penguin, 1973, 5.

ST MICHAEL'S WAY.

St Michael's Way was a mixed bag of work, including 3-D pieces, portraits (of Peter, a fisherman), landscapes, many seascapes, pictures of woods and trees, and some images of churches (including interiors). Pubs were another ingredient (they often feature in Kurt Jackson's art). The St Michael's Way route or path has been used since prehistoric times, and has recently been developed by Cornwall County Council.

IRELAND.

The *Ireland* show offered up some classic images of Ireland (many from 1999 and Kurt Jackson's artistic residences there) as a grey, green, misty, rocky, brooding place – the emerald isle of popular culture, the Celtic fringe. Some of the Irish pictures are misty and grey to the point of abstraction, recalling again the canvases of Agnes Martin or Jo Baer, American Minimal painters who explored the limits of grey-on-grey paintings.

SCILLY.

In the *Scilly* exhibition of 2002, virtually every image, as one would expect, was a seascape. There was:

(1) the sea at night, as in *Waning Moon* (1999),

(2) the sea with a shining backlight of sun, as in *The Old School* (2001), *St Mary's From Tresco* (2002), *Droppy Nose Point* (2000), and *Catch the Light* (2002), (

3) the sea a deep blue and turquoise, as in *Between Two Islands* (2002), *Late Sun On Bryher* (1999), *Low Tide and Still* (2001), *Night Islands* (2001), and *Low Tide, Hells Bay* (2001),

(4) the sea under moody skies, as in *S C 4, St Martin's,* (1998), *Scilly Dusk* (2000), and *Tean and St Martin's* (2002),

and (5) very rough seas, all grey and white and pale blues, as in *Rain, Gales and a Huge Sea* (2001), *Norrard Rocks From Droppy Nose Point* (2001), *Gweal Island, Big Sea* (2000) and *Storm At High Tide* (2000).

The *Scilly* show was one of Kurt Jackson's more appealing exhibitions, partly because most of the images were his favourite subject – the sea and sky – in one of his favourite places – the Isles of Scilly.

SOUTHERN EUROPE

Southern Europe was an exhibition of paintings from Kurt Jackson's travels in France, Spain and Greece. The Southern light, the Mediterranean light – you can see it immediately in the deep blues of the ocean, the luminous blues of the Middle Sea of myth and history in pictures such as *Church By the Sea, Hot and Still Cretan Sea,* and *Xiona, Hiona, Chiona the Cretan.*

This is a world away from the rocky, windswept cliffs and moorland of West Cornwall or Scotland (it's still cliffs, islands, seas and skies, though). It's a whole new palette of greens and blues, and new vegetation, new architecture, new environments.

SCOTTISH PAINTINGS.

The *Scottish Paintings* drew on images created in or about Kintyre, Mull, Jura, Arran and other Scottish locations. It was a series of sulky skies, steel grey clouds, lots of pale greys and blues, and some big skies, too, as in *Port Na Cuthaig, Early Evening Light On the Sea, Ailsa Craig, Arran From Kintyre,* and *Across to Arran.* There were moonlight pictures (*Full Moon Over Arran*), and pale, grey, misty seascapes (as in *Low Tide, Kintyre, Change In the Weather, Aird Croft,* and *Jura*).

The *Scottish Paintings,* like the later Scottish series *The Paps of Jura,* were pictures of emptiness, very Zen Buddhist or Existential, in a way – empty moorland, empty beaches, empty hills, empty woods, empty lochs. Total absence of humanity, of figures, and even of the marks of humanity. Characters out of Samuel Beckett's fictions might wander through these landscapes and seascapes. Wildernesses, wildnesses. Empty grassy promontories stretching out into lochs or inland seas. There's nothing here but the artist, working away on the edge of civilization.

THE PAPS OF JURA.

The Paps of Jura comprise some of the most appealing of Kurt Jackson's more recent works. They contain classic Jackson images of hot colours in the landscape (yellows in *Islay, Highland Cattle and Hebridean Black Sheep*, 2004, *Croft Ruins, Brailrinch*, 2004, and *Sitting Amongst the Bog Violets and Deer Poo*, 2004), collaged paper and mixed media (*Maol Nan Damh, Jura*, 2004), and expansive seascapes of pearly, smooth seas and mountains hovering on the distant horizon (as in *The Paps From the Mainland*, 2004, *Loch Tarbert, Jura*, 2004, and *Glas Bheinn From Traigh Na Mile*, 2004).

THE PAINTED ETCHINGS.

The Painted Etchings series (2004) is a good example of Kurt Jackson's mixed media experiments. Jackson took an etching he'd made of Priest's Cove (*Ebb and Flow, Priest Cove*, 1999) and applied colour and mixed media to it.[64] The original etching was a typical Jackson view of the ocean out from Priest's Cove, with white clouds flying above a calm sea. Onto the prints of the etching Jackson added acrylics, pastels, ink, crayon and media (including bits of cloth, plastic and feathers. Mixed media etchings included *Drift Plastic* and *Big Sea*).

The Painted Etching series turns out to be another exploration of the seascape looking out from Priest's Cove in a variety of moods and times of day: squally and overcast (*Spring Tides On an Autumn Day, Squall and Sunshine*); dusky (*Suddenly You Are Surrounded By the Sea*); bright sun (*Pools of Light* and *Mordros Whisper*); low sun (*Land's End*); and rough seas (*Morning Surf In the Cove*). The idea, Kurt Jackson said, was to have each worked-over etching express 'one idea from a stream of thoughts/ feelings/ visions that arise every time I visit Priest Cove'.

PORTH.

In Kurt Jackson's *Porth* show, which travelled around Great Britain in the 2000s, large-scale paintings were prominent. There was a

---

64 Over the years, Kurt Jackson has produced other prints and etchings of Priest Cove, including *Priest Cove, Fog and Sparkle* (1999) and *An Offshore Wind, Weak Sun, Priest Cove* (1999).

practical reason for this: Jackson had recently acquired a much larger studio, and so decided to work on a far larger scale than before. The biggest work was *Have You Ever Wondered What's Out There?*, a landscape-format painting of the sea at Cape Cornwall (like most of the other pieces in the *Porth* exhibition). Like *Have You Ever Wondered What's Out There?*, some of the other large-scale pieces in the *Porth* show were built from smaller panels (*Have You Ever Wondered What's Out There?* was built from four vertical panels). It was a technique which found its most refined expression in the 1960s, with the American Colorfield and post-painterly abstract artists (such as Robert Mangold and Frank Stella). In *Porth*, though, Jackson hadn't yet developed the concept of multi-part paintings nearly as strongly or richly as Brice Marden, Mangold or Stella (and he hadn't gone nearly as far as those painters into the realms of painterly abstraction). Jackson seemed, rather, to be using multiple panel paintings as simply a means of making very large works – i.e., by joining one panel to another. (Jackson worked on the floor in his large-scale pieces, using a step ladder to view them from above.)

All of the *Porth* paintings are seascapes, and Kurt Jackson has attempted to depict some of the power and light and movement of the ocean in them. *Moved By a Wave* (2002) portrays an enormous white foaming wave, while *Modros* (2002) shows white spray over a blue sky.

In *Art Review* magazine, Kurt Jackson explained what he was trying to do in his sea paintings:

> I am trying to catch that feeling of the light on the sea, the surface of the water, the wind's movement, the meeting of the water and rock (the soft and hard, the movement and the stillness), the colours of the granite. (1998)

TWO WOODS AND THREE WOODS.

Two Woods and later *Three Woods* were a series of works about forests – Ashcombe, woodland near Bath, the New Forest, one of England's great forest regions, and Skewjack in Cornwall. What unites these forests, grouped as *Two Woods* and then *Three Woods*? Autobiographical associations: Kurt Jackson had visited the New Forest as a child (like thousands of children before and after him – it's a favourite outdoorsy destination). There was also the link between Jackson's father and the artist Sven Berlin (1911-99), who had moved from St Ives to the New Forest (Jackson later met Berlin).

The images in the *Three Woods* series are dreamy, moody, silent or near-silent pictures, just wind noise and the rustle of leaves. Celtic twilight pictures, images which are lost in memories and thoughts of the past. J.K. Rowling has talked about forests being places to be alone.

In the *Three Woods* series, deep greens, pale greens, greys and pale blues predominate. Some of the paintings are very dark, among Kurt Jackson's darkest – for example, *Oak, Beech, Ash, Hazel* (2004) and *Roe Deer and Blue Tits* (2003). Some are night paintings, like *An Owl Calls In the New Forest* (2004). Figures appear in the distance in some of the *Three Woods* images (2005).

PONDS, POOLS AND PUDDLES.

The pools in *Ponds, Pools and Puddles* series were drawn from Kurt Jackson's regular haunts: the Isles of Scilly (*Sun's Over the Yard Arm,* 2006, *Western Rocks in the Haze,* 2006), West Penwith (*Scholars Settling Tank, Geevor,* 2006, *Marazion, a Few Gulls, a Heron,* 2006), and Priest's Cove (*Wrack, Periwinkles, Turkey Tops, Limpets, Whelks, Rock Pool,* 2006 and *Rock Pool At Low Tide,* 2001).

Most of the images in the *Ponds, Pools and Puddles* series were of water and reflections, with the pictures typically comprising a small pool in the foreground and middle ground, with the sky and sometimes the ocean beyond.

THE CORNISH CROWS.

The Cornish Crows (2007) is about birds. Well, not really, it's still landscapes and seascapes and poolscapes and hillscapes and treescapes and rockscapes and skyscapes. The birds – crows, magpies, buzzards, jackdaws and of course gulls – are little dots in the usual Kurt Jackson landscapes and seascapes. There are, though, one or two larger images of birds. *The Cornish Crows* also contains some wild seas, at Cape Cornwall, some tranquil seas, at Kynance, some very moody skies (at No Go By Lane), and a foggy, mizzily day (2007).

THE LIGHTS OF WEST CORNWALL.

One of Kurt Jackson's more recent shows, *The Lights of West Cornwall* (2008), took lighthouses around Cornwall as its starting point. But guess what? Most of the paintings were of skies and seas and pools, like most of Jackson's other exhibitions and images. The lighthouses featured mainly as slender white marks in the far distance, dwarfed by big seas and big skies.

The lighthouses Kurt Jackson painted in *The Lights of West Cornwall* included Wolf Rock, Bishops and Longships, in the sea to the West of Cornwall, and Pendeen and Godrevy on the North coast (Pendeen Watch is a lighthouse near St Just, and Godrevy, near St Ives, is supposedly the inspiration for Virginia Woolf's *To the Lighthouse*). All, like lighthouses tend to be, can be seen easily from land or sea.

Pendeen has a very impressive fog horn; I remember staying in a cottage at Pendeen during a foggy, misty and very dark night in the early Nineties, when the horn blasted out over the ocean. One of the strangest sound effects I've heard was the echo of the horn alarm being reflected back from the waves in the invisible sea below as it travelled away from the cliffs. Invisible sound in foggy blackness – impossible to paint, and impossible to describe.

The locations in *The Lights of West Cornwall* were familiar Kurt Jackson sites: the cliffs around Cape Cornwall, Pendeen, Land's End, Carn Gloose, Kenidjack, and of course the Isles of Scilly. There were quite a few pictures of Godrevy lighthouse and the St Ives region of West Cornwall, which hasn't featured nearly so much in Jackson's *œuvre* as it has in many other Cornish painters (that's maybe why Jackson has tended not to use the area as much as he might – it's been painted thousands of times).

So in *The Lights of West Cornwall* there was *Among the Pinks, Wild Carrot and Cress, Godrevy With Seals Snorting Below* (2007), a big picture depicting the cliffs strewn with flowers, *Across To Godrevy From Carbis Bay* (2007), *Godrevy 1 pm* (2007), *Godrevy – Hot Sun* (2007), *Godrevy, the Waves Crash Over the Rocks That Have People's Names Carved On Them* (2007), *I Am On Godrevy With the Gulls* (2007), and *To the Lighthouse* (2007).

The paintings in the show *The Lights of West Cornwall* were the usual Kurt Jackson ones: mainly seascapes and skyscapes, and mainly of West Cornwall (though some were of further afield, such as Brittany in France). Moody skies, blue skies, sunsets, bright light on the sea, rough seas, calm seas, stretches of beach, gulls, seals, boats, and plants.

The 2008 art show included mainly watercolour and acrylic pieces, with some bigger oil and mixed media paintings. The larger canvases tended to be seascapes – such as the ones of Pendeen lighthouse (2007), or Godrevy (2007), or Land's End or Scilly (2007). The bigger pictures seemed more opaque and less successful to me, although their size was impressive.

Like other Kurt Jackson shows, most of the work on display in *The Lights of West Cornwall* was recent, in this case from 2006 and 2007, but some came from earlier periods, such as 1998 (*From Pendeen Watch Lighthouse*) or 1999 (*Across the Cove To the Day Mark* and *Pendeen Watch*). *The Lights of West Cornwall* was a large exhibition, too, with 124 works in the catalogue, on show in two galleries in London's Cork Street. Jackson is certainly very productive.

Kurt Jackson is a popular painter, and plenty of viewers and critics like his work: 'he paints with passion and excitement, with bold marks and colours' (Vivien Blackburn);[65] 'a curious fierceness, pulsating with hidden energy' (John Russell Taylor);[66] 'a virtuoso performance. Jackson's technical mastery is a brilliant match for his wonderful intuition' (Marc Awodey).[67]

However, Kurt Jackson also has his critics – Michael Glover wasn't a fan of this particular London show: he wrote in *The Independent*:

> Yet the sad truth is that, as paintings of coastal scenes, they are not, in fact, very good at all. They often seem forced and tonally inconsistent, or tonally crude. Colours, and the way they are juxtaposed, jar more than please.
>
> Jackson often scratches into the surfaces of rocks to give them texture, but the scratches seem to hang there, unsatisfactory gestures towards a solution to a problem. Or the paint seems too thickly applied to no good end – look, for example, at *Dawn, Porthtowan to Godrevy Lights*. Does afternoon sunshine really stipple the sea molten? Do waves crash in bobbles? The effects, all too often, look neither consistent nor æsthetically right. There is a

65 V. Blackburn, Mch 22, 2007, vivienb.blogspot.com.
66 J. Taylor, *The Times*, Jan 14, 2004.
67 M. Awodey, *Seven Days*, June 26, 2002.

great deal of strained painterly rhetoric here, but the paintings seldom hit home.

RECENT SHOWS.

Other recent shows of Kurt Jackson's work have included: *Forest Gardens* (2009, London), *The Solent Project* (2008, Lymington), *The Still Lifes* (2009, Truro), *River Avon* (2009, Bath), *Enesow: An exploration of the islands of Cornwall* (2009, Truro), *Ardnamurchan* (2010, Edinburgh), *The Dart* (2010), *A Taste of Glastonbury* (2010, London), *Kurt Jackson at 50* (2011, Falmouth), *The Fort* (2011, Edinburgh), *Gwedhen/Tree* (2011, Truro), *The Catacol Series: Paintings On Arran* (2012, Edinburgh), *The Fishermen's Friend* (2012, National Maritime Aquarium, Plymouth), *This Place: St Just in Penwith* (2012, Truro), *A One-Mile Walk* (2013, Gloucestershire), *The Burn* (Glasgow, 2013), *The Blackberries* (2012-13, London) and *The Sketchbooks* (2012, London). And a book of poetry, *And* (2011).

The Dart (2010) was a show of work drawing on Dartmoor, the great, magical moorland of South-West Britain. It included works in metal and prints as well as paintings. Dartmoor has been the source of inspiration for 100s of artists – probably the most well-known is the artist-walker Richard Long.

A One-Mile Walk (2013, Gloucestershire) was yet another West Penwith show, business as usual for Kurt Jackson, featuring the usual Jacksonian motifs and themes, such as red-on-red bracken pictures, and numerous seascapes, such as *The Call of the Sea At Dusk* (2013), *Big Bottling Seal In the Surf, Porthmeor* (2012), and *A Beautiful Grey Atlantic* (2013).

The 2012 show at the Royal Cornwall Museum, *Kurt Jackson and St Just*, combined a selection from the museum's horde and a few of Jackson's paintings. *The Burn* (Glasgow, 2013) was a show of Scottish works, based a journey along the Tangy Burn, a small stream on the West coast of Kintyre.

This Place: St Just in Penwith (2012, Truro) featured the little town in West Penwith and its environs. Notable here were one or two images of the town itself, including (inevitably) the Star Inn (you can buy an etching for £400/ $600), plus the town's tiny centre (and Chapel Street, where Jackson used to live).

The Blackberries (2012-13, London) was a collection of small-scale works focussing on, yes, little blackberries that grow in hedgerows or stick out of Marmite jars and, according to Kurt Jackson in a rather pompous statement: 'they symbolise that contact, that connection with the seasonal rhythms of the countryside still hanging by a thread here in Britain'.

INDUSTRY

Industry has been a key element in Kurt Jackson's series of works: mines, miners and mining were the subject of an early Jackson series, based around the South Crofty mine in West Cornwall (one of the last working mines in the region). Jackson was there to document the miners at work (rather than as a tourist or visitor: Cornwall's mines have since become part of the heritage and tourist industry, like so much else in Cornwall).

Quarries were another subject for a groups of works (there are plenty in Cornwall, as pretty much everywhere in Britain). Quarries, as Kurt Jackson recognized, were ecologically problematic: they formed great big holes in the landscape, or giant mounds of earth (by-products of the china clay industry), and their products would be used for building roads (the eco movement in Blighty is often anti-roads, or anti-more roads). But there were pluses about quarries, such as the new little eco-systems of plants and animals.

The quarry paintings aren't particularly distinctive. Paintings such as *Crushing and Screening Plant* (1998), *Loading* (1998) and *4 p.m., Carnew, Low Sun* (1998) are among Kurt Jackson's least impressive works.

Another industrial link was the Tinner's Way group of works, which were based around a route taken by the tin mining industry. Fishing is a recurring theme in Kurt Jackson's art (and not just in his paintings made in the Scillies, or around Cape Cornwall). Jackson has made one of the fishing huts at Priest's Cove a studio for years, and has painted many times amongst the fishing boats, ropes, and tack.

Aspects of Cornwall's industrial past crop up in some of the later paintings: *China Clay Docks On the Fowey* (2004) and *Gig and Docks, Fowey* (2004). As Kurt Jackson acknowledges in *The Cornish Estuary*, most of the rivers and estuaries of Cornwall contain pleasure craft, not industry.

With all of Kurt Jackson's industrial series of works there is a melancholy, a nostalgia, because many of the industries Jackson has documented have been in sharp decline. They are all industries, too, associated with the working-class: fishing, quarrying, mining (rather than middle-class occupations like clerical or administrative work, for instance. I don't reckon that Jackson is likely to move into a block of offices in Penzance or Cornwall's county town of Truro and paint a pool of typists at work, or Bill from Accounts photocopying a spreadsheet).

And these industries also have an element of heroic, physical activity about them (and, crucially, masculinity). They are industries character-ized by men working down a mine in very dangerous conditions, or sailing on an ungovernable ocean, or hacking stone out of cliffs. These are industries, too, which are associated with the North of England, with coal mining districts like Nottinghamshire (think D.H. Lawrence) or Newcastle, or the cotton and wool towns of the North, or the great shipping port of Liverpool, or the steel city of Sheffield. And they are usually professions that work outdoors – but mowing the grass in the local park, fixing a roof, mending a road, digging drains, and collect-ing trash is also honest work done outside (but don't expect a Jackson exhibition about garbage men or sewage plants any time soon).

So Kurt Jackson's series of painting based on industries can be viewed as part of the left-wing/ liberal swansong for those dying (or dead) endeavours. Think of the 'kitchen sink' films of the early 1960s (Britain's answer to the Neo-realist cinema of postwar Italy, and the socialist-realist tradition of Russian cinema), or a late addition to the genre: *The Full Monty* (1997). And the artist's role in contemporary society is being renegotiated continually too.

In considering Kurt Jackson's pæans to the decline of industry in Cornwall, one should also point out that they are very poetic, romantic and painterly paintings. They are not in the style of socialist-realist art, and they are not paintings that function as documentaries in the conventional manner: *Long Hole Driller and Rig, Mine Labourers At Crowst, Jeff Tonkin In the Rig, Long Holer* and *Bernie Harradine Preparing the Drill* (all 1996). Compare them with industrial, State art of Russia made between 1925 and 1955 (the authorities of the Soviet Union in the Stalinist period would hate Jackson's art!).

When you look at the *South Crofty* paintings (1996), for instance, you see shadowy figures glimpsed in orangey darkness, but it's difficult to make out exactly what they're doing, or who they are. These are watercolour and ink paintings depicting glowing lights and shadowy figures in darkness. Kurt Jackson hasn't delivered a 'realistic' documentation of the workings of a tin mine (by 'realistic', many people would really mean 'photorealist' or 'superrealist'.[68] These paintings are the equivalent of a shaky, lyrical, poetic Super-8 film, part of alternative or underground cinema, rather than a brightly-lit, crisp video documentary which might appear on the BBC or PBS.)

But there's an ambiguity, too, because the industries of Cornwall have contributed towards the deterioration of the environment. Kurt Jackson has spoken of over-fishing, for instance, or the pollution from quarrying and mining.

PAINTING AND POLITICS.

A Marxist and materialist critic might carp that Kurt Jackson's art says nothing about the politics or ideology of contemporary life, and is only romantic escapism. A feminist might criticize Jackson's paintings because they don't say anything about women's issues. An ecologist might attack Jackson's art because it doesn't tackle the pressing issues of global capitalism, or consumerism, or tourism (an issue like tourism is big in Cornwall).

---

68 There are some more conventional images of South Crofty, such as the long distance view of the mine from Tuckingham Valley (1995).

I'd say: no, you've missed the point. Or it's another case of critics wanting art to be everything, to do everything. You don't expect Disney's movie *Snow White and the Seven Dwarfs* (1937) to offer a political deconstruction of the working conditions of miners! (Altho' some Marxist crrritics have derided the Disney corporation because it hasn't offered a satisfying critique of the American way of life in its movies. Yeah, but it never *intended to*!).

There *is* a political and ideological aspect to Kurt Jackson's work, though: it comes out strongest in the many references to declining or dead industries and ecologies. The fishing gear stuck onto the bottom of a painting, for instance, as a comment on the downturn in the fishing industry. The paintings about mines or quarrying. And Jackson has been linked to movements and charities like Greenpeace, Oxfam, VSO, Water Aid, Cornwall Wildlife Trust, Surfers Against Sewage, AIDS Relief, Woodland Trust, Survival International and Live 8, which demonstrates a keen committment to political causes.[69]

DANCE, RAVE, TRAVELLERS

Kurt Jackson's links to travellers (also known in earlier times as 'gypsies') includes the West Country itself, popular with hippies, and childhood links to the New Forest, and hearing stories about the Shave Green gypsy site (which Jackson discusses in *Three Woods*). Jackson has painted travellers' camps, such as in *Ding Dong Benders* (1993), *Travellers' Site* (1994) and *Ding Dong Travellers, Fog* (1993).[70]

In the 1990s, the 'crustie' entered the culture in Britain, and was defined by the rightwing media as a stereotype: a wasted, pallid, messy youth who trailed a dog on a bit of string. The crustie was linked (by

---

69 Kurt Jackson seems to be so right-on and green, politically, he worries about using renewable wood sources for his picture frames, and paper from sustainable sources (P, 31).
70 These sites at Ding Dong and Botallack Cliff are no longer used by travellers; Kurt Jackson's paintings are already historical.

the mainstream media, always keen to whip up fear and anxiety) with 'New Age travellers', the convoys of travellers, squatters, the homeless, the road warriors, the anarchists into green, ecological issues (issues included whales and dolphins, anti-nuke protests, road protests[71] and animal rights). Those were the days (which already feel prehistoric) when protesters camped in trees in order to prevent roads being built.

Crusties/ New Age travellers/ anarcho-activists were self-consciously political but a-social. They appropriated hobo culture, the age-old vagabond or wanderer culture of yore. Unlike the popular stereotypical hobo, who was a meths- and wine-sodden old codger, crusties/ New Age travellers/ squatters/ activists were young, educated and informed. They openly displayed themselves as social outcasts. They were not ashamed of their homelessness (rootlessness) or outsider nature. They were very visibly and determinedly socially different; they resembled the punks of the late 1970s, but they were also very much like the hippies of the late 1960s. Unlike punks, they did not go home to middle class houses and parents after a night sitting on benches and guzzling cider, and getting wasted on drugs. The crusties and New Age travellers were openly homeless or travelling, like gypsies.

New Age/ traveller/ crustie culture built on 1960s hippy idealism, but it became thoroughly cynical in the grasping Eighties. Instead of being 'anarchist', like punk, New Age/ crustie/ traveller culture was also deeply conservative, nostalgic and bucolic. It exalted rural camps, getting back to nature, which meant sitting around the fire, far away from cities. The modern primitivism, though, also embraced computers, cel phones and the internet. The New Age nostalgic looking back to an earlier Golden Age of utopian living, when people did not rely on late commodity capitalism with its masses of gadgetry, cars, telephones, computers, televisions, and i-Pods, and instead lived in pagan communes, was combined with the self-absorbed surfing of digital hyperspace and the internet.

Though the New Age travellers/ crusties rejected many of the trappings of Western commodity capitalism, and yearned for the communal living akin to Tibetan tribes in their *yurts* in the mountains, they also

71 Kurt Jackson has contributed paintings to political protests about road building (P, 18).

used used modern technology, such as CD players, TVs and computers. Plugging into the internet, cyperpunks and New Age crusties sat around a hyperspace campfire. The flickering computer screen replaced the flickering campfires. They communicated with other disaffected surfers in the information superhighway, in a virtual space that was the new commune and campfire. They also did not live entirely outside of towns and the establishment: they often relied on government financial benefits. Despising 'the system', they were also very much a part of it.

That's how 'New Age traveller' and 'crustie' culture was portrayed in the rightwing media (i.e., most of the media in Britain) during the 1990s. Moral panics grew up around 'New Age travellers' and 'crusties' – later the British press would move on to other targets, creating scares about young single mothers, or immigrants, or the Euro.

Meanwhile, the political elements shifted into anti-capitalism, anti-globalization and anti-American movements. Gestures such as the Live 8 concerts of 2005 were the official face of the ideological movements such as anti-capitalism and the cancelling the Third World debt.

On a more positive note, 'crustie' and 'New Age traveller' culture was deeply linked to music: we're talking Crass, Hawkwind, the Levellers, the Glastonbury Festival, Brighton, and rave and dance music. We're talking trance and techno and house, and the new Ecstasy drug (but also plenty of pot, LSD and speed), and trippy videos on *Top of the Pops* and MTV (and the rise of the superclubs when dance and rave culture became establishment). We're talking two thousands people in a field swaying to techno music and high on Ecstasy. It was Sixties psychedelia reborn, convoys on the M25 driving out to some secret rave, avoiding the police and getting raided.

The 'passive' aspect of rave culture is one of the most interesting things about it: rave culture was a return to the womb and the maternal realm, to an enclosed, secure, pre-œdipal, pre-sexual stage. The imagery of rave, as with indie pop, was of childhood: rave culture favoured ice lollies to help dancers chill out and cool down (news-papers ran reports of youths dying from going without liquids while on E); there were dummies, whistles, pacifiers, glow-in-the-dark collars, primary colours, stocking knot-top caps, stripey and 'childish' clothes, and samples from kids' shows such as *The Magic Roundabout, Dr Who,* and *Sesame Street.*

Rave culture extolled the merits of fairy tales, J.R.R. Tolkien, and all the festivals and motifs of a pseudo-pagan religion: the Summer Solstice[72] at Stonehenge, Glastonbury, Avebury, etc. Rave parties typically took place in the most 'pagan' part of Britain, the South-West, a coach drive from London (Wiltshire, Somerset, sometimes Cornwall). Rave/ dance culture embraced the marginal/ occult/ paranormal aspects of culture: the 'Celtic' festivals of Hallowe'en and the Solstices; UFOs; crop circles; mythic sites such as Glastonbury and Avebury; astral planing; Tarot; astrology, etc.

The rave culture return to the Mother was part of the revival of the Goddess cult in techno-pagan music, dancing to the 120-130 bpm baby's heartbeat rhythms might be like dancing in the same womb: the rave hangar was like a New Age womb. The ravers were new pagans dancing like mæands high on hallucinogens, rave dancing as modern day rituals of delirium, the rave party as a rediscovered rite of social cohesion, the revivified dream of a quasi-spiritual unity. The music of dervishes and shamans who fling themselves about until they reach ecstasy and alpha-wave experience.

Rave was the flipside of aggressive, macho rock: it was 'passive', 'feminine', Goddess culture (as opposed to the exaltation of masculine pursuits of street violence, wielding guns, tupping prostitutes and killing policemen in gangsta rap and hiphop). Rave culture looked back to the oceanic music of the late 1960s and early 1970s, the synth washes of Tangerine Dream, the hypnotic pulse of Fleetwood Mac's 'Albatross', the New Ageism of Steve Hillage and Gong, the Gaia imagery of Weather Report and Return to Forever.

Just as significant as the absorption of Oriental musics in ambient house – the lengthy drones of Hindu sacred music, for example – was the idea of the vast blue ocean, particularly the Pacific (again, think of Kurt Jackson's dreamier seascapes). Pacific, pacify, passive – the Hawaiian guitar of early Pink Floyd (on *Atom Heart Mother* and

---

72 Kurt Jackson has referenced the solstices in his paintings.

Meddle) became the gliding guitar of indie and 'shoegazer' music and the Vangelis-like synth glissandos of ambient and rave music. Acts like Banco de Gaia, Future Sound of London, the Aphex Twin (Richard James was from Cornwall), the Orb and Paul Van Dyk produced what was termed 'progressive house', or 'prog dance', or 'ambient house'; it took part of its inspiration from the prog rock of the early 1970s: witness the steals and homages to bands like Pink Floyd (especially), Genesis, Fleetwood Mac, Brian Eno and Tangerine Dream.

What has this to do with Kurt Jackson? Well, I reckon there is a nostalgic desire for the natural world in Jackson's art, a back-to-nature yearning which manifests itself in Jackson pursuing notions of 'wilderness' and 'wildness' in nature. And Jackson has been part of some political music gestures, such as Live 8 (as artist in residence) at the Eden Project in Cornwall (what a terrific concert that was!). As a child he said he was taken on political demonstrations by his parents, as well as attending lectures. Jackson said he'd inherited his parents' left-leaning, libertarian politics, and was, if anything, even more radical than them – especially about issues relating to the environment.

And Kurt Jackson's popularity in the U.K. must have something to do with the subjects he's portraying – the seas, the trees, the skies, the landscapes that people in Britain revere so much. Never forget how much the Brits love the countryside (and their pets), how they flock to National Trust country houses and English Heritage castles, to gardens, to parks, to out-of-town DIY stores and gardening centres. And the sea! Every day, up and down the land, thousands of Britons will be sitting in their cars staring at the sea. And some of the really adventurous ones will even get out of their cars and sit on a bench. Or maybe – 'watch yourself, Bert!' – 'I am, Ethel, I am!' – roll up their trousers and dip their ankles in the cold surf.

And dance and rave music and culture is part of the cultural background of the period – late Eighties to late Nineties – when Kurt Jackson was developing some of his most significant artworks. Music is an under-rated factor, I think – artists glean inspiration from all sorts of sources, not only visual ones. Poetry was vital for J.M.W.

Turner, for instance (and James Thomson in particular).[73] And it's significant that Jackson has forged links with musical enterprises such as Live 8 and the Glastonbury Festival (and some of the other causes he has supported have associations with pop music: Friends of the Earth, Greenpeace, AIDS Relief, etc).

---

73 Turner would often quote poets beside his paintings (as well writing own poetry, *Fallacies of Hope*, in imitation of the poets he loved, like Thomson).

7

ASPECTS OF
KURT JACKSON'S ART

PAINTING AND WRITING

A recurring motif in Kurt Jackson's art is writing on the surface of his paintings, or collaging pieces of text into the paintings. Some of this appears to be autobiographical: the phrases are a reminder for the artist of his surroundings, his feelings. They are a personal record of particular days, or who was with him when he made (part of) the picture. (They are also a way of recording things which cannot be put into a conventional landscape painting: the date, for instance. The season – Autumn, say – might be obvious from a painting, but not whether it was a Wednesday or a Sunday, or whether the painting was completed at noon or four in the afternoon). The writing came about partly through the frustration of titling paintings (the ubiquitous title of modern art and contemporary art is of course *Untitled,* which many painters have employed for a variety of reasons, but one reason is certainly to avoid coming up with titles).

So in Jackson's paintings there'll be references to his children, or his wife Caroline, or a friend, or someone he's known. Or a shopping list. Birds, clouds, the weather, the tide, and animals are among the phenomena Jackson records in his paintings.

Note that Kurt Jackson nearly always includes the place in the title or in his writing on the picture. Clearly *place* is vitally important for Jackson. It's essential to know, for the artist, if a painting was produced in the Isles of Scilly or the New Forest, for instance.

The tide is often recorded in the texts and titles of Kurt Jackson's paintings, for obvious reasons: it's impossible to miss the uncontrollable, relentless rhythm of the tides when you're working around the coasts of Cornwall. And at one of Jackson's favourite spots, Priest's Cove, the sea often comes in with an incredible force, so thunderous it threatens to sweep everything away before it. The beaches of this part of Cornwall, even the small stony, rocky ones, are very different at low tide compared to high tide.

Kurt Jackson often discusses plants, birds and animals in his art – don't forget that he studied zoology at university in Oxford, and has been interested in the natural world since childhood (P, 9). He's an artist who likes to identify particular plants or birds, which find their way into the titles of his paintings as well as the paintings themselves.

It should be noted, too, that Kurt Jackson isn't always located down on the beach when he's producing sea paintings: plenty of his work is viewed from the vantage points of the tops of cliffs (such as near Carn Gloose), or from up the valleys of Kenidjack and Cot, or looking down at Zawn an Bal (1997), or from the fields around Kenython Lane (near Jackson's home), where the sea can be a distant blue or grey blur.

❖

One of the ways that Kurt Jackson says he gets started on a work is by collecting material to use as a collage. He might then use watercolour washes, and continue by adding acrylics, ink, maybe pastel, or pencil, and more watercolours. The traditional watercolour techniques of lifting off or scraping away layers is employed.[74] It goes without saying that working in watercolour and other water-based media means you've usually got to work quickly.

THE SEXUALITY OF SURFACES

The surfaces and textures of Kurt Jackson's paintings are an important ingredient in the success of his art among art lovers. Why? Because surfaces and textures are part of the erotic appeal of paintings, along with colour, light, composition and all the other technical and formal aspects – irrespective of subject matter – we're talking an erotic approach to making art and the eroticism of the art object itself (consider the work of Michelangelo Merisi da Caravaggio or Gustave Moreau or Max Beckmann). Jackson doesn't paint nudes, or sex acts, but that doesn't mean there isn't an erotic element to his art. There is, and it partly resides in the textures and surfaces.[75]

It's important, for instance, that Kurt Jackson's paintings are not smooth and blemishless in terms of surface or texture. Rather the paint is scumbled, layered, and textured. Sometimes Jackson draws the end of the paintbrush through the wet paint. Sometimes he uses watercolour techniques, like lifting off wet paint with a cloth and repainting over an area. Sometimes he lets pigment dry, other times he works wet-in-wet. And occasionally, when frustrated, he says he has stomped on a painting (P, 29).

The eroticism of painterly surfaces and textures has one of its most impressive manifestations in contemporary art in the work of Jasper

74 Technique was important, Kurt Jackson said, but it wasn't what his paintings were about. Other aspects were more significant, such as the subject (P, 22).
75 The sensuality of surfaces, of textures, of brushwork, of the artist's sense of touch, is crucial to the 'greatness' of art, as Lynda Nead writes: 'the artist's subjectivity that is registered by the brushwork and surface is sexualized. Art criticism writes sex into descriptions of paint, surface and forms.' (Female Nude: Art, Obscenity and Sexuality, Routledge, London, 1992, 58)

Johns, for instance, with his oil and encaustic and wax technique: Johns' American flags and targets are among the sexiest examples of contemporary painting.[76]

Other painters in this same vein of supersensual surfaces include the German painters Gerhard Richter and Anselm Keifer, and semi-abstractionists such as Thérèse Oulton.[77] In canvases like *Wayland's Song (With Wing)* and *Margarethe*,[78] Keifer fixed a number of elements to his pictures. Robert Rauschenberg, a contemporary (and one-time lover) of Jasper Johns, is one of the undisputed masters of sticking whatever takes his fancy onto a painting. (Seeing some Rauschenberg works recently in L.A., New York and Washington reminded me again just how incredibly good Rauschenberg is. Rauschenberg reminds you that *anything is possible*, and not to be afraid – *of anything*. Jackson is a fan of his art).

Kurt Jackson has moved further into the mixed media field in his later work, with newspapers and magazines and printed material a favourite device. Sometimes Jackson will do a rubbing of a sign that's near the location of the painting to enhance the sense of place (P, 28).[79] Jackson's collaging of words and images has plenty of forebears: it goes back to the Cubists, to Pablo Picasso and Georges Braque (Jackson's habit of working fragments of newspapers and headlines into his paintings inevitably recalls the Cubists); to the Surrealists' collages; and to the photo montages of John Heartfield.

But the true ancestors are the artists of the 1960s like Jasper Johns and Tom Phillips, particularly in the way they fused typography and pigment using smearing, layering, and overlapping (again, Kurt Jackson's collaging of printed material in his art is far less radical (or interesting) than that of many other artists).

Part of Kurt Jackson's penchant for writing and texts is also

76 Jasper Johns: *Flag*, 1955, Museum of Modern Art, New York.
77 Others might include: Christopher Le Brun, Lance Smith, Hughie O'Donoghue, R. B. Kitaj, Jim Dine, Richard Diebenkorn, Sean Scully and Howard Hodgkin.
78 A. Keifer: *Wayland's Song (With Wing)*, 1982, oil, emulsion, straw on photo, on canvas with lead; *Margarethe*, 1981, oil and straw on canvas, 9'2" x 12'6", Saatchi Collection, London.
79 And including the signs, such as 'dangerous cliff', over a picture of the sea was meant to show how 'inappropriate and intrusive' the signs can be (P, 28).

decorative and calligraphic: he simply likes how words look on a painting (the writing, though, isn't meant to be the subject of the painting, although it can take over with very small works. Rather, the handwriting becomes a faint line when seen from a normal viewing distance [P, 28]). Indeed, some critics have dubbed it Disneyesque and gimmicky.

You'll notice, though, that Kurt Jackson doesn't include just *any* newspaper in his paintings. Not *The Guardian, The Times, The Sun* or, heaven forfend!, the *Daily Mail* or *Daily Express*, rightwing tabloids. No, not national newspapers (products from 'up country'), but local newspapers: the *Hayle Times* or, if he's in Scotland, the *West Highland Free Press.*

Kurt Jackson sometimes uses his feet to make marks with, as well as his hands and paint brushes. Sometimes he flicks paint onto the canvas, rather like Jackson Pollock (indeed, Pollock's techniques of painting are the forerunners of the methods of so many contemporary artists: working on the floor, working large, using spontaneity and accidents, emphasizing gesture, and being involved very physically with the piece, etc. Pollock continues to be a hero to many artists).

SHAPES, FRAMES AND EDGES

Kurt Jackson favours regular rectangular formats for his paintings, and they tend towards squares. Shapes that are very narrow are not used, and neither are irregularly-shaped canvases – triangles, say, or arches (some of Jackson's works are not regular rectangles – sometimes the edges of paintings are left ragged, sometimes due to the shape of the paper or support). Smaller works might twelve by twelve inches, and larger works 36 by 36 inches. Larger paintings than that are much rarer; 6 feet would be about the biggest, with 48 inches square being typical; Jackson hasn't gone in for the really large scale of much of contemporary painting, for instance.

When it comes to edges and frames, Kurt Jackson tends to allow his paintings to fray or spread around the edges. This is a common device in modernist art – an art which self-consciously alludes to its facture. Often the edges of Jackson's paintings are hard lines, with the mixed media worked up to the edge. Often, though, the pigment and materials fade out before reaching the edge.

This relates directly to framing, of course: some art consumers will buy paintings and have them framed *inside* the painting's area, so the ragged edges are cut off. That makes a painting look neat, with regular edges. Some artists build their own frames, of course, and deliberately mount the paintings to retain the ragged edges.[80] Many of Jackson's works are on paper rather than canvas or wood or other solid supports, so it's easy to choose between a frame which draws attention to the ragged edges and a frame which hides them.

HORIZONS

Notice that Kurt Jackson nearly always includes the horizon in his art. Is that significant? Well, it means that his paintings remain in a figurative or representational mode, referring to the world outside. If you can see the sky, and if that patch of blue or grey is meant to be the sky, the artwork is clearly representing the world or relates to the world. If you can't see the horizon, the painting might have more chance of being interpreted as abstract.

For instance, works such as *Bramble Flowers and Blackberries* (1992) and *Nancherrow Stream* (1996) are views of the landscape which leave out the sky and the horizon and move towards abstraction (although it still possible to discern the things that the artist is depicting). Whereas *The World of Ours* (2004), *The Gorse, the Cottage, the Hedge, April*

---

80 Kurt Jackson frames his pictures with his wife Caroline (P, 31).

Showers (2005), *Towards Land's End From Carn Bosavern, Warm Sunshine* (2001) and *Prehistoric Hedges Above Sennen Beach* (2005), like most of Jackson's paintings, all contain the sky and the horizon, anchoring the images on the Earth, and in the realm of representation.

And when Kurt Jackson is painting the sea, the horizon is just about always included: there are very few Jackson paintings with the viewpoint tilted down into the water (easy to do on those Cornish cliffs, looking down at the ocean, or those rockpools). So if the horizon is included, that means that Jackson is *always painting the sky*. The sky is the one recurring element in all of Jackson's art.

INTO THE LIGHT

Some of the most appealing Kurt Jackson paintings are the ones that take a viewpoint from high up and far off, so the ocean is spread below the artist from up on the cliffs. With the sun high, the water is side-lit or back-lit, and the sea becomes shiny, silvery, and luminous – as in *On Botallack Head* (1999), *Big Silver Sea From Carn Gloose, Bottom of Carn Gloose, Low Tide* (1996), *Priest Cove, Hot Day, Priest Cove* (1997), *Blackbird Watching the Sun On Cape Cornwall* (2001), and *Afternoon On the Cliffs, Wind and Sun* (1995),

Sometimes Kurt Jackson paints the path of light on the sea, the narrow column of shining light that stretches from the shore up to the horizon. You see it in *Nanquidno, Low Tide* (1996), *Sealight, Chloe, Nanquidno, Low Tide* (1996), *The Sun Comes Out, the Tide Comes In* (1999), *Tide Coming In Fast* (1996), *Backalong* (2001), and *November Butterflies At High Tide* (2006).

7 a.m., Penlee Point To the Lizard, Sun (1996) is one of my favourite Kurt Jackson images, an appealing two-foot square rendition of a brooding grey sky and an open sea from up on the cliffs. It's really only sunlight on water again, one of Jackson's primary subjects, but it's beautifully done. It's not about colour (greys, blues and blacks predominate), but about light, the way the light falls on the ocean and is separated into patches of light and dark by the clouds.

A distinctive, instantly recognizable feature of Kurt Jackson's sea paintings is the way he paints the light on the sea: he often leaves the white watercolour paper or canvas showing through, to represent the light reflecting on the waves, as in *On Botallack Head* (1997), *Land's End From Priest Cove* (1998) and *Just Before an Evening Pint* (2004). The large areas of white speckles on blue give Jackson's paintings a particular look, which few other painters among his contemporaries use.

When Kurt Jackson sets himself down on the West-facing coast of Cornwall, in West Penwith, he's in a prime position to paint countless sunsets. But another feature of Jackson's art that's striking is how often he *avoids* your typical sunset picture, the ones you see on tourist postcards and leaflets, the sunsets with plenty of reds, oranges, yellows, lilacs and purples in them. Although Jackson's art is full of deeply romantic and very lyrical images of the sea and the sun setting, he doesn't often deliver the chocolate box, twee sunsets that dominate travel brochures and tourist material.

There are some splashes of hot colours at sunset, though, in Kurt Jackson's art: the band of luminous yellow in *Above the Crowns, Botallack* (1996), *Loch Diabaig, The Sun Comes Out After a Wet Afternoon* (2005), the gold cloud in *One of Caroline's Winter Afternoons* (2001), and *Dusk, Seacroft* (1997). Other pictures with warm sunset elements include: *Pond At Dusk* (2005), and *Once the Sun Has Set Behind a Bank of Cloud the Sea Starts To Glow* (2005),

❖

One aspect of Kurt Jackson's seascapes one can't help noticing, although it's so obvious it seems too simple to mention, is that he prefers the sea to be blue, pale blue, or grey, and only occasionally does Jackson paint the sea as green, or allow green to take precedence. The sea in Kurt Jackson's art is every shade of blue, and frequently shifts into purples, and at the other end of the scale, into greys and whites. But there's plenty of green in the real sea around Cornwall – not only turquoise, which Jackson often employs, but vivid greens. A painting such as *Treen Cliff* (1996) contains the kind of green I'm talking about, a green of watery translucence.

SQUIGGLY LINES

Another distinctive element of Kurt Jackson's art which the viewer spots immediately is the use of squiggly black lines, usually included to represent or suggest plants – trees, brambles, gorse bushes, hedgerows. *Lowe Pool Oaks* (2004), *Red Sandbank, Low Tide, Fal Estuary* (2002), *Birch* (2005), and *Allt Na Diabaig* (2006) are typical works. Jackson said he didn't like to produce straight lines, but preferred the arc of a brush, or to drip or throw paint to create a straight line (P, 22).

Paintings such as *Above the Loch Amongst the Birch and Oak* (2005) and *Birch Wood, Moss, Rock, Diabaig* (2005) are dense with black lines. Some are achieved with narrow skeins of paint, and some by dragging the end of the brush over wet paint. The flattened space in these images of trees against lakes and skies and the twisted, squiggly twigs and branches recall the landscape paintings of Egon Schiele (such as Schiele's *Four Trees* [1917] and *Autumn Trees* [1911, private collection]). (An earlier version of this format of bare spines and twigs against the sky occurs in *Out of the Woods* [1996], painted at the small inland Drift reservoir, and the small painting *Cottage In the Woods* [1999]).

Trees, flowers and plants are a challenge for a landscape painter: do you go in close and attempt to render every detail (like Claude Lorrain)? Or do you stay back and offer impressions or suggestions of shapes, patterns, colours and details (as Jean Baptiste Camille Corot liked to do)? Kurt Jackson's solution is to explore the borderline between abstraction and figuration. His art is wholly figurative or representational, but he does occasionally move into more abstract approaches. Jackson's is an art of feelings, as he says – an art of experiences and responses. So, faced with a bunch of trees or hedgerows or flowers, Jackson isn't interested in rendering them 'accurately' or 'realistically', but subjectively and imaginatively.[81]

In paintings such as *Cot Valley* (1995), *Hot Afternoon In Kenidjack* (2000) and *Rain, Oaks, Birch, Diabaig Stream* (2005), Jackson suggests trees and plant stalks with clusters of jagged vertical lines, scratched in the wet paint, or with thin lines drawn over orangey-red areas. Very often, trees and leaves are rendered in Jackson's art by hundreds of dabs of paint spread evenly over the paper, as in *Fig Tree Outside the Monastery, Agia Agathia* (1997), *A Few Boats, Low Tide, Malpas Creek* (2004), *Summer Plants* (1997) and *Kenidjack Stream* (1995). Some of *The Cornish Hedge* works – such as *An Ke Kernewerk* (2005), *Campion, Foxgloves, Sorrel, Nettle, Bracken, Bramble, Gorse, Navelwort, Stonecrop, Hogweed, Buttercup, Stitchwort, Bluebell* (2005) and *This World of Ours* (2005) – are nothing but hundreds of dabs of paint, recalling Georges Seurat, Paul Signac and Camille Pissarro and the Post-Impressionists (a.k.a Neo-Impressionists), and their technique of pointillism or divisionism.

Kurt Jackson is fond of splitting the horizon of his compositions with a bold diagonal form, often a tree or a bush, leaning over in the wind, or a tree or bush that's grown at a slant due to the prevailing wind. If Jackson sets up his vantage point below the horizon, looking up at the sky and the plants and trees, he'll pick a single tree or bush that will break the horizon and dominate the upper half of the painting, as in *Winter Sunshine In Harvey's Field* (2005), *Two Snipe Fly Over Followed By Two Fieldfares* (2004), and *Treligga Slate and Blackthorn* (2005).

---

81 And Kurt Jackson is also keen to avoid being 'twee' or cute or 'pretty'. So fields full of daffodils or crocuses or roses or bluebells are out. Occasionally Jackson has painted bluebells – as in *Down To Botallack* (1998) and *Early Evening* (1997).

Night paintings are a recurring subject in Kurt Jackson's art: for instance: *Botallack Head In the Light of a Waxing Moon* (1998), *Full Moon Over Warren's Pool* (2005), and *Full Moon Over Warrens Pond, 5.30pm.* (November, 2005).

Kurt Jackson said he painted at night partly to avoid being disturbed by passers-by, and to find new ways of looking at familiar places (P, 17). It also meant interesting things could happen with the materials in the dark. The British artist Hamish Fulton, who makes art from walks, sometimes walks along a familiar route at night, because at night things are different (Fulton also walks without sleeping, which alters perception).[82]

Blue predominates, as one might expect, and many of Kurt Jackson's night paintings are moonscapes – *Full Moon Over the Scillies* (1998), *Full Moon Rising Over Scilly* (1998), and *Full Moon Rising Over the Gump* (1999).

Dusk is another favourite time of day for Kurt Jackson – *Gear Lane Totem Pole* (1999), *Allt Na Diabaig* (2006), *The Gloaming* (2006), *A Game of Frisbee On the Beach At Dusk, Scilly* (1998), *Jura, a Heron At Dusk* (2004), *Inverlussa Beach, Dusk, Sun Sinking* (2004), *Dusk Towards Lelant Saltings* (2002), and *Towards the Turkish Coast, Dusk* (1997). Jackson said he painted during a day's work until the light faded, so twilight is going to feature from time to time in his art.

A painting that Kurt Jackson told me was a favourite with people was *Dusk, Seacroft* (1997), a small watercolour and ink image of Jackson's house near St Just-in-Penwith (it's the frontispiece of the book *Paintings of Cornwall and the Scillies*). It's one of those watercolour paintings where the artist has worked the colours wet-in-wet, allowing them to spread and merge, with blues, yellows and blacks pre-dominating. Dashes of red and green enhance the composition in the centre. *Dusk, Seacroft* is closer to abstraction than Jackson's usual

---

82 Such as Hamish Fulton's walk along the Pilgrims' Way in Southern England between December 21st and 23rd, in 1991, a 125 mile continuous walk without sleep. Or his *Seven Walk Without Sleep*. Fulton likes to toy with the hallucinations and altered states that sleep deprivation brings (i.e., it can be a walk along a familiar route, but it's a completely different experience because the artist-walker's gone without sleep).

paintings, with only the house and telegraph pole on the right giving an idea of the setting. Without those marks of humanity, it might be a sunset on the Russian tundra.

WILDERNESS

> I often do paintings of the open sea with no land visible; the last wilderness here [Cornwall] is the sea. You can look out there to the Atlantic and there is no visible sign that we have done anything to it, although we know we have. That's the fascination with it and why I paint it over and over again – big expanses of open sea and open sky.

Kurt Jackson (*Paintings of Cornwall and the Scillies*, 12)

One of Kurt Jackson's appealing concepts is that the ocean is one of the last true wildernesses left on the planet. It's an idea that I found very interesting when he explained it to me when we first met in St Just. I took it that he meant a *spiritual* as well as ecological or physical wilderness. Jackson's art can thus be seen as an art that is exploring the border region between humanity and nature, between culture and nature, as well as literally tackling that area – the coast – which is neither land nor sea. Note that Jackson is always facing *outwards* from the land, and looking *towards* the ocean, not painting with his back to the sea, and looking towards the land (and notice that the many boats and ships and helicopters and such in this area are left out of the paintings, too). So Jackson's *Porth* series, about Priest Cove, and all of his sea paintings, are very important in his art in articulating this idea of the ocean as the last wilderness.

'Have you ever wondered what's out there?' is a question that Kurt Jackson asks (it's the title of one of his major paintings, too – the centrepiece of the *Porth* series). Related paintings include *Endless* (2000), another Priest Cove picture. Jackson has repeated the question over a number of related works: the title of two 2004 works is *The Last*

Wilderness In Western Europe? This was painted on Jura, and both pictures are consciously emptied of human marks – just empty moorland and a delicate blue sky.

An earlier picture, part of the *Cape* series, was entitled *Do You Ever Wonder What's Out There?* (1999) – an unusual composition in the Kurt Jackson *œuvre* which puts the horizon very high, and focusses on a dark blue ocean flecked with white spray.

The point, of course, is that *anything* can be out there, because the ocean is a mirror, a wish-fulfilment, a fantasy. And the sea is of course the symbol of the unconscious *par excellence*. The sea can symbolize or represent anything you like: birth, rebirth (the birth of Venus), death, plenitude, the mother, the Goddess, the origin of life, change, transformation, time, cycles (the tides), the moon, food, and so on. For the fishing industry, the sea's a rich source of product to be harvested (as well as a place of danger). For the military it's a zone that needs to be continually policed, and sea lanes kept open (there are surveillance devices positioned in the seas around Britain, for instance, to warn of submarines and vessels). For the British government it's a border between Britain and Everywhere Else that has to be carefully controlled. For holiday-makers it's something cold and wet to dip into occasionally, and makes a pleasant backdrop to an afternoon's sunbathing. For artists, the ocean offers astonishingly varied phenomena, which can be the subjects or starting-points for creative works.

Kurt Jackson isn't that interested in many of the connotations of the ocean – the moon, time, goddesses, rebirth (though moons do appear in his art from time to time). He's not really interested in religious or pagan or magical symbols in that way. So Jackson doesn't (usually) load the sea in his paintings with symbolism or metaphor or allegory (though viewers can – and no doubt do – read anything they like into his sea pictures). And he's not that interested in shipping, fishing, and all things maritime, like J.M.W. Turner was.

But when Kurt Jackson asks a question like 'have you ever wondered what's out there?', and considers the sea as one of the last wildernesses, that alters the interpretation of his sea paintings. It doesn't apply to all of them, though: in plenty of paintings (and not only the smaller or more modest ones), Jackson is not thinking in terms of big themes. But when he titles a painting *Have You Ever Wondered What's Out There?* (and writes the title in big letters across the painting), it's clearly intended to resonate in the viewer at a deeper level.

OUTSIDE

Much is made in publicity and reviews of Kurt Jackson's method of working *en plein air*, in the tradition of the painters in the French sense of both painting out of doors, and of paintings which give the impression of being painted outside. The whole *en plein air* thing is really overdone – with regard to many artists, not just Jackson.

You might have seen the video documentary of Kurt Jackson at work which's part of his exhibitions, where the artist is portrayed making a painting on a canvas laid out on the ground on the cliffs above the sea (Jackson often paints on the ground). It's looks great, but the practicalities of creating a painting like that in those circumstances must be, as other artists have commented, difficult. The truth is, that sort of imagery is significant in the part it plays in the marketing or visual representation of the artist in the media and in information related to the exhibitions (it's the kind of set-up scene that TV documentaries like to stage. It makes the act of painting more dramatic because, let's face it, unless you're Michelangelo Buonarroti working on the Sistine Chapel ceiling, painting can be a boring thing to watch).

Of course, Kurt Jackson does a lot of work outside – or *seems* to – that's easy to see from any of his paintings. The big paintings, though, are likely created back in the studio. But the sketchbook, the water-colour paper pad, the leaves of Arches paper, those seem to have been taken outdoors sometimes and worked on (even if only for the initial sketch). (Jackson has 100s of sketchbooks, like many artists; and works made in the sketchbooks, which are a visual diary, could be every bit as significant as a big oil painting, he said [P, 21]. Jackson published a selection from his sketchbooks, in 2004). Jackson says that if the painting's made *in situ*, the bulk of the work will have been done on the spot, with only a few marks added in the studio. (But even if a painting *wasn't* made outside, some consumers prefer to *think* that it was).

The sketchbooks include drawn maps, collages of found objects, pencil sketches of people, flowers, and olive groves, but mostly the sketchbooks contain watercolour and acrylic paintings of seascapes and skyscapes. Most of Kurt Jackson's sketches contain writing – notes, ideas, titles, and records of what's in front of him. These examples of Jackson's writing on his sketches are typical:

Cot stream onto Nanven cove, morning sun on my back, sea breeze in my face.
[Above a watercolour painting of the Cot stream as it enters the ocean]

Towards the coast, late afternoon, dark landscape, hundreds of birds, gulls, rooks, jackdaws.
[Below a watercolour of the sea]

I saw my first redwing eating the last blackberries
I heard a woman say, 'I think I'll go on the Atkins diet'
I saw a bare-chested man wearing a skirt and sun hat
I heard a man say, 'but surely we can afford day-boarding?'
I heard a peregrine's rush as it chased a pipit
I felt the stillness and silence of Samson
[Under a pencil and ink sketch of the Scillies][83]

But even Britain's greatest painter – J.M.W. Turner – wasn't able to create finished oil paintings *in situ*. No, Turner did that back in the sanctuary of his studio (and, famously, he was working on his oils right up to the last minute during those varnishing days at the Royal Academy in London: the image of Turner, smartly dressed, in a top hat, standing on a box – he wasn't a tall man – to apply the finishing touches to his paintings, is one of the great images of British art).

But J.M.W. Turner did of course produce sketches and watercolours (including his *Colour Beginnings* watercolours) as he travelled around – a series of thousands of works which are one of the most remarkable

83 Included in *Sketchbooks 2003-2004*.

outpourings of creativity in the whole 100,000 year history of art (and one could argue that, alongside, say, Leonardo da Vinci's notebooks, Turner's sketchbooks are one of *the* great artworks).[84] Turner also famously had a brilliant memory: observers recalled how he would pop his head out of a moving carriage, to sketch a sky or a storm, then reproduce the event months later in a big painting.

While talking about J.M.W. Turner, it should be noted that Britain's greatest painter got there *first* in every respect: he toured Britain and Europe painting sea, skies, rivers, towns, everything; he produced near-abstract watercolours; he worked non-stop, creating thousands of works; he did *absolutely everything* a painter could do, and today he's still way ahead of everybody else.

No one can touch him. In a way, all landscape painters after J.M.W. Turner are working in his shadow (or should that be in his dazzling light?) – including Kurt Jackson.

Back to the painting-in-open-air issue: I think it's more that art lovers would like to think that Kurt Jackson made those paintings outside. Why? A romance with nature, of course (never under-estimate how much Brits love nature – and gardens, and their pets), and the idea that an artist is 'in touch' with their subject matter (i.e., he's not making paintings of the sea in the middle of a city), and that image of the artist at work out of doors gives a heroic, romantic edge to the artist's identity. The artist isn't sitting in a warm, comfy studio, reclining in a armchair, clad in a black lounge suit, while he sips port and makes polite conversation with his maiden aunt, and occasionally rises to dab some paint on a canvas balanced on an antique easel.

No, the public maybe prefers to think of the landscape painter as a hiker/ walker/ climber/ hunter character, tough, rugged, but oh so sensitive, oh so romantic. And they're out there, in the real world (as if the real world were only *outside*, as if we aren't part of nature too, wherever we are), painting the hills and rivers and fields and trees and oceans.

It's the same with other contemporary artists: take British artists Andy Goldsworthy and Richard Long. Goldsworthy, a hugely popular

---

84 'Turner's watercolour sketches I adore', commented Kurt Jackson (P, 20).

artist in the Western world, creates sensitive, intimate responses to the natural realm in the form of sculptures constructed from stones, branches, leaves, flower petals and the like. He could've built those ephemeral artworks in his studio in Scotland and taken them outside and photographed them (or he could've built sets in his studio, or faked them with montage and digital techniques). But the art audience I'm sure prefers to imagine that Goldsworthy was really out there in the natural world, reacting to it and creating his sculptures.

Similarly with Richard Long, an artist who founds his entire output on the art of walking. A Richard Long exhibition usually comprises framed photographs and pieces of text (always in Gill Sans font), with one or two stone rings or rows on the gallery floor. Long walks in wildernesses usually – we're talking the Bolivian desert, or Lappland, or the mountains of Nepal. And very often in Dartmoor in dear old England. But the textworks and photoworks could be fiction: a novelist makes up stories, why not a visual artist? But, again, the art public appreciates some degree of 'authenticity', some real, physical link with the subject matter.

And it's the same with Kurt Jackson. So that's one reason why the exhibition catalogues and the video and TV documentaries and the other information surrounding Jackson always shows the artist sitting in a field or by the sea, with a sketchbook in hand. He could be photographed in his studio, or on the phone discussing insurance for a future exhibition, or chatting with folk on Facebook or Twitter, or whatever. But the image of the artist presented in the secondary material is that heroic, romantic one. This isn't about the artists themselves, it's about how audiences like to see artists.

If you wander around this planet you might have seen a painter at work. It's a very rare sight, though. More common is a photographer (and with digital cameras and cel phones, photographing anything and everything is even more common. Anyone with a cel phone can be a photographer. In theory, that is – but not everyone with a cel phone is Ansel Adams!). But I bet you've never seen a sculptor working on a clay model in the landscape. Or a composer with a portable electronic piano set up in a field, like a scene out of a Ken Russell movie. Nope:

ballet dancers, sculptors, musicians, rap stars, clay potters and the like simply don't work out of doors in front of an inspiring landscape. So the idea that a landscape painter has to be out of doors in all weathers and all hours painting and sketching is ridiculous. But the image persists.[85] (One of the other reasons is that many artists don't like to be seen at work, and neither does Jackson. When he's down at Priest Cove, for instance, he prefers to find a spot that's out of sight of passers-by.)[86]

FIGURES IN A LANDSCAPE

Kurt Jackson's family sometimes appear in his paintings – standing by the sea, as in *Zinzi and Chlöe, Sandy Cove* (1997), *Seth, Sandy Cove* (1997), *Sealight, Chlöe* (1997), and *Zinzi and Chlöe Playing Catch* (1998). Paintings such as *Sealight, Chlöe, Jumping Off Black Rock* (1997) and *Porthcressa, St Mary's Scilly* (1997) are archetypical Jackson figurative paintings – or rather, paintings of figures: a person seen against the ocean. (Many of the images of Sennen, one of the closest big sandy beaches to Jackson's home in St Just (many beaches are rocky), have people in them – it's rightly one of the most popular beaches in the area: as in *Sennen, 19.9.98, 3 p.m., Surfers Rushing Into the Sea*, 1998, and *Sennen*, 1994).

Kurt Jackson is a figurative painter, but not a painter of figures. He sticks wholly to landscape art, but people do crop up in his work from time to time. There are occasional self-portraits (such as the ones at Priest Cove). There are images of his family. And sometimes other figures. (Jackson has done life drawings, including female nudes, at life

---

85 I have seen painters only very, very occasionally at work in the landscape (in pretty towns you sometimes see a painter painting). I met a painter out in the middle of Dartmoor, in 2006, during a hike. We got talking and it turned out that Stewart Edmondson was a big fan of Kurt Jackson's art, and travelled to his exhibitions. Edmondson has his own website and can also be found at the D'Art Gallery in Dartmouth.
86 Observers have noted that Jackson will enlist family or friends to help ward off onlookers as he's painting.

drawing classes in St Just, but prefers not to exhibit them. He also feels uneasy about being 'a male artist who draws female nudes' [P, 30]).

Figures feature more prominently in Kurt Jackson's sketchbooks rather than in finished or published paintings. There are drawings of people reading, musicians, kitchens, dinners, picnics, blackberrying, doing homework, watching TV. Many of the sketches of people depict modest, domestic scenes.[87] Needles to say that Jackson's wife Caroline appears in most of the images of people.[88]

Why figures? Because there are pictures which seem to require the human figure to complete them, Kurt Jackson explained, so he'll include a little vertical figure against the landscape (which also help to give a sense of scale, and break up the horizontality of most of Jackson's pictures).

'Figures in a landscape' is a huge genre in the history of art, but Kurt Jackson's pictures are not like the usual figures in a landscape image. In the paintings of Claude Lorrain and Nicholas Poussin, for example, the figures typically have a mythological or historical significance. In the art of J.M.W. Turner, they might be mythological or small-scale, social and local. Caspar David Friedrich is one of the great painters of figures in a landscape, and his images have religious and Romantic themes.

In Kurt Jackson's art, though, the figures don't have any of those weighty historical or mythological aspects to them (though the figures of miners or fishermen or quarry workers do have a political dimension). Rather, the kids playing frisbee or catch, or diving off rocks seem to have wandered into the composition, into the space in front of the painter, and might wander out again at any moment. They are down at the foreshore, next to the water, and they'll scoot along to the next bit of beach seconds later.

Kurt Jackson has produced paintings of towns in the area, such as Trewellard and St Just itself (*Levant Road, Trewellard,* 1998, and *Trewellard Hill,* 1998), but not as many as artists like Gill Watkiss (her strange visions of a dream-like St Just populated by a recurring cast of

87 There are images of Jackson's children – Zinzi, Seth, Chloe. And some of them are drawn in the act of drawing – maybe dad's been encouraging them.
88 Caroline Jackson sitting by the sea at Sennen, Caroline at Nanquidno, Caroline on the train to Worcester, Caroline on the couch with flu.

odd characters are instantly recognizable and unsettling).

It's been a great pleasure following Kurt Jackson's artistic career, and to see his work reaching a wider audience. One imagines, though, that Jackson would continue to paint, with or without the success his art has brought him. He is a painter who likes to paint.

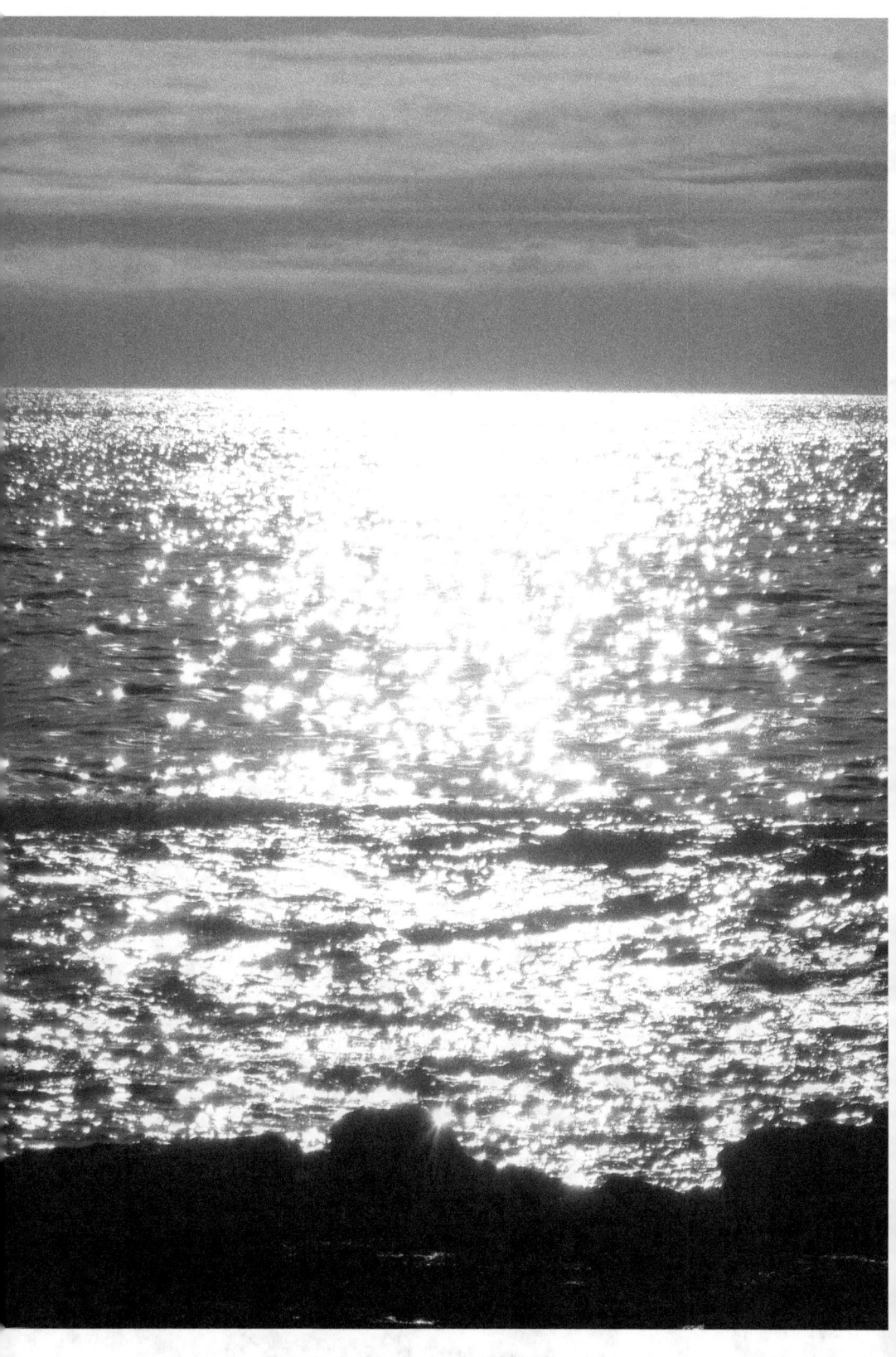

You are here. You have always been here.
Cot Valley, West Penwith, Summer, 2013

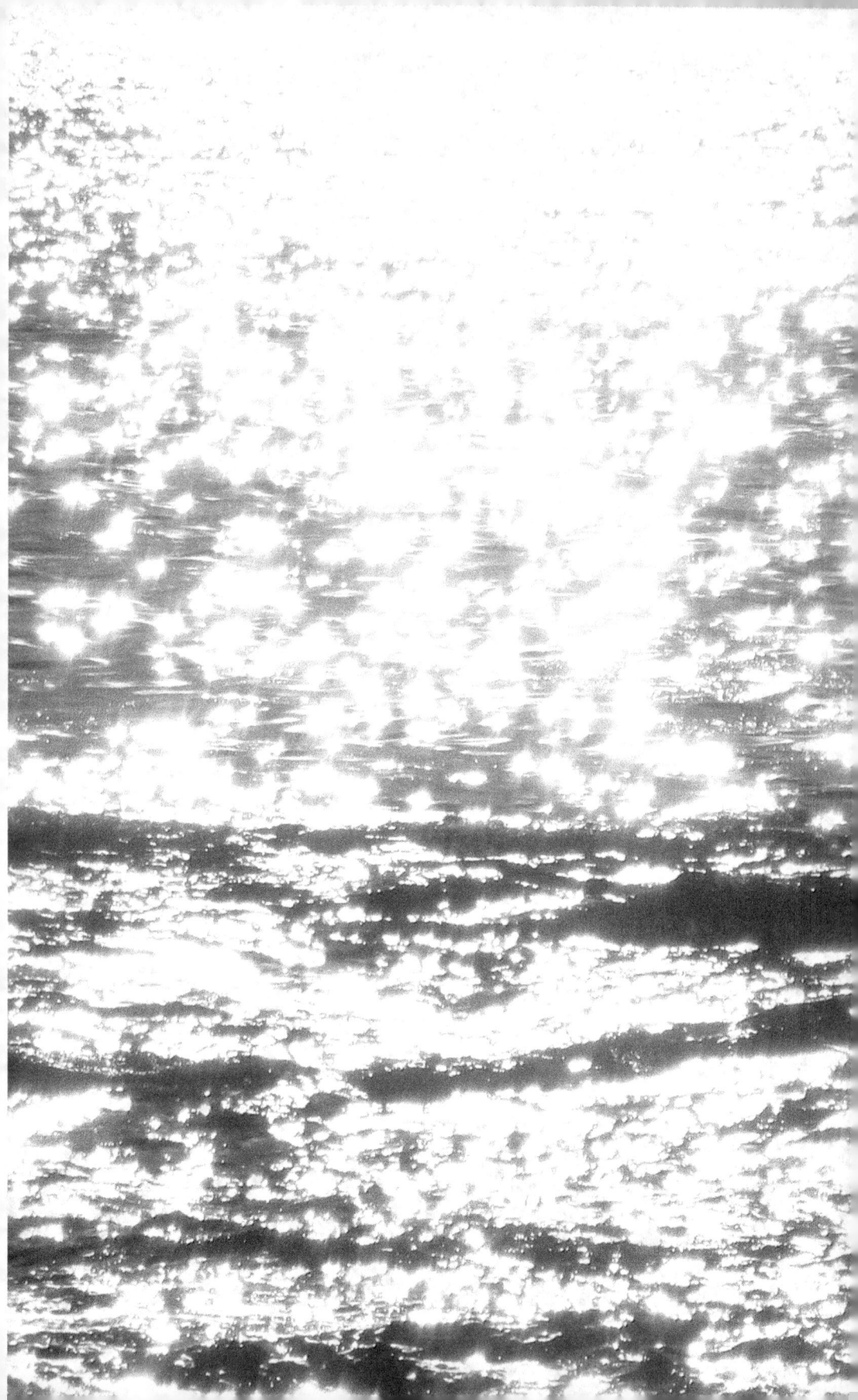

BIBLIOGRAPHY

KURT JACKSON

Kurt Jackson, privately published, essay by J.A. O'Brien, 1995

An Irish Sketchbook, Origin Gallery, Dublin, 1997

Kurt Jackson: South Crofty, Cambourne School of Mines and touring exhibition, 1996

Between Earth and Sky , John Davies Gallery, Stow-On-the-World, Glos., 1998

Kurt Jackson: Both Ends of the Brush, David Messum Gallery, London, 1998

Turn Left At the Clocktower: Five St Just Artists, Great Atlantic Map Works, St Just, Cornwall, 1998

The Next Generation: Jeremy Annear and Kurt Jackson, David Messum Gallery, London, 1998

"Kurt Jackson – Artist's Eye", *Art Review*, June 1998

Between Dawn and Dusk, John Davies Gallery, Stow-On-the-World, Glos., 1999

Crossing the Peninsula: Painting the Path of Totality, Great Atlantic Map Works, St Just, Cornwall, 1999

Follow the Light, Great Atlantic Map Works, St Just, Cornwall, 1999

Kurt Jackson, Great Atlantic Map Works, St Just, Cornwall, 1999

Carnsew: a working granite quarry in Cornwall, Falmouth Art Gallery, 1999

A3071: The Road to St Just, Great Atlantic Map Works, St Just, Cornwall, 2000

Paintings of Cornwall and the Scillies, White Lane Press, Plymouth, Devon, 2000

Kurt Jackson, David Messum Gallery, London, 2001

From Penwith to Las Alpujarras, John Davies Gallery, Stow-On-the-World,

Glos., 2001

Delabole Slate Quarry , Great Atlantic Map Works Publications, St Just, Cornwall, 2001

Tinner's Way, Great Atlantic Map Works Publications, St Just, Cornwall, 2001

The Long Field, Great Atlantic Map Works Publications, St Just, Cornwall, 2002

The Cape, with R. Gaskell, Truran, 2002

Kurt Jackson, David Messum Gallery, London, 2002

Priest Cove, Lemon Street Gallery, Truro, Cornwall, 2002

Scilly, Lemon Street Gallery, Truro, Cornwall, 2002

Kurt Jackson in Scotland, Lemon Street Gallery, Truro, Cornwall, 2002

Kurt Jackson, David Messum Gallery, London, 2003

St Michael's Way, Lemon Street Gallery, Truro, Cornwall, 2003

The Paps of Jura, Lemon Street Gallery, Truro, Cornwall, 2004

Sketchbooks 2003-2004, Truran, 2004

The Cornish Estuary, Lemon Street Gallery, Truro, Cornwall, 2004

Porth, Lemon Street Gallery, Truro, Cornwall, 2004

Kurt Jackson, David Messum Gallery, London, 2004

Two Woods, Victoria Art Gallery, Bath, 2004

The Cornish Hedge, Lemon Street Gallery, Truro, Cornwall, 2005

Kurt Jackson, David Messum Gallery, London, 2005

The Painted Etchings, Lemon Street Gallery, Truro, Cornwall, 2005

Three Woods, St Barbe Museum and Art Gallery, 2005

Neil's Place, Dundas Street Gallery, Edinburgh, 2006

The Thames Project, Lemon Street Gallery, Truro, Cornwall, 2006

Kurt Jackson, David Messum Gallery, London, 2006

Kurt Jackson, David Messum Gallery, London, 2007

The Lights of West Cornwall, David Messum Gallery, London, 2008

Below the Cairngorms, Dundas Street Gallery, Edinburgh, 2008

The Young Liffey, Lemon Street Gallery, Truro, Cornwall, 2008

The Solent Project, Lymington, Hants., 2008

The Mining Project, Geevor Mine Gallery, Penzance, 2008

The Tamar Project, Lemon Street Gallery, Truro, Cornwall, 2008

Forest Gardens, David Messum Gallery, London, 2009

OTHERS

M. Awodey. "Piece of the Rock", *Seven Days*, Vermont, June 26, 2002

M. Cocker. "The Vision of Kurt Jackson", *Granta*, 102, 2008

P. Davies. *St. Ives Revisited*, Old Bakehouse, Abertillery, Gwent, 1994

M. Glover. "Kurt Jackson", *The Independent On Sunday*, Feb 4, 2008

P. Redgrove. *The Black Goddess and the Sixth Sense*, Bloomsbury, London, 1987

—. *The Best of Peter Redgrove's Poetry: The Book of Wonders*, ed. J.M. Robinson, Crescent Moon, 2007

—. *Sex-Magic-Poetry-Cornwall: A Flood of Poems*, ed. J.M. Robinson, Crescent Moon, 2007/ 11

Cat Rogers. "Painting to the Beat", *The Scotsman*, April 23, 2002

"Shedding Light on Ancient Ways", *Daily Telegraph,* August 7, 1999

Marion Whybrow: *St Ives 1883-1993: Portrait of an Art Colony,* Antique Collector's Club, 1994

CRESCENT MOON PUBLISHING

web: www.crmoon.com e-mail: cresmopub@yahoo.co.uk

ARTS, PAINTING, SCULPTURE

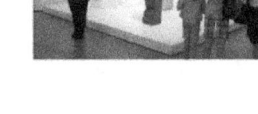
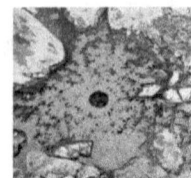
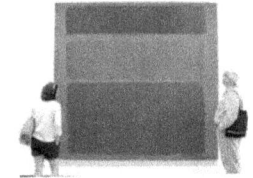

The Art of Andy Goldsworthy
Andy Goldsworthy: Touching Nature
Andy Goldsworthy in Close-Up
Andy Goldsworthy: Pocket Guide
Andy Goldsworthy In America
Land Art: A Complete Guide
The Art of Richard Long
Richard Long: Pocket Guide
Land Art In the UK
Land Art in Close-Up
Land Art In the U.S.A.
Land Art: Pocket Guide
Installation Art in Close-Up
Minimal Art and Artists In the 1960s and After
Colourfield Painting
Land Art DVD, TV documentary
Andy Goldsworthy DVD, TV documentary
The Erotic Object: Sexuality in Sculpture From Prehistory to the Present Day
Sex in Art: Pornography and Pleasure in Painting and Sculpture
Postwar Art
Sacred Gardens: The Garden in Myth, Religion and Art
Glorification: Religious Abstraction in Renaissance and 20th Century Art
Early Netherlandish Painting
Leonardo da Vinci
Piero della Francesca
Giovanni Bellini
Fra Angelico: Art and Religion in the Renaissance
Mark Rothko: The Art of Transcendence
Frank Stella: American Abstract Artist
Jasper Johns
Brice Marden
Alison Wilding: The Embrace of Sculpture
Vincent van Gogh: Visionary Landscapes
Eric Gill: Nuptials of God
Constantin Brancusi: Sculpting the Essence of Things
Max Beckmann
Caravaggio
Gustave Moreau
Egon Schiele: Sex and Death In Purple Stockings
Delizioso Fotografico Fervore: Works In Process 1
Sacro Cuore: Works In Process 2
The Light Eternal: J.M.W. Turner
The Madonna Glorified: Karen Arthurs

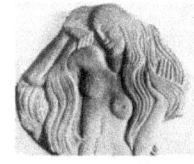
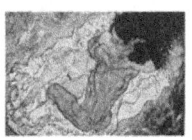
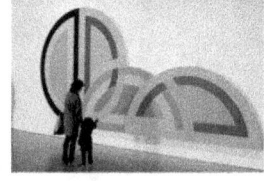
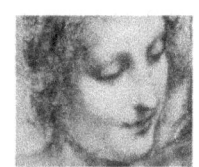
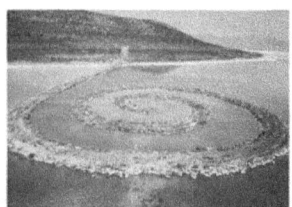

LITERATURE

J.R.R. Tolkien: The Books, The Films, The Whole Cultural Phenomenon
J.R.R. Tolkien: Pocket Guide
Tolkien's Heroic Quest
The *Earthsea* Books of Ursula Le Guin
Beauties, Beasts and Enchantment: Classic French Fairy Tales
German Popular Stories by the Brothers Grimm
Philip Pullman and *His Dark Materials*
Sexing Hardy: Thomas Hardy and Feminism
Thomas Hardy's *Tess of the d'Urbervilles*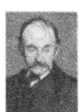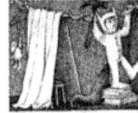
Thomas Hardy's *Jude the Obscure*
Thomas Hardy: The Tragic Novels
Love and Tragedy: Thomas Hardy
The Poetry of Landscape in Hardy
Wessex Revisited: Thomas Hardy and John Cowper Powys
Wolfgang Iser: Essays and Interviews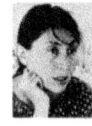
Petrarch, Dante and the Troubadours
Maurice Sendak and the Art of Children's Book Illustration
Andrea Dworkin
Cixous, Irigaray, Kristeva: The *Jouissance* of French Feminism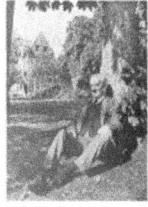
Julia Kristeva: Art, Love, Melancholy, Philosophy, Semiotics and Psychoanalysis
Hélene Cixous I Love You: The *Jouissance* of Writing
Luce Irigaray: Lips, Kissing, and the Politics of Sexual Difference
Peter Redgrove: Here Comes the Flood
Peter Redgrove: Sex-Magic-Poetry-Cornwall
Lawrence Durrell: Between Love and Death, East and West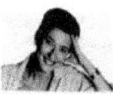
Love, Culture & Poetry: Lawrence Durrell
Cavafy: Anatomy of a Soul
German Romantic Poetry: Goethe, Novalis, Heine, Hölderlin
Feminism and Shakespeare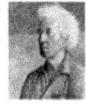
Shakespeare: Love, Poetry & Magic
The Passion of D.H. Lawrence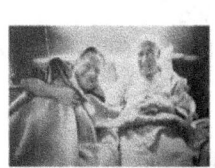
D.H. Lawrence: Symbolic Landscapes
D.H. Lawrence: Infinite Sensual Violence
Rimbaud: Arthur Rimbaud and the Magic of Poetry
The Ecstasies of John Cowper Powys
Sensualism and Mythology: The Wessex Novels of John Cowper Powys
Amorous Life: John Cowper Powys and the Manifestation of Affectivity (H.W. Fawkner)
Postmodern Powys: New Essays on John Cowper Powys (Joe Boulter)
Rethinking Powys: Critical Essays on John Cowper Powys
Paul Bowles & Bernardo Bertolucci
Rainer Maria Rilke
Joseph Conrad: *Heart of Darkness*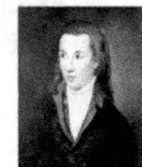
In the Dim Void: Samuel Beckett
Samuel Beckett Goes into the Silence
André Gide: Fiction and Fervour
Jackie Collins and the Blockbuster Novel
Blinded By Her Light: The Love-Poetry of Robert Graves
The Passion of Colours: Travels In Mediterranean Lands
Poetic Forms

POETRY

Ursula Le Guin: Walking In Cornwall
Peter Redgrove: Here Comes The Flood
Peter Redgrove: Sex-Magic-Poetry-Cornwall
Dante: Selections From the Vita Nuova
Petrarch, Dante and the Troubadours
William Shakespeare: Sonnets
William Shakespeare: Complete Poems
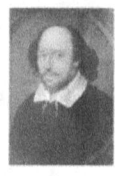
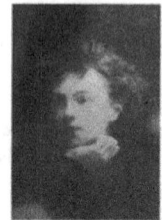
Blinded By Her Light: The Love-Poetry of Robert Graves
Emily Dickinson: Selected Poems
Emily Brontë: Poems
Thomas Hardy: Selected Poems
Percy Bysshe Shelley: Poems
John Keats: Selected Poems
Joh n Keats: Poems of 1820
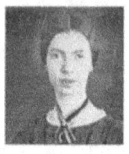
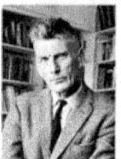
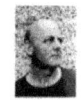
D.H. Lawrence: Selected Poems
Edmund Spenser: Poems
Edmund Spenser: Amoretti
John Donne: Poems
Henry Vaughan: Poems
Sir Thomas Wyatt: Poems
Robert Herrick: Selected Poems
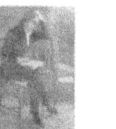
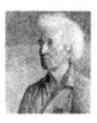
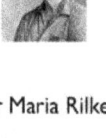
Rilke: Space, Essence and Angels in the Poetry of Rainer Maria Rilke
Rainer Maria Rilke: Selected Poems
Friedrich Hölderlin: Selected Poems
Arseny Tarkovsky: Selected Poems
Arthur Rimbaud: Selected Poems
Arthur Rimbaud: A Season in Hell
Arthur Rimbaud and the Magic of Poetry
Novalis: Hymns To the Night
German Romantic Poetry
Paul Verlaine: Selected Poems
Elizaethan Sonnet Cycles
D.J. Enright: By-Blows
Jeremy Reed: Brigitte's Blue Heart
Jeremy Reed: Claudia Schiffer's Red Shoes
Gorgeous Little Orpheus
Radiance: New Poems
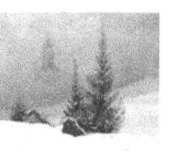
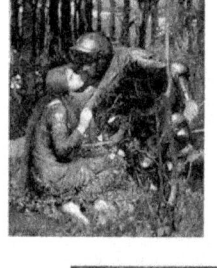
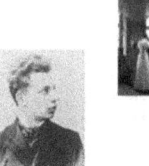
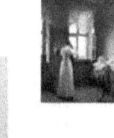
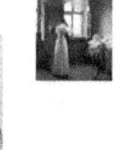
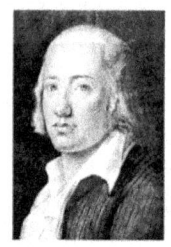
Crescent Moon Book of Nature Poetry
Crescent Moon Book of Love Poetry
Crescent Moon Book of Mystical Poetry
Crescent Moon Book of Elizabethan Love Poetry
Crescent Moon Book of Metaphysical Poetry
Crescent Moon Book of Romantic Poetry
Pagan America: New American Poetry
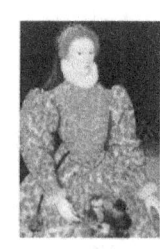

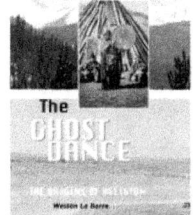
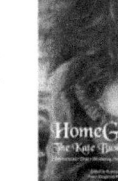
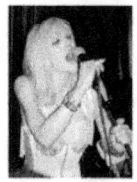
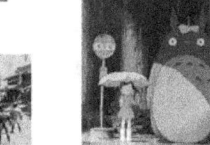
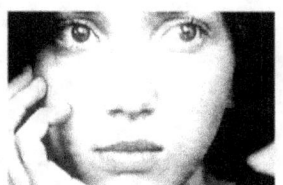

The Light Eternal is a model monograph, an exemplary job. The subject matter of the book is beautifully
organised and dead on beam. (Lawrence Durrell)
It is amazing for me to see my work treated with such passion and respect. (Andrea Dworkin)

CRESCENT MOON PUBLISHING
P.O. Box 1312, Maidstone, Kent, ME14 5XU, Great Britain. www.crmoon.com

cresmopub@yahoo.co.uk   www.crescentmoon.org.uk

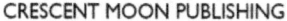